DIVORCED FROM REALITY

FAMILIES, LAW, AND SOCIETY SERIES
General Editor: Nancy E. Dowd

Justice for Kids: Keeping Kids Out of the Juvenile Justice System
Edited by Nancy E. Dowd

Masculinities and the Law: A Multidimensional Approach
Edited by Frank Rudy Cooper and Ann C. McGinley

The New Kinship: Constructing Donor-Conceived Families
Naomi Cahn

What Is Parenthood? Contemporary Debates about the Family
Edited by Linda C. McClain and Daniel Cere

In Our Hands: The Struggle for U.S. Child Care Policy
Elizabeth Palley and Corey S. Shdaimah

The Marriage Buyout: The Troubled Trajectory of U.S. Alimony Law
Cynthia Lee Starnes

Children, Sexuality, and the Law
Edited by Sacha Coupet and Ellen Marrus

A New Juvenile Justice System: Total Reform for a Broken System
Edited by Nancy E. Dowd

Divorced from Reality: Rethinking Family Dispute Resolution
Jane C. Murphy and Jana B. Singer

Divorced from Reality

Rethinking Family Dispute Resolution

Jane C. Murphy and Jana B. Singer

NEW YORK UNIVERSITY PRESS

New York and London

NEW YORK UNIVERSITY PRESS
New York and London
www.nyupress.org

References to Internet websites (URLs) were accurate at the time of writing. Neither the author nor New York University Press is responsible for URLs that may have expired or changed since the manuscript was prepared.

Library of Congress Cataloging-in-Publication Data
Murphy, Jane C., author.
Divorced from reality : rethinking family dispute resolution / Jane C. Murphy and Jana B. Singer.
pages cm. — (Families, law, and society series)
Includes bibliographical references and index.
ISBN 978-0-8147-0893-4 (cl : alk. paper)
1. Family mediation—United States. 2. Dispute resolution (Law)—United States. 3. Domestic relations courts—United States. I. Singer, Jana B., 1955– author. II. Title. III. Series: Families, law, and society series.
KF505.5.M868   2015
346.7301'5—dc23   2014050100

New York University Press books are printed on acid-free paper, and their binding materials are chosen for strength and durability. We strive to use environmentally responsible suppliers and materials to the greatest extent possible in publishing our books.

Manufactured in the United States of America

10 9 8 7 6 5 4 3 2 1

Also available as an ebook

CONTENTS

ACKNOWLEDGMENTS

This book grew out of the authors' conversations over many years about how to improve family dispute resolution and the family justice system. We came to this work with different perspectives and experiences. We both have a foot firmly in the theory and practice of family law, but Jane's many years in clinical education and Jana's strong focus on scholarship brought different strengths and orientations to the work. This resulted in a collaboration that was, at times, challenging but always rewarding; we believe it made the book more balanced, thoughtful, and grounded in the real world. Both authors' views were enriched and changed by the process of writing this book.

We thank Nancy Dowd for inviting us to contribute to the Families, Law, and Society series, and the editors and staff at NYU Press for their encouragement and patience. We also thank the anonymous reviewers whose thoughtful comments improved the book, as well as the family law colleagues who read and commented on drafts of the various chapters. These valued colleagues include Andrew Schepard, Jane Spinak, Leigh Goodmark, Karen Czapanskiy, Mike Millemann, and Theresa Glennon. We thank the University of Baltimore and the University of Maryland Francis King Carey Schools of Law and their library staffs for their sustained support for this book, as well as the many students, lawyers, mental health professionals, judges, and court administrators with whom we have worked over the years to improve the family justice system.

In addition, Jane wishes to thank the many fine research assistants who worked on this book at various stages: Catherine Bouldin, Peggy Chu, Hannah Dawson, Amy Lazas, and Victoria Narducci. She also appreciates the support of Deans Phil Closius and Ron Weich as well as colleagues Rob Rubinson, Dan Hatcher, Melissa Breger, Elizabeth Samuels, Lydia Nussbaum, Pamela Ortiz, and Dave Jaros for their help in reviewing drafts, discussing ideas, and offering support in a variety of ways. Jane's administrative assistant Shavaun O'Brien's energy, good humor, and management skills were invaluable over the course of writing this book. Finally, Jane deeply appreciates the enthusiasm, support, and patience that her family—especially her husband and children, Chris, Brendan, Katie, Margaret, Cat, and Gracie—demonstrated for this book and everything she does.

Jana wishes to thank her colleagues at the University of Maryland Carey School of Law for their ongoing engagement and intellectual support. She would also like to thank Deans Karen Rothenberg and Phoebe Haddon for their support and Jillian Chieppor for her excellent research assistance. Finally, Jana would like to thank her family—especially Larry, Michael, and Josh—for their sustaining love and support that make academic work both possible and worthwhile.

Introduction

Over the past three decades, there has been a profound shift in the way the legal system approaches and resolves parenting disputes. This shift has replaced the law-oriented and judge-focused adversary model with a more collaborative and interdisciplinary regime that deemphasizes legal norms and discourages third-party decision-making. Although the paradigm shift has focused largely on divorce-related parenting disputes, it has both borrowed from and influenced other areas of family law, including juvenile justice and child welfare proceedings.

Over this same thirty-year period, the structure and composition of American families has changed dramatically. Divorce rates have leveled off and even begun to drop, while the number and percentage of children born and raised outside of marriage has increased sharply. Moreover, legal developments at both the federal and state levels have greatly increased the likelihood that disputes involving never-married parents will end up in family court. As a result, the families who experience the new dispute resolution paradigm have become more diverse and their legal situations more complex.

This book examines the late twentieth-century paradigm shift in family dispute resolution and juxtaposes it with more recent changes in the structure and composition of today's families. Focusing on disputes among family members, we ask whether the current dispute resolution regime responds adequately to the needs of the families it purports to serve. Our answer is a qualified no. While the new paradigm may represent an improvement over its more adversary predecessor, it is built largely around the model of a divorcing nuclear family—a model that fits poorly with the more complicated realities of today's disputing families. Moreover, the new paradigm largely fails to acknowledge that some parents and children need the protections afforded by traditional legal processes and authoritative third-party decision-making. We also find that the legal profession has been slow to adapt both to the new dispute resolution paradigm and to more recent changes in family structure. As a result, a majority of today's disputing families must navigate a complicated and tiered judicial system without adequate access to legal information or advice—a state of affairs that jeopardizes the ability of today's dispute resolution regime to achieve durable or just results for many families, particularly families without substantial means. The recommendations we offer at the end of the book are designed to address these shortcomings.

Chapter 1 traces the doctrinal and procedural antecedents of the late twentieth-century paradigm shift and introduces several themes that inform the remaining chapters. These include the close connection between changes in substantive family law doctrine and changes in family dispute resolution processes; the shifting boundary between the public and private aspects of family dispute resolution; and the differential treatment by the family court system of families with and without financial means.

Chapter 2 lays out the critique of adversary family justice made by proponents of the new paradigm and explains how the current family dispute resolution regime developed as a response to this critique. It also describes the concerns raised by some commentators about the retreat from adversary procedures. Chapter 3 explores a paradox that lies at the heart of the new paradigm. The new paradigm expands the vision and role of family courts at the same time that it reduces the primacy and relevance of legal norms in resolving disputes about children. The result is a more powerful family court system that is less constrained by legal limits than its more traditional predecessor. While such an expanded and expansive court system may benefit children and families in need of services, it also poses substantial risks, both to the family members it serves and to the larger society.

Chapter 4 focuses on recent changes in the structure and characteristics of the families who interact with the new paradigm. These changes include the decline of marriage and the resulting increase in nonmarital families with parenting disputes; the prevalence of stepfamilies; the increase in grandparent and other non-parental caretakers of children; the rise of gay and lesbian families; and the sharp increase in *pro se* parties in family court. This chapter also explores the mismatch between the complex realities of today's families and the more simplistic assumptions that underlie the new paradigm.

Chapter 5 explores the changing roles of lawyers and judges in the new family court system. It describes how these changes have reduced the distinctions between judging and lawyering and blurred the roles of judges, facilitators, and attorneys. The chapter explores the implications of these new and expanded roles for families and family dispute resolution, as well as the challenges they create for traditional understandings of professional and ethical norms.

Chapter 6 explores how international and comparative law developments have influenced the development of the new paradigm in the United States. It focuses, in particular, on reform efforts in Australia that have shifted family dispute resolution away from the court system and into the community, and on the implementation of the mandate of the United Nations Convention on the Rights of the Child that children have the opportunity to participate in legal proceedings that affect them.

Chapter 7 shifts our lens from analytic to prescriptive. It offers a series of recommendations designed to address the disconnect between the new paradigm and today's families, and to adjust the balance between court-based and community-based approaches to family dispute resolution. The goal of these recommendations is to look forward, rather than backward, and to use the insights of the new paradigm to build a more just and effective twenty-first-century family dispute resolution regime.

1

Historical Overview

The paradigm shift that we describe in this book is principally a contemporary phenomenon, but it has a number of historical antecedents. These precursors include important doctrinal developments in both the nineteenth and twentieth centuries, which expanded and transformed the judicial role in divorce and custody disputes, ultimately making courts the primary guardians of children's welfare in the face of family breakdown. In addition, the therapeutic underpinnings of progressive-era juvenile justice reform migrated in the mid-twentieth century from the delinquency to the divorce and custody context. Although these therapeutic principles initially foundered on the shoals of no-fault divorce, their migration from juvenile to family court paved the way for many of the dispute resolution reforms we analyze in this book. Finally, the shift from a fault-based, sole custody regime to a no-fault co-parenting model in the 1980s and early 1990s simultaneously undermined the efficacy of traditional adversary processes and invited ongoing court involvement in families affected by divorce and parental separation—both important elements of the new paradigm.

This chapter will examine these historical antecedents and explore their impact on today's family dispute resolution system. This historical excavation will reveal three themes that inform the remainder of our analysis: the close connection between changes in substantive family law doctrine and changes in family dispute resolution processes; the shifting boundary between the public and private aspects of family dispute resolution; and the differential treatment by the family court system of families with and without economic means. While previous family law scholars have emphasized the disparate legal treatment of poor and wealthy families, they have tended to focus on differences in the substantive legal doctrines applied to these two groups;[1] our examination indicates that the disparities extend as well to the impact of the processes and court practices used to resolve family disputes.

Colonial America and the Unified Patriarchal Family

During the colonial period, the American legal system viewed the marital family as a unified and cohesive entity.[2] Divorce was rare and generally required a special enactment by the legislature. Mirroring the society around it, the colonial family was both hierarchical and patriarchal. Male heads of household exercised legal control over the women and children in their families, and represented those families in the public sphere.[3] As historian Michael Grossberg has written, "The community charged each male governor with the duty of maintaining a well-ordered home and sustained his authority by granting him control of its inhabitants as well as of family property and other resources. Women and children, as subordinates and dependents in the corporate body, had limited capacity to engage independently in community life."[4]

Consistent with this view, eighteenth-century Anglo-American law granted fathers an almost unlimited right to the custody of their minor, legitimate children. Children were viewed as paternal assets, and the legal rules governing the care and control of children reflected this property orientation. Married women had no legal right to custody of their children during marriage or in the unlikely event of divorce. Moreover, although a mother was assumed to be the natural guardian of her children upon the death of her husband, a father could overcome this assumption by appointing someone else as a guardian in his will, and the courts were bound to respect his testamentary wish.[5]

Because divorce was rare during the colonial era and women lacked independent legal status, the judiciary's role in resolving disputes between parents was extremely limited. Courts became involved in disputes regarding the custody and control of children principally when they were asked to approve contracts for indenture or to resolve disputes between masters and fathers regarding the treatment of childhood apprentices.[6] Although children were the subjects of these contract-based disputes, their welfare was not a primary consideration for the courts.

Colonial courts intervened more actively in the lives of poor children and their families. Following the tradition of the English poor laws, fathers who could not adequately maintain their families risked losing custody of their children to poor law officials. With the consent of the appropriate court or magistrate, these officials were authorized to "bind out" the children to a master who could support them.[7] Impoverished widows and unwed mothers faced similar court-supervised intervention and forced separation from their children. Once a child was involuntarily "bound out," the parents, if still alive, lost any claim to custody.[8]

Thus, during the colonial era, white families that were "well governed" and headed by a male patriarch faced minimal judicial scrutiny, while families that lacked an effective male governor were subject to considerably greater judicial control. Moreover, where the judicial system did intervene in family matters, its primary purposes were to preserve paternal rights and to protect the community's economic interests, not to promote the welfare of children.

For black families in the colonial era, slavery made formation of legally recognized families impossible. Colonial and state laws considered slaves property, not legal persons who could enter into marriage or other contracts.[9] Many enslaved adults considered themselves married and, along with their children, functioned as families. But the vast majority of African Americans could not legally marry until the end of slavery in 1865. Thus, while oppression by the state through slavery was a central feature of African American family life, the judicial system had little contact with African American families during this period.

Judicial Authority and the Republican Family

A series of changes in the post-Revolutionary era challenged this unitary and hierarchical vision of family, and significantly expanded the judiciary's role in resolving intra-family disputes. One important influence was a new domestic egalitarianism based on the ideology of domesticity and separate spheres. This ideology emphasized the separation of work and home and assigned sharply differentiated roles to women and men; while men enjoyed primacy in the public realm of work and politics, women were the central actors in the private domain of home and family.[10] The ideology of domesticity also identified the family as a key locus for the transmission of moral values and the education of future citizens—tasks for which women were now primarily responsible. Domesticity thus gave women and men complementary, as opposed to hierarchical family roles—women were now viewed as different from men, but not necessarily inferior to them, particularly with respect to family governance.

The importance that domesticity placed on the role of mothers significantly enhanced women's ability to obtain custody of their children after separation, divorce, or death of a husband. Judges in contested custody proceedings increasingly cited the distinctive role of mothers as grounds for overcoming the father's common law right to control and custody of his children. In addition, women used their enhanced status within the family to seek divorce or judicial separation when husbands behaved inappropriately or refused to live up to their proper role as economic provider.[11]

Domesticity did not eliminate women's formal legal disadvantages, including the doctrine of coverture, which granted husbands control of their wives' labor and property. Moreover, judges who awarded child custody to women did not do so on grounds of women's equal rights, but rather based on the judicial view that placing young children in their mothers' care was in the best interests of children. As Joel Bishop's 1852 treatise on marriage and divorce law explained, a father's right to custody "is not an absolute one, and is usually made to yield when the good of the child, which especially according to the modern American decision, is the chief matter to be regarded, requires that it should."[12] Thus, judicially inspired limitations on paternal custody and guardianship rights shifted child placement authority to the courts more than they changed the subordinate status of married women.[13] For this reason, many feminists were ambivalent about these legal developments, advocating instead for legislation that would formalize women's equal custody rights. These advocacy efforts were largely unsuccessful; in 1900 only nine states and the District of Columbia gave mothers the statutory right to equal guardianship of their children.[14] By refusing to formalize maternal custody rights, legislators left the issue to the discretion of the courts, ensuring that judicial judgments of parental fitness and child welfare—as opposed to notions of gender equality—would determine custody rights.[15]

The ideology of domesticity also had a class dimension. Courts and social reformers used its precepts to critique the child-rearing practices of poor and immigrant women and to assert control of children whose mothers failed to live up to middle-class notions of maternal virtue. Historians have documented how social reformers and government authorities used the language of domesticity to control the behavior of poor families, including those who peddled and scavenged in city streets, declaring that children should be off the streets, wives and mothers at home, and husbands and fathers gainfully employed. Judges played an active role in these social reform efforts, using their expanded power to determine custody to remove children from allegedly harmful parental influences and place them in more "wholesome" environments, away from their families of origin.[16]

A new perception of childhood also contributed to the republican-era redefinition of the home. "During the nineteenth century, children came to be seen more explicitly than ever as vulnerable malleable charges with a special innocence and with particular needs, talents, and characters."[17] The colonial view of children as economic assets gave way to a more romantic view of children who no longer belonged to their fathers or masters, but instead were deemed to have interests of their own—interests that became increasingly identified with a nurturing mother.

As children began to be viewed as persons, rather than as property, the legal community took a more active interest in their well-being. Reflecting this child welfare orientation, "custody rulings increasingly devalued paternally oriented property-based standards, and instead emphasized maternally based considerations of child nurture."[18] Thus, a father's traditional entitlement to custody gradually evolved from a property right to a trust tied to his responsibilities as a guardian: his title as father thus became both more transferable and more subject to judicial control. For wealthy families, the primary impact of this shift was to enhance the status of mothers in contested custody proceedings; for poor families, by contrast, the effect was often to transfer authority from a child's parents to the state.

The community's growing interest in child welfare also affected the legal treatment of children born outside of marriage. Rejecting the common law's treatment of such children as *filius nullius*, with no legally recognized family ties, nineteenth-century legal reformers deemphasized criminal penalties for bastardy and gave formal legal recognition to the bond between mothers and their nonmarital children.[19] Fathers retained the obligation to support their nonmarital children, but lost their superior right to custody. However, harsh economic realities often diluted women's and children's enhanced legal status. Although bastardy reforms halted the previously widespread practice of separating unmarried mothers from their children solely on the basis of the child's place of birth, these changes did not protect a mother from losing her child because of poverty.[20] The judiciary played a major role in these developments, using its newfound emphasis on child welfare to support the custody claims of financially solvent mothers and to validate the community's interest in children whose parents could not support them.

Thus, although the community's enhanced interest in the well-being of children reduced fathers' custody rights, it did not necessarily enhance maternal power. On the contrary, judicially created standards of child welfare reduced the rights of parenthood generally, particularly for poor parents, and substituted judicial for paternal determinations of child well-being. As historian Michael Grossberg has concluded, "Courts applied judicially created standards of child welfare and parental fitness in order to take the ultimate decision of child placement out of the hands of both parents."[21]

The rise of domesticity and its accompanying emphasis on children's interests also led to a rethinking of the unitary vision of the family that had characterized colonial-era family jurisprudence. While eighteenth-century domestic relations law had conceived the family as an organic unit with a male householder at its head, republican-era legal reforms reenvisioned the family as a group of connected individuals, each with his or her specialized role and duties. Not only did men and women have different family roles, but children, too, had distinctive interests that warranted deference and protection. As a result, the legal system could no longer presume that a father adequately represented the interests of all family members before the law. Once traditional paternal governance lost its privileged legal position, the authority and legitimacy to oversee domestic relations shifted to the newly expanded republican state. Where family members were in conflict, the judiciary increasingly assumed the role of arbitrating among the various interests at stake.[22]

The shift from legislative to judicial divorce also enhanced the role of the courts in resolving disputes between family members. Starting soon after independence, the New England and mid-Atlantic states shifted jurisdiction over divorce from the legislatures to the judiciary. The Southern states moved more slowly, but as the number of divorce petitions rose, legislative divorce proved too costly and inefficient for even its staunchest Southern supporters.[23] By 1867, thirty-three of the thirty-seven American jurisdictions had substituted judicial for legislative control over divorce.[24]

A significant rise in divorce rates during the latter half of the nineteenth century also enhanced the judiciary's role in resolving intrafamily disputes. According to family historians, divorce rates rose at a rate of over 70 percent during the last decades of the nineteenth century. By 1900, American courts were handing down more than fifty-five thousand divorce judgments each year, and about 10 percent of all marriages ended in divorce.[25] Although these figures seem insignificant when compared to twentieth-century divorce rates, they created national consternation and fierce public debate, including significant efforts to address the "divorce problem" at a national level.[26] While efforts to nationalize divorce law ultimately failed, these public discussions underscored the impact of divorce on society and further enhanced the role of courts in protecting the welfare of children affected by divorce and parental separation.

Despite this expansion of the judicial role, nineteenth-century divorce remained an adversary process. Rarely did specific procedural instructions accompany the granting of enhanced domestic relations authority to the courts. Hence, the major procedural aspects of divorce and custody cases tracked the adversary processes applicable to other litigation.[27] Moreover, "[f]ault both heated and illuminated formal divorce policy, and divorce grounds and defenses orbited around the concept of guilt."[28] To obtain a divorce, a claimant generally had to prove that her spouse had committed a narrowly defined marital offense and that she was innocent of marital fault.[29] Standards for awarding custody reflected this fault-based orientation. Divorce statutes in a number of states directed courts to award custody to the party who was not at fault in a divorce.[30] Courts also used fault to judge parental fitness, particularly with respect to mothers. Women who committed adultery or who left their husbands for reasons deemed insufficient by a court risked losing custody of their children, despite the general judicial preference for maternal custody of children of tender years. Thus, while nineteenth-century judges significantly expanded their authority to resolve divorce and custody disputes, they continued to exercise this authority within a traditional adversary framework.

Progressive-Era Juvenile Justice and the Birth of the Therapeutic Ideal

The initial challenge to the use of adversary procedures to resolve family matters came not from domestic relations law itself, but from progressive-era juvenile justice reforms. The establishment of juvenile courts in cities across the United States was one of the earliest social welfare reforms of the progressive era and represented a major change in the way that the legal system dealt with wayward children. Juvenile court reformers rejected both the limited role of the state in protecting children and the use of traditional adversary procedures to handle court cases involving young people. As the Supreme Court explained in *In re Gault*, the reformers "were profoundly convinced that society's duty to the child could not be confined by the concept of justice alone. They believed that society's role was not to ascertain whether the child was 'guilty' or 'innocent,' but 'what is he, how has he become what he is, and what had best be done in his interest and in the interest of the state to save him from a downward career.'"[31]

Pursuant to this philosophy, progressive reformers—including leading legal minds like Roscoe Pound[32] and prominent first-wave feminists like Jane Addams[33]—rejected the emphasis of adult criminal courts on formal public trials in which certain punishment followed findings of guilt. In contrast, the new juvenile courts were intended to reflect the reformers' view that wayward children needed protections and interventions different from adult criminals. While adult criminals were morally blameworthy, the reformers viewed children as products of their environment, who needed to be helped rather than punished.[34] "The child—essentially good, as they saw it—was to be made 'to feel that he is the object of [the state's] care and solicitude,' not that he was under arrest or on trial. The rules of criminal procedure were therefore altogether inapplicable. . . . The child was to be 'treated' and 'rehabilitated' and the procedures, from apprehension through institutionalization, were to be 'clinical' rather than punitive."[35]

This view of the state's role in protecting and rehabilitating children produced changes in the court system that were both substantive and procedural.[36] Because juvenile court proceedings were not considered criminal, early juvenile courts did not distinguish between "dependency" cases, where children were at risk of parental abuse or neglect, and "delinquency" cases, where a minor's unlawful act triggered the judicial intervention. All children in need of "saving" were treated as a single group, whether the condition that brought them to the court was delinquent conduct or dependent status.[37] Indeed, "the critical philosophical position of the [juvenile] reform movement is that no formal legal distinctions should be made between the delinquent and the dependent or neglected."[38]

Juvenile court processes also reflected the reformers' philosophy that cases involving children were not primarily legal events, but rather occasions for beneficent court intervention. Children's cases were heard in closed hearings and the records were kept confidential.[39] The closed proceedings were also informal, heard largely before judges rather than juries, often in chambers.[40] Most children in juvenile court appeared without a lawyer, and legal norms played a minimal role.[41] As one of the leading juvenile court judges of that era explained, "a child's case is not a legal case" and "therefore it [is] not necessary for the child to be legally represented."[42] Other reformers called "for the juvenile court bar to trade its adversariness for a role as 'participant decision maker,' part of the 'dispositional team,' including behavioral scientists and the court, all sharing the aim of rehabilitating the child."[43]

Informal juvenile court processes permitted the introduction of a wide range of testimony and information to assist judges in reaching a disposition. Judges consulted extensively with court personnel—social workers, probation officers, and other personnel vested with broad decision-making authority. These nonlegal players assumed a critical role in juvenile cases, assisting judges in investigating the "character and social background of both 'pre-delinquent' and 'delinquent' children."[44] Evidentiary rules, strictly followed in criminal cases, were largely inapplicable in juvenile court because judges viewed such rules as inconsistent with their therapeutic role and as impediments to learning all facts necessary to determine the individualized treatment designed to rehabilitate the minor.

Juvenile court judges also had broad discretion over the type and length of sentences or "dispositions," as they were called in this court. Indeterminate sentences were the norm because the time needed to rehabilitate varied with each juvenile. Social workers and probation officers were key players in this process, making recommendations to judges about the appropriate disposition of cases. Typical dispositions involved some period of probation to which a variety of "voluntary" conditions were imposed, such as the youth's agreement to stop drinking alcohol, to attend school, or to find employment.[45] Judicial outcomes were not limited by the nature of the offense that brought the child to court. If, during the course of the court's "examination," the judge learned that the child was having trouble in school or had bad habits, the child might be sent to a reform school for months despite the minor nature of the underlying offense.[46] This focus on the child's "needs," rather than the seriousness of the underlying offense, often led to sentences that were disproportionate and could last the length of the child's minority.

While the bulk of the juvenile court caseload dealt with delinquent children, a significant portion was devoted to dependency, which included parental neglect, abuse, and abandonment. Indeed, with the initiation of the first juvenile court in 1899, jurisdiction over dependent and neglected children was fairly rapidly transferred out of the regular court system to the juvenile courts, on the theory that the causes of delinquency were closely tied to those of neglect.[47] Laws giving these courts the power to remove children from their parents and to make them wards of the state were often loosely written, granting significant authority and discretion to juvenile court judges as guardians of children's welfare.

Fueled by a coalition of social workers, politicians, and activist judges who believed that the judicial system could be used to strengthen families, juvenile courts spread rapidly throughout the country. By 1925, barely twenty-five years after the establishment of the first juvenile court in Chicago, every state except Maine and Wyoming had one.[48] Although there were efforts to extend these courts into rural areas, they were primarily a phenomenon of cities, where large concentrations of immigrants and other poor families lived at the turn of the century.[49] This was not a coincidence. To a significant extent, these courts were designed to deal with the perceived problems of poor and immigrant families. As family historian Lynne Carol Halem has written, "The early twentieth century family courts were, in fact, tribunals for the poor, geared toward protecting lower class children from the baneful influences of their home and community and indoctrinating them into the values and standards of the middle class."[50]

From their inception, problems plagued the juvenile courts. Most juvenile courts were poorly funded and many lacked the social workers and other trained personnel deemed central to their "child saving" mission. A 1963 survey found that one-third of juvenile judges had no probation officers or social workers attached to their courts, and between 80 and 90 percent had no available psychologist or psychiatrist.[51] The quality, training, and commitment of the judges themselves also left much to be desired. Although the reformers' original understanding called for dedicated, highly trained judicial specialists, in practice, assignment to juvenile court was considered the lowest rung of the judicial ladder, and work as a juvenile court judge was "not regarded as desirable or appropriate for higher judgeships."[52] The exclusion of lawyers from the juvenile court lowered the visibility of juvenile issues in legal academia and the organized bar, and "the confidentiality of juvenile court proceedings exacerbated the lack of public and professional attention to these issues."[53] As legal historian J. Herbie DiFonzo observed, "in many ways, these once revolutionary courts had slipped into the backwater of the law."[54] High rates of recidivism also undermined reformers' claims that informal processes and individualized attention were effective means of reducing crime or rehabilitating wayward juveniles. Indeed, by the mid-1960s "practically every significant aspect of the juvenile legal process [was] under heavy attack."[55]

The Supreme Court's landmark decision in *In re Gault* further undermined the therapeutic premises of the juvenile court movement. In holding that juvenile delinquency proceedings were constrained by fundamental due process guarantees, the Court acknowledged that "the highest motives and most enlightened impulses" had led to the creation of the juvenile court.[56] It cautioned, however, that "[t]he absence of substantive standards has not necessarily meant that children receive careful, compassionate, individualized treatment. The absence of procedural rules based upon constitutional principle has not always produced fair, efficient, and effective procedures."[57] Instead, the *Gault* court concluded that "Juvenile Court history has again demonstrated that unbridled discretion, however benevolently motivated, is frequently a poor substitute for principle and procedure."[58] Although the Court cautioned that its decision in *Gault* was not meant to address "the totality of the relationship of the juvenile and the state," its opinion underscored the point that, where individual liberty was at stake, benevolent therapeutic intentions were no substitute for fundamental due process guarantees. As historian J. Herbie DiFonzo put it, "the juvenile court was, in short, ordered to act more like a court and less like an omnipotent and irresponsible social agency."[59] Thus, by the mid-twentieth century, the optimism of the early juvenile court reformers about the therapeutic potential of courts had given way to serious reappraisal.

From Juvenile Justice Reform to Therapeutic Divorce

The juvenile court movement was directly linked to broader efforts to reform the family court system. Indeed, many of the key architects of the juvenile court movement were also proponents of administering therapeutic divorce through reconstituted family courts. These reformers consciously sought to apply the therapeutic and rehabilitative ideals of the juvenile court movement to divorcing and separating spouses, whose behavior they viewed as both psychologically and socially irresponsible. As leading juvenile court reformer Paul W. Alexander explained, "Since the problems in a divorce case are so much more social than legal, why not take the embattled spouses out of the antiquated old divorce mill with its creaking legalistic machinery and put them into a socialized court, as we have done with the juvenile."[60]

Proponents of therapeutic divorce viewed most divorce seekers as sick or mentally unstable. Troubled marital partners were impulsive and vulnerable, often pursuing divorce out of immaturity or an inability to cope.[61] In their view, a petition for divorce was not a request for a legal remedy but rather a cry for help, to which the judicial system should respond by offering an array of remedial services. Thus, like the reformed juvenile court, the new family tribunal would substitute diagnosis and therapy for guilt and punishment. It would handle ailing marriages and disputing spouses "much as we handle our delinquent children— for often their behavior is not unlike that of a delinquent child and for much the same reasons."[62] Instead of looking only at the guilt of the defendant, the reformed family court would examine the whole marriage, endeavor to discover the basic causative factors, and seek to remove or rectify them, enlisting the aid of other sciences and disciplines and of all available community resources. Its overriding mission—like that of the reformed juvenile court—would be both protective and restorative: "Just as the fundamental purpose of the juvenile court is to protect children and restore them to society as healthy, happy, law-abiding future citizens, . . . so the outstanding objective of the family court is to protect the family and restore it to society as a healthy, law-abiding unit, the basic unit of our society."[63]

Established organizations such as the National Probation and Parole Association and the American Bar Association endorsed this importation of therapeutic principles from juvenile to family court. As early as 1917, the National Probation Association adopted a resolution recommending the organization of family courts on the juvenile court model.[64] Similarly, in a 1948 report prepared for the National Conference on Family Life, the American Bar Association (ABA) urged, "Instead of determining whether a spouse has misbehaved and . . . 'punishing' him by rewarding the aggrieved spouse with a divorce decree we would follow the general pattern of the juvenile court and endeavor to diagnose and treat, to discover the fundamental cause, then bring to bear all available resources to remove, or rectify it."[65]

Family court reformers also postulated a strong link between divorce and future delinquency, asserting that the children of broken marriages were doomed to be neglected as a result of their parents' breach of the familial bond.[66] This asserted link between divorce and childhood crime provided an additional rationale for modeling the proposed family tribunals after the reconstituted juvenile courts. Moreover, the link between delinquency and parental neglect empowered courts not only to judge the actions of youthful offenders, but also to determine, often without the safeguards of a formal trial, the fitness of the child's home and parents.[67]

Many attributes of the proposed therapeutic family tribunals were borrowed directly from earlier juvenile court reforms. Like the reformed juvenile court, the family tribunal would strive to "wed the legal and social sciences."[68] Its staff would include trained technicians and skilled specialists, such as social workers, clinical psychologists, marriage counselors, and custody investigators. Specially trained judges would work closely with these mental health professionals to serve the best interests of the family unit—conserving the marriage if at all possible and protecting the most vulnerable family members in cases of irreconcilable conflict.[69] As Herma Hill Kay has explained, both juvenile and family court proponents relied heavily on three key techniques: "a specialist judge to direct the court; a professional staff that will gather information as well as diagnose, prescribe treatment for, and sometimes actually treat, the emotional difficulties of the court's clientele; and the substitution of a non-adversary 'therapeutic' environment for the law's traditional adversary procedures."[70]

In addition to the goal of reducing the incidence of divorce, some reformers had a broader conception of the function of a therapeutic family court. These reformers posited that court-connected clinical services would help prepare divorcing partners for more successful remarriages, at the same time as the court's conciliatory atmosphere would reduce the likelihood of post-divorce conflict, particularly if children were involved. Thus, where a marriage could not be saved, divorce counseling could help the spouses gain insight into the reasons for their marriage failure so that they could avoid repetition of the disastrous pattern in their next relationship.[71] Like the wayward youth rehabilitated by the juvenile court, divorcing spouses would leave a therapeutic family court psychologically stronger and more intact than they had entered it. To achieve these broader therapeutic objectives, reformers urged judges to shift their focus from the divorce determination itself to the underlying causes and consequences of marital dissolution.

Some reformers were unsatisfied with separate juvenile and family courts, even if both pursued therapeutic goals. "For these reformers, the answer to juvenile crime, parental neglect or mistreatment, and divorce and marital instability seemed to lie in a singular family court with broadly based powers to try all criminal and civil cases related to domestic affairs."[72] Responding to these sentiments, a few jurisdictions created comprehensive family courts with jurisdiction over both juvenile and divorce matters.[73] The reach of these tribunals was expansive and their rationale mirrors more recent calls for unified family courts: "The court will undertake to deal more effectively with the family which produces the neglected or delinquent child, who is merely a chapter in the larger and more complicated problem. . . . It will be vested with both equitable and criminal jurisdiction and will deal with all charges against minors, with neglected children, and with all cases such as divorce, adoption, etc., in which the custody of children is in question."[74]

The early family court movement was largely unsuccessful in achieving either its instrumental or its therapeutic goals. Divorce rates did not decline during the early part of the twentieth century. Nor did the process of marital dissolution become noticeably less traumatic. In part, this was because the new court-connected services continued to operate within the established fault-based paradigm. Because the legal grounds for divorce in most states continued to require the identification of one guilty and one innocent party, adversary procedures remained primary and courts continued to stress the punitive aspects of the law in the award of child custody, alimony, and child support.[75] Moreover, the Supreme Court's rejection of the therapeutic underpinnings of the juvenile court movement undermined support for the early family court ideal.[76]

The conventional wisdom is that the therapeutic divorce movement "blossomed quickly, bloomed brightly, then died abruptly."[77] But our examination suggests that this tells only half the story. It is true that the no-fault divorce revolution largely rejected the claim that courts could—or should attempt to—save broken marriages. But the belief that courts can save children has proven more resilient. Indeed, many of the ideas that animated the movement for therapeutic divorce would resurface several decades later as elements of the new paradigm in family dispute resolution. Moreover, although the Supreme Court and other critics undermined the therapeutic premise of the early juvenile court, the juvenile court movement succeeded in legitimizing the hope that courts could function as curative agents.[78] That hope, in turn, became a prime catalyst for the creation of therapeutic tribunals in a number of areas, including the resolution of divorce-related parenting disputes.

From Fault and Sole Custody to Post-Divorce Co-parenting

The final two antecedents that paved the way for the contemporary paradigm shift in family dispute resolution were the widespread adoption of no-fault divorce and the accompanying shift from a sole custody regime to a post-divorce co-parenting model.

The shift from fault to no-fault divorce took place across the United States with remarkable speed. Indeed, one author has described the transformation as a "silent revolution" that occurred without extended public debate or significant political controversy.[79] In 1969, California became the first state to eliminate fault-based grounds for divorce. By 1976, forty-six other states had effectively removed fault impediments to dissolution, either by replacing their fault-based divorce statutes with pure no-fault legislation or by adding no-fault provisions to their existing grounds for divorce. By 1985—only sixteen years after California's pioneering divorce legislation—not a single American jurisdiction retained a pure fault-based system of divorce.[80]

The elimination of fault as a prerequisite to divorce significantly undermined the utility of traditional adversary procedures for resolving divorce-related matters. No longer was it necessary for a court to determine whether a spouse had engaged in actionable behavior or to ascertain who was responsible for the breakdown of a marriage— backward-looking tasks for which the adversary process was arguably well suited. Instead, the primary role of the divorce court—in cases where the parties were not already in accord—was to determine the financial and parenting consequences of the marital dissolution. For these more forward-looking tasks of family reorganization, adversary procedures were, at best, unwarranted.

Moreover, the deregulation of intimate relationships that accompanied the no-fault divorce revolution provided an important impetus for the adoption of non-adversarial dispute resolution processes such as mediation. With the shift from fault to no-fault divorce, the court system largely abandoned its role as the moral arbiter of marital behavior and ceded to divorcing couples themselves the authority to determine whether and how to end their union.[81] Unlike formal adjudication, mediation offered divorcing couples a way to exercise this authority privately and to order their own post-divorce affairs. Where parties could not agree, however, the prevailing best interests standard allowed courts to continue to consider fault, as well as any other factors the judge deemed relevant to the child's welfare.

Perhaps even more important than the shift from fault-based to no-fault divorce was the displacement of the prevailing sole custody regime in favor of post-divorce co-parenting. Under the fault-based divorce system, the job of the court in resolving contested custody cases had been to identify a single, preferred custodian and assign that parent primary legal rights to the child. As Andrew Schepard has explained, the court system:

conceived of a custody dispute much like a will contest. The parents' marriage, like the decedent, was dead. Parents, like the heirs, were in dispute about the distribution of one of the assets of the estate—their children. The . . . court's role was, after trial, to determine which heir/parent was more morally or psychologically worthy to control the children. . . . Once the court distributed custody rights, its role in facilitating the ongoing process of reorganizing the child's relationships with both parents was over, except for enforcement or modification of its initial award, tasks also accomplished through adversary process.[82]

Prevailing psychological theory supported this sole custody model. In their influential book *Beyond the Best Interests of the Child*, Professors Goldstein, Freud, and Solnit asserted that the interests of children would be best served if courts ensured the continuity of the child's relationship with one "psychological parent" to whom the child was already attached.[83] Indeed, the authors placed such importance on the stability of this primary custodial relationship that they advocated granting the psychological parent the power to preclude visitation by the other parent, for fear that it would be emotionally disruptive.[84] Although no court took the policy of stability this far, the authors' emphasis on a child's relationship with a single psychological parent provided an important justification for the sole custody model.

The sole custody model also cohered with then-prevailing gender roles within the family—roles that were reflected in the tender years doctrine applied, either formally or informally, in many states. The doctrine identified mothers as the preferred custodians for young children upon divorce, unless a mother could be proven unfit. This emphasis on the mother–child bond discouraged some divorcing fathers from seeking custody at all; where custody disputes did occur, the focus on maternal fitness turned them into intense adversarial contests, involving claims and counter-accusations of unfitness that would have qualified as grounds for divorce under the fault-based regime.[85]

The legal and social movement for gender equality that began in the 1970s undermined both the tender years doctrine and the sole psychological parent model.[86] Faced with constitutional challenges to gender-based classifications, courts abandoned reliance on the tender years doctrine that many had used to operationalize the best interests of the child standard in disputed custody cases. At the same time, more fathers began to contest custody, often asserting claims based on equal parenting rights. Custody courts were thus faced with a burgeoning caseload at the same time as they lost the "lodestone doctrine" that had provided certainty in decision-making and limited the number of custody contests.[87]

At the same time, prevailing psychological theory shifted away from Goldstein, Freud, and Solnit's emphasis on a single psychological parent, in favor of the view that even young children were capable of forming close emotional attachments to more than one parent. These new theories coincided with growing research on the importance of fathers in a child's life. This research fueled an emerging mental health consensus that children generally do best if they are able to maintain ongoing relationships with both parents following divorce or parental separation—a result that the sole custody model failed to facilitate. Thus, a legal regime originally designed to effectuate the best interests of children was now subject to critique as failing to serve children's needs.

The legal response to these developments was the widespread endorsement of joint custody—a development that commentators have described as a "small revolution . . . in child custody law."[88] The core premise of this revolution is that, while divorce may terminate the spousal bond, it does not dissolve the parenting partnership.[89] As family law scholar Patrick Parkinson recently explained, "The history of family law reform in the last twenty years could be said to be the history of abandonment of the assumption, fundamental to the divorce reform movement of the early 1970's, that divorce could dissolve the family as well as the marriage when there are children."[90]

States have embraced the shift from sole custody to post-divorce co-parenting in a variety of ways. Virtually all states now authorize courts to award joint custody—both legal and physical—following a divorce or parental separation. A number of states have adopted a preference for some form of joint custody, particularly in cases where both parents consent. Some states allow for such an award over the objection of one or even both parents.[91] Other states have adopted so-called "friendly parent" provisions, which give priority in contested custody proceedings to the parent who is more likely to encourage the other parent's involvement in the child's life. An increasing number of states have rejected entirely the traditional labels of custody and visitation and have replaced them with terms such as "time-sharing" or "parenting time" that reflect the parents' equal legal status and ongoing joint involvement in a child's post-divorce life.[92]

The shift from sole custody to joint parenting required a rethinking of the procedural role of the custody court. Under a post-divorce co-parenting regime, the court's job is no longer to make a one-time custody allocation, but rather to supervise the ongoing reorganization of a family. As Andrew Schepard has written, a custody court in a co-parenting regime:

> can be analogized to a bankruptcy court supervising the reorganization of a potentially viable business in current financial distress. The business is raising children and the parents—the managers of the business—are in conflict about how that task is to be accomplished. The court's aim is to get the managers to voluntarily agree on a parenting plan rather than impose one on them. . . . The court has an ongoing role in managing parental conflict; parents have continuing access to the settlement processes if future disputes arise or modification of the parenting plan is necessary because of changed circumstances.[93]

Neither adjudication nor adversary procedures are well suited to accomplishing these forward-looking, managerial tasks. Moreover, because joint custody works best when parents are able to cooperate and make decisions together, divorcing and separating families are best served by judicial processes that reduce, rather than exacerbate, conflict. These are precisely the type of interventions envisioned by the paradigm shift in family dispute resolution.

Conclusion

This brief historical explanation demonstrates the close connection between changes in substantive family law doctrine and changes in family dispute resolution. In the nineteenth century, the shift from legislative to judicial divorce and the rejection of patriarchal custody rules in favor of a judicially determined "best interests of the child" standard expanded and transformed the judicial role in resolving intra-family disputes. To be sure, judges initially exercised their expanded powers within a traditional adversary framework. But twentieth-century doctrinal changes fundamentally undermined this adversary regime. In particular, the shift from fault to no-fault divorce and the endorsement of post-divorce co-parenting transformed the role of the custody court and undermined the utility of adversary procedures in effectuating this new role. The rise of the new paradigm is largely a response to this transformation.

Our historical examination also shows the overlap and shifting boundary between the public and private aspects of family law. The therapeutic and rehabilitative ideals that originated in the public realm of juvenile justice migrated in the twentieth century to the more private context of divorce and custody disputes. Although no-fault divorce statutes initially rejected the notion of therapeutic divorce, more recent family court reformers have enthusiastically embraced therapeutic approaches to handling divorce-related parenting disputes. Similarly, the notion that courts play an important role in promoting children's welfare initially gained traction in the public realm of child abuse and neglect proceedings; more recently, it has come to dominate judicial approaches to custody disputes between private parties. Recent calls for unified family courts similarly draw on the efforts of early juvenile court reformers to link parental separation with both child neglect and juvenile delinquency.

Finally, our historical analysis reveals that changes in family dispute resolution affect families quite differently, depending on their social and economic circumstances. For example, the enhanced judicial attention to child welfare that characterized nineteenth-century family law had quite different consequences for families with and without financial means. For wealthy families, the primary impact of the increased emphasis on children's interests was to shift power in family disputes from husbands to wives and from fathers to mothers. For poor families, by contrast, the primary impact of the enhanced judicial role was to transfer child-rearing authority from parents to the state or other third-party caretakers. Similarly, whereas middle- and upper-class women were able to use the discourse of domesticity to defeat their husbands' traditional child custody rights, lower-class women risked losing custody of their children if they failed to exhibit the feminine virtues associated with domesticity.

The socioeconomic status of the perceived targets of family reform also affected the success of these reform efforts. For example, the early juvenile court movement spread rapidly, in part because its therapeutic orientation was viewed as a desirable way of "rescuing" lower-class children from the unhealthy influences of their homes and communities. By contrast, the movement for therapeutic divorce in the 1960s foundered, in part because the increasing numbers of middle- and upper-class divorce seekers were unwilling to subject themselves and their social peers to state-mandated judicial therapy. As succeeding chapters will explore, similar socioeconomic factors continue to influence the impact and direction of contemporary family court reforms.

the Adversary System and the
as a Response

Today's family dispute resolution regime rests on a sharp and success-ful critique of adversary family justice. That critique highlighted the detrimental impact of adversary processes on children and on disput-ing families. It also emphasized the burdens that the adversary regime imposed on the judicial system and the negative impact of adversary practice on family lawyers and on the legal profession more generally. The paradigm shift in family dispute resolution developed largely as a response to this critique. This chapter examines the late twentieth-century critique of adversary family justice and explains how it has shaped today's dispute resolution regime.

Adversary Processes Harm Children

Critics argued first and foremost that reliance on adversary processes to resolve family disputes harms children. They pointed to exten-sive social science research, which shows that children are adversely affected by parental conflict during and after separation and divorce. While experts disagree about the magnitude and long-term effects of divorce on children, virtually all researchers acknowledge that "paren-tal conflict is toxic for children in divorce."[1] The higher the levels of parental conflict to which children are exposed, the more negative the effects of family dissolution.[2] Children "caught in the crossfire of parental acrimony" are at increased risk for a myriad of emotional, behavioral, and psychological problems.[3] Moreover, although actual litigation is the exception and settlement of parenting disputes the norm even under an adversary regime, "the hostile and competitive attitude which prospective litigation creates pervades the entire pro-cess of negotiating a settlement."[4]

Critics also noted that reliance on adversary procedures strains parent–child relationships at a time when children are most in need of effective and consistent parenting. "As the parental alliance weakens, the behavior standards for the children decline. If parents quarrel openly in front of the children, and show contempt for each other, the atmosphere of mutual respect that underlies their joint authority and effective co-parenting is seriously weakened."[5] While studies indicate that a strong parent–child relationship can buffer children from inter-parental conflict, high levels of divorce-related conflict tend to erode both the ability of parents to cooperate and their capacity to parent effectively. "As a consequence of divided parental authority and lack of respect for each other, parenting tends to become more problematic: discipline is more coercive, and expectations are more inconsistent, all of which are predictive of more negative and distant parent–child relationships and an increase in children's emotional and behavioral problems."[6] Children who are caught in the middle of their parents' conflict, or who are pressured to side with one parent or the other, are particularly vulnerable.

Critics emphasized that reliance on adversary procedures to resolve parenting disputes at best fails to mitigate parental conflict; at worst, it exacerbates and prolongs discord. For example, traditional adversary tactics such as advising a client not to talk to the other spouse, making extreme demands to gain leverage in negotiations, and filing pleadings that characterize the other parent in a negative light, diminish the prospects for future cooperation, even if the dispute settles, rather than proceeds to trial. Moreover, when a custody case does go to trial, the evidence and counterevidence of bad behavior and deficient parenting typically introduced to buttress a client's position exacerbates existing hostility and engenders long-term mutual distrust. As one critic colorfully put it, "the formal nature of the courts pits the parties against one another like two scorpions in a bottle, at a time when they are most angry and hostile toward one another."[7] Thus, participation in litigation or adversary negotiations pushes parents into antagonistic positions which imperil children and from which it can be difficult to retreat.[8]

Critics also pointed out that adversary procedures do little to teach parents how to manage their conflict or to relate to each other after the court process is over. Where parties are represented by counsel, direct communication between parents is often discouraged, and lawyers generally conduct negotiations with little participation by the parents themselves. Children are similarly absent from the dispute resolution process, save for the unusual case where children are separately represented by counsel or interviewed by fact-finders. Moreover, because of ethical constraints and confidentiality concerns, therapists who interact with only one of the parties to the divorce conflict "can encourage uncompromising stands, reify distorted views of the other parent, write recommendations, and even testify on behalf of a parent with little or no understanding of the child's needs, the other parent's position, or the couple and family dynamics."[9] Thus, even where cases settle without resort to a contested trial, the adversary paradigm in which such settlements occur leaves many parents ill equipped to manage the day-to-day challenges of post-divorce child-rearing.

Because adversary procedures encourage and prolong parental conflict, and because such conflict harms children, critics argued persuasively that reliance on such practices to resolve parenting disputes disserves children and undermines family law's purported goal of fostering children's best interests.[10]

Adversary Processes Harm Parents and Families

Reformers also argued that adversary processes harm parents and families in several ways. First, reliance on adversary procedures strains family relationships and has a detrimental impact on parents' ability to cooperate after divorce or separation. As critics have pointed out, where children are involved, divorce does not dissolve the family, but rather transforms it; while divorce may terminate the spousal bond, it does not dissolve the parenting partnership.[11] Thus, divorce today "is not the end of a relationship but a restructuring of a continuing relationship."[12] The use of adversary procedures at the time of divorce or parental separation impedes and distorts this transformation process. As a leading divorce researcher has explained: "The basic nature of the adversarial process pits parents against each other, encourages polarized and positional thinking about each other's deficiencies, and discourages parental communication, cooperation, and more mature thinking about children's needs at a critical time of change and upheaval. Possible future constructive relationships between parents are often thus destroyed."[13]

In addition, critics argued that the win/lose orientation of traditional, adversarial procedures denigrates and diminishes the role of the "losing," noncustodial parent, 70 percent of whom are men.[14] Relegated to the role of a visitor, noncustodial parents too often react by distancing themselves from their pre-divorce family and eventually dropping out of their children's lives, to the detriment of both themselves and their children.[15] Although contact between nonresidential fathers and their children has increased over the past decade, many noncustodial parents remain absent from their children's lives. As Robert Emery notes, the modal level of contact between divorced, nonresidential parents and their children ranges between every other weekend and several times a year, and the frequency of this contact drops off sharply over time, particularly in conjunction with events such as remarriage or relocation.[16] Research involving noncustodial fathers suggests that the win/lose orientation of adversary divorce procedures contributes significantly to this disengagement process.[17]

Critics also emphasized that adversary procedures are expensive and time-consuming; they thus divert both financial and other parental resources that would be better spent directly on children, at a time when children are likely to need extra care and parental attention, and when family budgets must stretch to cover the expenses of two households.[18] Moreover, the delay inherent in the litigation process is especially detrimental to a child's sense of time. Depending on a child's age, what seems like a short amount of time to an adult involved in a custody dispute can seem like an eternity to a child.[19] Children are also less capable than are adults of dealing with the uncertainty and emotional turmoil associated with prolonged custody litigation.[20]

Some research also indicates that inter-parental conflict may be detrimental to parents' physical and emotional health. At least one study found a strong correlation between inter-parental conflict and parents' emotional problems; other studies suggest that high-conflict parents are at increased risk for severe psychopathology and substance abuse.[21] Thus, critics argued that adherence to a procedural regime that fails to mitigate conflict may endanger the health of parents as well as children.

Critics of traditional processes also cautioned that parents may be less invested in custody arrangements imposed by judges or negotiated by lawyers in the shadow of the courthouse than they would be in arrangements crafted as part of a more collaborative and participatory process.[22] Mediation research supports this assertion. Most studies report higher rates of compliance with mediated parenting agreements than with resolutions reached through the adversarial process.[23] Thus, reliance on adversarial processes may decrease the durability of post-divorce parenting arrangements and increase the likelihood of relitigation.

Critics also pointed out that adversarial procedures tend to focus on which parent will receive custody, rather than on the day-to-day details of children's lives. As a result, adjudicated and attorney-negotiated custody orders are often phrased in general language such as "primary custody to mom, with liberal visitation rights to dad"; mediated agreements and agreements reached through a collaborative process, by contrast, are much more likely to include specifics about children's schedules, parental communication, and child-related decision-making. Studies indicate that spelling out such details in advance helps minimize post-divorce conflict and may encourage more stable parenting arrangements.[24]

Recent research suggests that the use of mediation and other, less adversarial dispute resolution processes can mitigate some of the detrimental effects of divorce and parental separation on children and families. In a twelve-year follow-up study of high-conflict families who were randomly assigned either to mediate or to adjudicate their custody disputes, Robert Emery and his colleagues found that parents who mediated reported significantly less parental conflict and significantly more involvement by noncustodial parents in their children's lives than the adversary group. Nonresidential parents who mediated were also better parents, according to ratings given by the child's residential parent. Thus, twelve years after being randomly assigned to mediation, residential parents reported that the nonresidential parent was significantly more likely to discuss parenting problems with them and to have had a greater influence on child-rearing decisions, in comparison to parents in the adversarial group. Nonresidential parents who mediated were also significantly more involved in the children's discipline, moral training, school events, recreation, and vacations. Despite this greater degree of co-parenting, parents who mediated reported significantly *less* post-divorce conflict than did parents who litigated. Thus, relative to adversary settlement, mediation produced *both* higher levels of nonresidential parental involvement *and* less co-parenting conflict—both of which have been identified as beneficial to children.[25]

Emery's findings are consistent with those of earlier studies, which suggested that "divorce education, custody mediation and mediation/ arbitration interventions for parents in high conflict are often effective in reducing conflict and promoting communication between parents during and after separation or divorce."[26] On the other hand, Emery's study found no significant differences in the mental health of children whose parents mediated, as compared to children whose parents did not—a result that is also consistent with prior research.[27] Thus, while mediation may reduce parental conflict and enhance post-divorce cooperation, these benefits may not translate directly into tangible measures of child well-being.

Adversary Processes Harm the Judicial System

In addition to harming children and families, critics of the adversary paradigm argued that overreliance on adversary processes to resolve parenting disputes imposes significant costs on the judicial system. In particular, critics noted that contested custody cases consume disproportionate amounts of court resources and are emotionally draining for judges. Indeed, many judges identify custody trials as among the most difficult and least satisfying aspects of their work.[28]

Litigants, too, tend to express dissatisfaction with the adversary process, even when they prevail at trial. For example, between 50 and 70 percent of participants in a nationwide study of custody cases in the mid-1990s characterized the adversarial system as "impersonal, intimidating and intrusive."[29] Similarly, 71 percent of divorcing parents in a Connecticut study reported that the court process escalated their level of conflict and distrust "to a further extreme."[30] More generally, although participant involvement in the process is an important factor in achieving a durable divorce or custody resolution, "the complexity of litigation leaves many individuals feeling lost, confused and uninvolved."[31]

Proponents of the new paradigm also cite studies that indicate higher levels of participant satisfaction with mediation than with litigation or adversary settlement. For example, in their study of divorcing families randomly assigned either to mediate or to continue with adversary procedures, Emery and his colleagues found that, on average, parents who mediated were more satisfied than parents who litigated, both with respect to their participation in the process and with respect to the protection of their rights.[32] Moreover, these results were consistent across time: parents were happier with mediation than with adversary settlement when they were first queried six weeks after dispute resolution, a year and a half later, and again twelve years after the initial settlement.[33] These results are consistent with other studies which have found that divorcing parents generally report high levels of satisfaction with mediation, and that satisfaction levels are higher following mediation than they are following adversarial settlement.[34]

There is one important caveat to these findings. Several studies, including Emery's research, suggest that women who litigate custody disputes may be more satisfied with the outcomes than mothers who mediate, at least under the judicial custody standards that prevailed during the 1980s and 1990s. Emery suggests that this finding reflects the fact that mothers in his adversary settlement group almost always won full legal and physical custody, while mediation gave fathers more of a voice and was more likely to result in joint legal (but not joint physical) custody arrangements.[35] Other studies have found no significant gender differences and have reported that both mothers and fathers were more satisfied with mediation than with adversary resolution of their disputes.[36]

Research indicates that mediation and other collaborative processes help parents settle their disputes without appearing in front of a judge.[37] To be sure, most contested custody cases eventually settle; however, mediation appears to increase the likelihood of settlement. Mediated cases are also likely to settle earlier in the process and without resort to multiple pretrial hearings. In Emery's recent study, for example, 72 percent of cases randomly assigned to continue with adversary processes appeared in front of a judge, compared to only 11 percent of cases randomly assigned to mediation. Put another way, cases randomly selected to continue with litigation were nearly seven times more likely to be resolved by a judge than were cases randomly assigned to mediation. Moreover, even when mediation did not end in a settlement, parents in

Emery's study often settled subsequently outside of court, with the aid of their lawyers. Proponents of the new paradigm point to these and similar results to suggest that moving away from adversary procedures will benefit the judicial system by increasing settlement rates and decreasing the need for costly trials.

Adversary Processes Harm Lawyers and Decrease Confidence in the Legal System

Finally, critics and court reformers argued that reliance on adversary processes to resolve family disputes negatively affects lawyers and decreases public confidence in the legal profession. Critics have noted the sharp increase in *pro se* representation in family cases, even by some parties who can afford legal representation.[38] Couples who wish to divorce cooperatively are wary that lawyers will aggravate and prolong conflict and that seeking legal representation will impede their ability to control the dispute resolution process.

Parents who do engage counsel often express dissatisfaction with their attorneys. A 1999 survey of divorcing parents and their children in Connecticut validates these concerns. Parents and children reported that their attorneys failed to provide adequate guidance, information, or quality of services. They also complained that the adversary divorce process took control of their lives and that it was too long, too costly, and too inefficient.[39] Court reformers have also noted that divorce lawyers are on the receiving end of more ethics complaints than lawyers in other fields of practice.[40] Although most lawyers are exonerated, reformers claim that the number of complaints initiated is another reflection of public dissatisfaction with the adversary process.

Finally, family lawyers themselves have noted the toll that practicing within an adversary paradigm can impose. They point to high levels of frustration and burnout among family practitioners, who are more likely than attorneys in other specialties to face malpractice suits and fee complaints from dissatisfied clients. "Clients are almost never happy, and often their frustration and dissatisfaction are directed at the lawyer who was supposed to make it all better. Lawyers who went into the domestic practice to help people with real life problems often become bitter, cynical, and unhappy with their work."[41] Family lawyers also complain that traditional models of zealous client advocacy constrain their ability to consider the well-being of children or to pursue the best interests of the family as a whole.[42]

Lawyer dissatisfaction with traditional adversary processes has led some family lawyers to develop new models of practice, including collaborative law in which lawyers and their clients sign a binding agreement to attempt to resolve divorce-related issues without resort to court proceedings.[43] If settlement efforts are unsuccessful, the collaborative attorneys must withdraw from representing the clients in litigation. The rapid growth of collaborative family lawyering "epitomizes the deep discomfort with the traditional adversarial model experienced by many lawyers and clients."[44] As collaborative family practitioners, lawyers who have become disillusioned with traditional adversary practice can maintain their identity as attorneys, while offering their clients a more holistic and less adversarial model of representation.[45]

The New Paradigm as a Response to the Critique

The paradigm shift in family dispute resolution responds directly to this critique of adversary family justice. Its primary target is parental conflict and its focus is to enhance the well-being of children and families by reducing the conflict associated with parental separation and divorce. To this end, the new paradigm seeks to educate parents about the detrimental impact of separation-related conflict and the importance of developing a positive co-parenting relationship. Parents are urged to separate their ruptured bond as spouses or romantic partners, from their ongoing affiliation as parents. To reduce the confining influence of law on this renegotiation project, the new paradigm reconceptualizes family disputes as ongoing social and emotional processes, rather than discrete legal events. "Thus recharacterized, family disputes call not for zealous legal approaches, but for interventions that are collaborative, holistic and interdisciplinary, because these are the types of interventions most likely to address the families' underlying dysfunction and emotional needs."[46]

Family court systems across the country have embraced this recharacterization. As a result, they have adopted an array of educational and settlement-oriented interventions that deemphasize adjudication and backward-looking judgment in favor of planning and capacity-building processes that emphasize family reorganization and that seek to empower parents to resolve their own family disputes. Increasing numbers of family lawyers have retooled themselves as mediators, collaborators, and dispute resolution advocates in order to participate in these less adversarial processes and reorient their practices away from litigation.

Critiquing the Critique

Although the critique of adversary family justice has been widespread, it has not been unanimous. A handful of judges and academic commentators, as well as many family lawyers, have defended the value of adversary procedures and have cautioned against their complete rejection in resolving intra-family disputes.[47] Critics have also questioned whether courts are capable of achieving some of the more expansive goals of the new paradigm. "While there are those that believe family courts can reach the lofty goals of making parents and children better, courts are not generally able to meet those goals because the judiciary rarely has control over resources."[48] Other scholars have suggested that asking courts and judges to address the complex dynamics of family reorganization may compromise their ability to achieve other important goals, such as fairness, finality, and timely resolution of disputes.[49] Still others have suggested that the lack of lawyers in most family cases has undermined the functioning of the adversary system, which is built on the assumption that both parties will have legal representation.[50] Finally, several family law scholars have drawn cautionary parallels between the therapeutic ambitions of today's problem-solving family courts and the excesses of the juvenile court movement of the early 1900s.[51] Proponents of the new paradigm have largely discounted these concerns.

Conclusion

The new paradigm in family dispute resolution rests on a thoroughgoing critique of adversarial family justice. Proponents of the new paradigm have argued forcefully that our traditional reliance on adversary processes to resolve disputes about raising children disserves the interests of children and their families. Reformers have also highlighted the costs of adversary justice to the court system and to lawyers and the legal profession. The new paradigm attempts to address these shortcomings by reframing and expanding the role of family courts, while simultaneously reducing the primacy of legal norms and procedures. The next chapter examines this paradox.

3

Expanded Courts with Diminished Legal Norms

At the heart of the paradigm shift in family dispute resolution is a striking juxtaposition. The new paradigm expands the vision and role of family courts at the same time as it reduces the primacy and relevance of legal norms. The result is a more powerful court system that is less constrained by legal limitations than its more traditional predecessor. While such an untethered court system may benefit families and children in need of services, it also poses substantial risks, both to the individuals and families it serves and to the larger legal system.

The Expanding Vision of Family Courts

A core element of the new paradigm is a significantly expanded vision of the role of family courts. According to this expanded vision, resolving disputed legal issues is too narrow an objective for an effective family court. Rather, to achieve its mission, an effective family court must address not only the parties' immediate legal needs, but also the underlying family dynamics and future well-being of the children and families who appear before it. Moreover, because divorce and parental separation no longer signal the end of a relationship, but rather the restructuring of a continuing parenting partnership, both the range of relevant issues and the potential duration of court involvement in family life have expanded dramatically.

Central to this expanded vision is the belief that most family disputes are not discrete legal events, but ongoing social and emotional processes.[1] As such, family disputes call *not* for narrow, time-limited judicial decision-making, but for court interventions that are comprehensive, holistic, and interdisciplinary, because these are the types of interventions most likely to address the families' underlying needs.[2] Understanding family conflict as primarily a social and emotional process, rather than a legal event, also reduces the primacy of lawyers in handling these disputes and enhances the role of nonlegal professionals in the family court system.

This new understanding of family disputes has led to a reformulation of the goals of legal intervention in the family. Traditionally, legal intervention was a backward-looking process, designed primarily to assign blame and allocate rights. Under the new paradigm, by contrast, judges and affiliated court personnel assume the much more forward-looking task of supervising a process of family reorganization. As Andrew Schepard has noted, family court judges no longer function primarily as faultfinders or rights adjudicators, but rather as ongoing conflict managers.[3] As a result, "the primary role of family courts has shifted from adjudication of disputes to proactive management of family law-related problems of individuals subject to their jurisdiction."[4]

The therapeutic jurisprudence movement embodies this forward-looking orientation. From a therapeutic perspective, legal intervention in the family strives not merely to resolve disputes, but to improve the material and psychological well-being of individuals and families in conflict.[5] Effective family court systems embrace this therapeutic role by attempting to understand and address underlying family dynamics and by using judicial authority "to motivate individuals to accept needed services and to monitor their compliance and progress."[6] Moreover, to achieve these therapeutic goals, family courts have adopted systems that deemphasize authoritative, third-party dispute resolution in favor of capacity-building processes that seek to empower family members to manage conflict and to develop positive post-separation relationships. Proponents of the new paradigm urge that these nonlegal services be court-based to facilitate accessibility and accountability.[7] As the American Bar Association, a major proponent of model family courts, explains, the court's mission is to provide families with "comprehensive services . . . for children and families in the courts."[8]

The court system's perceived responsibility to children provides strong support for this expanded vision. Historically, the legal system advanced children's interests primarily by adopting child-focused substantive legal rules, most notably the "best interests of the child" standard, to resolve contested cases about children—particularly custody disputes between parents. Under the new paradigm, by contrast, the "best interests of the child" has evolved from a legal standard used to resolve contested cases to the overriding mission of the family court. Consistent with this fundamental mission, the primary goal of court involvement is to protect and promote children's well-being, and both the processes and the outcomes of family law are increasingly measured against this goal.

As proponents of the new paradigm have emphasized, a cardinal threat to children's well-being is prolonged parental conflict, both during and after divorce or separation. In order to serve children's interests, therefore, family courts must help parents ameliorate and manage conflict, rather than simply resolving their immediate disputes. To do this, judicial processes must shift their focus from past events to future well-being and must help parents modify their behavior and retool their relationship in order to facilitate an optimal environment for children. "Addressing the best interest of children requires all possible efforts to reduce—or better, resolve conflict between their parents, thereby creating the highest possible level of family functioning in the post-separation family environment."[9] Only if courts embrace this overriding mission of conflict management will children be shielded from the most hazardous risk factors of separation and divorce, and only then will their best interests be served.[10]

Some commentators have argued that the vision of family courts should expand beyond managing the parties' post-separation behavior, to address their emotional relationships as well. For example, one noted legal scholar recently argued that family law doctrines and court processes should cultivate forgiveness, as a way of reducing inter-parental hostility and conflict after divorce or separation. Drawing on a growing body of literature on the role of emotions in law, Soledad Maldonado argues that fault considerations should be excised from all aspects of divorce proceedings, and that high-conflict divorce and custody litigants should be required to participate in a court-connected forgiveness education program.[11] Similarly, Clare Huntington has proposed a "reparative model" of family law and practice that would "facilitate better relationships between former family members" by fully "embracing the emotional life of familial disputants."[12] Along the same lines, Marsha Freeman has advocated that family courts apply the concepts and methods of therapeutic jurisprudence and restorative justice in order to encourage parties to "accept their own responsibility in bringing about the dissolution and learn to forgive (if not forget) the other's role in it, simultaneously accepting the value of learning to live effectively as a post-dissolution family unit."[13] What animates these and similar proposals is the conviction that, to achieve their mission of serving children and families, family courts must move beyond legal boundaries to address the underlying emotional and psychological needs of the individuals and families who appear before them.[14]

The role and vision of the family court has expanded in time as well as in scope. Unlike the clean-break philosophy that animated early no-fault divorce reform, the new dispute resolution paradigm is committed to the idea that, while divorce may terminate the spousal bond, it does not dissolve the parenting partnership.[15] In popular parlance, "parents are forever."[16] Thus, divorce and parental separation no longer signal the end of a relationship, but instead entail the restructuring of an on-going—if sometimes contentious—parenting partnership. The court system plays an important role in managing that restructuring process.

The shift from a sole custody to a joint parenting regime frames the court's restructuring project. Under the old, sole custody model, the court's job in resolving divorce-related parenting disputes was to identify a single, primary custodian and to grant plenary authority to that parent, with the goal of ensuring stability for the child and minimizing the need for future judicial involvement.[17] The working assumption was that both parents should be able to reorganize their lives with only residual ties to their former partner and limited opportunity for further discord. To be sure, this model left room for some post-divorce disputes—for example, petitions to modify custody or to enforce child support obligations, but courts were generally reluctant to intervene, and the standard for modifying custody was quite high.

Under today's joint parenting regime, by contrast, divorced and separated parents are expected to collaborate on major decisions involving their children, as well as manage the frequent and continuing contact with both parents that the joint parenting model envisions. As a result, the lives of the parents remain deeply entwined, and opportunities for disagreement abound. While most divorced and separated parents are able to negotiate these disagreements without further resort to court processes, a substantial minority are not.[18]

Not surprisingly, the rise of the new paradigm has coincided with a sharp increase in post-dissolution parenting litigation. Courts are now routinely called on to decide such child-rearing issues as where a child should attend school, what medical care a child should receive, and whether a child should participate in a particular extracurricular activity. While a few commentators have argued that courts should refuse to entertain these post-separation disputes,[19] others have disagreed, and family courts are understandably reluctant to block the courthouse door. Instead, courts have adopted a variety of programs and services designed to reduce conflict and help parents manage their post-separation relationship.[20] These services include mandatory parenting education classes designed to enhance communication and problem-solving skills; supervised visitation programs, which ensure the safety of children visiting parents where past abuse or violence is a concern; and quasi-judicial parenting coordinators, who are appointed to help high-conflict families adhere to concrete parenting plans and resolve ongoing disputes arising under these plans. While these services are designed to avoid adversarial litigation, they also result in protracted court involvement in the post-separation lives of families and children.[21]

Coinciding with the new paradigm, post-divorce relocation disputes have also risen dramatically in recent years.[22] This is not surprising. Under the former, sole custody regime, a custodial parent had the presumptive right to choose or change a child's residence, and a nonresidential parent had little authority to challenge that decision.[23] Under today's joint parenting regime, by contrast, a parent who seeks to change a child's principal residence must generally seek the agreement of the other parent. If the nonresidential parent does not consent to the move, the residential parent must obtain judicial permission to relocate.[24] Often that permission is not forthcoming or is granted with significant strings attached.[25]

Moreover, states have adopted a "bewildering variety of approaches" to deciding relocation disputes. Indeed, one noted scholar has described the current state of relocation law across the United States as a "hodgepodge of presumptions, burdens, factors and lists."[26] In recent years, the trend has been to move toward an open-ended best interests of the child test—a standard that minimizes predictability for litigants and grants maximum discretion and oversight to judges.

Remarriage and stepparenthood further increase the opportunities for post-separation parenting disputes. As chapter 4 details, stepfamilies formed by marriage or by cohabitation have become America's fastest growing family form;[27] indeed, it is estimated that one-third of U.S. children will live in a remarried or cohabiting stepfamily before reaching adulthood.[28] These stepfamily relationships are often impermanent, as divorce and separation rates for stepfamilies are significantly higher than for first marriages. While traditional family law doctrine generally refused to recognize any legal ties between stepparents and children after the termination of the stepparent's relationship with the child's biological parent, modern courts are increasingly likely to consider stepparents' claims for visitation and custody, based on their relationship with the child. These developments are consistent with the more general trend of granting judicially cognizable rights and obligations to adults who function as parents, regardless of their biological or marital status. Recognition of such "de facto parenthood" is based on the belief "'that disruption of a child's preexisting relationship with a non-biological parent can be potentially harmful to the child,' thus warranting State intrusion into the private realm of the family."[29] While such judicial recognition arguably serves the best interests of the children involved in these cases, it also expands the category of post-dissolution disputes eligible for judicial intervention and increases the number and types of families subject to ongoing court supervision.

An expanded vision of the role of courts is thus central to the new paradigm in family dispute resolution. Because child well-being is the overriding goal, and family disputes are understood as ongoing processes rather than discrete legal events, courts must deploy a broader and more enduring array of tools and services to achieve their mission. The goal of these expanded court-based interventions is not merely to resolve existing legal disputes, but to supervise the ongoing reorganization of family relationships in order to minimize parental conflict and to promote the well-being of children.

The Diminishing Role of Legal Norms in Resolving Family Disputes

The new paradigm, then, embraces an expanded vision and includes an ambitious set of goals for family courts. At the same time, however, it envisions a diminished role for legal norms in the resolution of parenting disputes. As one British legal scholar described the late twentieth-century family court movement in the United States and Britain: "Moves away from adversary justice and towards a family court are in effect moves towards the delegalization of family dispute settlement."[30] Several elements of the new paradigm contribute to this delegalization process, which is far more pronounced for parenting disputes than for other types of family cases, where legal norms remain important. While the delegalization of parenting disputes offers potential benefits for families and children, it also poses significant risks, particularly when coupled with the ambitious agenda of today's family courts.

Recharacterization of Family Disputes

The recharacterization of parenting disputes from legal events to ongoing, multifaceted processes diminishes the importance of legal norms in family dispute resolution. This reframing shifts the court's focus from applying legal standards to adjudicate conflicting claims, to providing families with tools and services related to child well-being and co-parenting after divorce or separation.[31] These new tasks call not for authoritative legal norms, but rather for expertise from the fields of mental health and child development. As a result, courts increasingly turn to nonlegal staff—professional and nonprofessional—to perform a variety of court-connected functions. These functions include parent education, mental health assessment, and parenting evaluation, designed to assist parties and provide information to the court on issues related to child well-being and family relationships. Although judges still serve as the ultimate backstop if other dispute resolution mechanisms fail, decision-making functions are increasingly delegated to nonlegal staff who rely on party self-determination or staff evaluation that draws more on psychology and social work than on legal doctrine.

These changes mark a partial return to the philosophy and ambitious agenda of progressive-era juvenile courts and early advocates of therapeutic divorce.[32] Indeed, one of the leading juvenile court judges of that era justified the absence of lawyers in juvenile court by explaining that "a child's case is not a legal case."[33] Advocates of the new paradigm similarly justify the enhanced role of nonlegal professionals in family court by asserting that family disputes are occasions for therapeutic interventions rather than legal judgments.[34]

Mid-century proponents of therapeutic divorce made similar claims about the nonlegal nature of marital dissolution. Those claims, however, were temporarily eclipsed by the enthusiasm for private ordering that characterized early no-fault divorce reform.[35]

However, the shift from fault-based to no-fault divorce in the 1960s and '70s laid the groundwork for the modern reemergence of this view of family conflict. The related shift in custody law from presumptions based on gender and parental behavior to the "best interests of the child" standard also reframed and broadened the focus of child access disputes.[36] The best interests standard requires a decision-maker to look explicitly at the open-ended and future-oriented question of child well-being—a question that many judges and commentators believe calls primarily for nonlegal expertise.[37] Judges deciding custody disputes thus moved from the application of a limited number of legal presumptions to an individualized inquiry that invites deference to mental health experts about the child's psychological well-being and relationship with both parents. The twenty-first-century family court's embrace of child well-being as an overriding mission brings this trend to its full expression.

Reliance on Nonlegal Staff Diminishes Importance of Legal Norms

The role of legal norms has also been diminished by the shift in the family court's primary function from the backward-looking task of authoritatively applying legal standards to the forward-looking role of planning for the post-divorce family. This forward-looking orientation has also increased reliance on mental health professionals and other nonlawyers. As one early commentator on this trend noted, "professional language of the social workers and mediators has progressed to become the public, then the political, then the dominant rhetoric. It now defines the terms of contemporary discussions about custody and effectively excludes or minimizes contrary ideologies and concepts."[38] Professor Fineman attributed this shift, in part, to the willingness of judges and lawyers to cede authority because of doubts about their ability to make judgments regarding the best interests of children. More recently, Elizabeth Scott and Robert Emery have argued that a misplaced faith in the judgments of mental health professionals helps explain the "puzzling persistence" of the best interests standard in resolving contested custody cases.[39]

The expanded vision of today's family court has also enhanced the court's reliance on nonlegal personnel. As it embraced "a more rehabilitative, service-oriented model," the twenty-first-century family court required staff to "manage cases, provide court-connected services, and assist fact finders and decision makers in reaching settlements or decisions."[40] To provide these services, some existing court staff, such as court clerks, intake coordinators, and case managers, have assumed new and broader functions, including advising the burgeoning numbers of unrepresented litigants.[41] In addition, the roles of additional court-connected personnel, such as custody evaluators, parenting coordinators, and mediators, have become more regularized and standardized.[42] And new players have materialized—most without a legal background—who are performing new functions. For example, some family courts have added "parenting plan consultants" and "child specialists" to their staffs, despite the lack of any clear consensus about qualifications or functions.[43] What most of these players have in common is that they are nonlawyers drawing on expertise and techniques from other disciplines. As two family court observers have noted, "the family court of the early twenty-first century is often an interdisciplinary enterprise, where psychologists, social workers, non-lawyer mediators and others may wield extraordinary power."[44]

While not a zero-sum game, the enhanced importance of nonlegal staff has resulted in a diminished role for lawyers. To be sure, attorneys still help clients "navigate the often bewildering world of mandatory mediation, mandatory divorce education, court-appointed custody evaluation, parenting coordination, and more."[45] But they play a much narrower role in the processing and resolution of disputes. In particular, as nonlegal staff manage, investigate, and facilitate party-centered decisions, the traditional role of lawyers in speaking and advocating for clients becomes less central.

This is particularly true in the range of mediative settings in which many family cases involving children are now resolved. Attorneys have not traditionally played a central role in mediation. In part, this reflects the attitude and practices of most attorneys. Unless confronted with a court order for mediation, attorneys rarely mention mediation as an option for clients facing family breakup, either through divorce or child welfare proceedings.[46] Although some legal commentators recognize the important role attorneys can play, both in preparing clients for mediation and in the mediation sessions themselves,[47] the prevailing view is that attorneys add little value to mediation.[48] Many mediators share these views. Indeed, some mediators actively discourage the participation of attorneys. Without evidentiary rules or procedural complications, mediators argue, parties can navigate the mediation process themselves, and the presence of attorneys is likely to detract from party empowerment and ownership of the process. Attorneys have little or no role under this conception of family mediation.

This increased reliance on nonlegal staff echoes the reliance of progressive-era juvenile courts on social workers and probation officers who were the primary contacts for families entering that court system. One commentator's description of the early juvenile and family court system reflects this emphasis: "one expert judge, assisted by capable female social workers, with the combined resources of Chicago's private social agencies behind them, could hear all of the city's domestic relations cases and develop a plan of treatment for troubled working class home life."[49] Although the rhetoric of today's family courts is less gendered and perhaps less patronizing, it reflects a similar confidence in the ability of nonlegal personnel to address a family's legal problems.

New Processes De-emphasize Legal Norms

The embrace of alternative processes for family dispute resolution has also reduced the primacy of legal norms in the new dispute resolution paradigm. One of the centerpieces of the new paradigm is a shift away from adjudication to a reliance on private ordering through facilitated agreements negotiated by the parties to the dispute. As two leading family court reformers put it, "in the last quarter century, the process of resolving legal family disputes has, both literally and metaphorically, moved from confrontation toward collaboration and from the courtroom to the conference room."[50]

Although traditional lawyer-directed negotiation still accounts for many settlements in family cases, family mediation—both voluntary and compelled—is increasingly the preferred option for both parties and courts to resolve parenting disputes. In family mediation, a neutral third party helps disputants articulate their interests, improve their communication, and reach an agreement with respect to their future relationship. In some cases, parties with means choose and hire their own mediators to facilitate an agreement outside of court. For the vast majority of parties who lack the resources to engage their own dispute resolution experts, court-based programs encourage or require the use of mediation for child access disputes. In many of these court-based programs, mediation is a prerequisite to a judicial hearing. In the last three decades, nearly all states have enacted statutes or rules establishing court-connected mediation of parenting disputes.[51] Encouraged by judges and court administrators who welcome both the reduction of cases on their dockets and the avoidance of difficult child placement decisions, mediation has assumed a central place on the family dispute resolution continuum.

In addition to "traditional" mediation to develop an initial parenting plan, reformers have deployed a variety of other mediative processes to address particular stages in the separation and post-divorce parenting process. These include "parenting coordination," which is used when parties continue to experience conflict after they have implemented a parenting plan.[52] Other variations include "impasse-directed mediation" for high-conflict families,[53] and "mixed" or "hybrid processes" of mediation and evaluation, ranging from early neutral evaluation,[54] mediation–arbitration, and mediative evaluations.[55]

The relevance and role of legal norms declines dramatically when dispute resolution moves from the courtroom to the mediation table. There is no fact-finder or decision-maker apart from the parties in mediation. Rather, a mediator helps the parties to resolve their disputes, largely without resort to law or legal standards.[56] Mediating parties "may address any issue they wish, not limited to legal causes of action; they may bring in any information they wish, not limited by rules of evidence and procedure to probative evidence, relevant to legal causes of action and meeting evidentiary requirements for authenticity and accuracy."[57] While legal rules may constrain mediation in limited areas such as child support, parties are largely encouraged to generate their own norms. Even in so-called evaluative mediation, which uses legal norms to inform agreements, the sessions are private and informal with few rules governing the scope of discussions or exchange of information, other than mediator-developed rules of civility. As two mediation scholars explain, "The ultimate authority in mediation belongs to the parties themselves and they may fashion a unique solution that will work for them without being governed by precedent or by concern for the precedent they may set for others. The parents may, with the help of the mediator, consider a comprehensive mix of their children's needs, their interests and whatever else they deem relevant, regardless of rules of evidence or strict adherence to substantive law."[58]

The new paradigm also encourages private norm creation through the use of parenting plans. Parenting plans were developed as a way to "neutralize the framework of the adversarial system of divorce" by changing the question from Who is the better parent? to What plan can the parties develop for parenting their children after separation or divorce?[59] A central purpose of the parenting plan process is to replace the legal designations of "custody" and "visitation" with detailed, party-generated designations of the child's residential time with each parent, the allocation of decision-making responsibilities between parents, and any other issues the parents wish to include about post-separation parenting. Legislation or court rules have encouraged the use of parenting plans in many states; in some jurisdictions they are now mandatory.[60] Similarly, the American Law Institute's *Principles of the Law of Family Dissolution* endorses individualized parenting plans as an alternative to judicial custody rulings.[61]

Even in cases that remain contested, despite the range of available settlement processes, judicial custody determinations rely less on lawyers and legal norms than they did in the past. Many courts now rely on a process broadly referred to as custody evaluation to reach a decision without an extended adversarial process. While the practice of custody evaluation varies widely, it generally involves an assessment by a court-connected mental health professional, which provides the court and the parties with detailed information to guide decision-making based on an assessment of the "psychological best interests of the child."[62] In theory, of course, the judge is responsible for making the ultimate custody decision where the parties have been unable to agree; in practice, today's family court judges rely heavily on nonlegal assessments to determine which parenting arrangement will serve the child's best interests.[63]

Many of the processes of the twenty-first-century family courts are reminiscent of the pronounced informality of the early juvenile courts. Like their juvenile court predecessors, today's family court processes eschew reliance on legal norms in favor of more interdisciplinary and holistic approaches to family problems. Moreover, like the early juvenile courts' private, off-the-record "hearings," both mediation and custody evaluation take place outside of public view, and both accord nonlegal decision-makers broad discretion to fashion solutions that accord with the decision-maker's sense of what would best rehabilitate the child and family. Individualized and therapeutic assessments, rather than legal norms, drive the decision-making process.

Consequences of the Expanded Vision and the Diminished Role of Legal Norms

Benefits

The expanded vision of the family court and the diminished role of legal norms have had mixed consequences for families and for the broader legal system. Families benefit in concrete ways from the court's expanded vision of its role. Many family members appearing in family courts will present with a range of treatable problems, ranging from drug addiction to lack of parenting experience. They are, perhaps for the first time, a "captive audience" for potentially beneficial services and treatments. While studies have not yet established the efficacy of court-ordered family services, research shows that, where funding is available, growing numbers of litigants each year are using the services.[64]

The de-emphasis on legal norms and the introduction of nonlegal players also has obvious benefits to both families and the judicial system. Cases can proceed more quickly without the complexity and constraints of substantive doctrine and formal procedures. This is often critically important in child access cases where lingering uncertainty about post-separation parenting roles can add to children's trauma. Informal processes may also be more accessible to participants who are often lost in formal court proceedings. Thus, procedural informality and a de-emphasis on substantive rules of law may ultimately improve access to family dispute resolution.[65] This is particularly true when parties lack legal representation, which is increasingly the case for family litigants.

Further, the participation and input of nonlawyer child development experts should improve the content and durability of post-separation parenting arrangements, particularly those that present complex issues.[66] And many of the critiques leveled against the outsized role of nonlegal experts in the juvenile courts and the early family tribunals will have less force in twenty-first-century family courts as standards, ethical rules, and roles are clarified for mediators, custody evaluators, and other nonlawyer participants in the new paradigm.[67]

Reliance on a less adversarial dispute resolution continuum also benefits families. Alternative processes such as mediation and collaborative law can diffuse conflict and have the potential to generate agreements that more accurately represent the needs and values of family members.

Parties have the ability to customize decisions that best fit their circumstances. This is particularly true as family composition becomes more diverse, and as legal norms fail to account for this diversity or to recognize new family members. In appropriate cases, mediation can also empower parties, enhance their ability to work together in the future, and promote flexible and creative problem-solving. This has particular value in parenting disputes, where processes that strengthen, rather than harm, relationships can facilitate ongoing cooperation after family breakup.[68]

The court system itself may benefit when a significant percentage of cases resolve through mediation and other non-adjudicative processes. Studies analyzing ways for courts to respond to deep budget cuts have increasingly focused on "moving" and "clearing" dockets more quickly, and mediation can help accomplish those goals.[69] Judicial resources are also conserved when cases resolve through mediation sessions, rather than contested hearings. And, to the extent that voluntary agreements reduce the likelihood of post-judgment litigation, more judicial resources are saved. Judges can then focus on high-conflict cases where parties are unable to reach agreement and authoritative judicial resolution is essential.

Some judges have also reported higher levels of satisfaction when serving in the expanded world of the new family courts. Like their counterparts in the early juvenile courts, many judges seem to prefer the role of "team leader" administering therapeutic justice, to the traditional role of decision-maker in the adversary system.[70] This may bode well for attracting more informed and engaged judges for family courts and divisions that have long been plagued by disinterested and inexperienced judges.

Risks to Families and the Legal System

However, the combination of a more expansive but less constrained family court system also poses risks to individuals, families, and the legal system as a whole. With respect to individual litigants, many researchers have expressed a concern that reliance on informal processes and nonlegal staff increases the danger that parties will leave the court system without the legal remedies they need and are entitled to under existing law.

When formal procedures and legal rules are jettisoned in favor of consensus and party self-determination, parties risk entering agreements that waive important rights. The risk increases when parties lack information about legal norms that may govern should they fail to reach agreement. In mediation, for example, attorneys who do not participate in mediation sessions may not play an effective role in advising clients about their rights and interests. For unrepresented parties, now the norm in family cases, the risk of loss of rights in the mediation process is significantly greater.[71] Even if the attorney does not attend the mediation, the represented party has far greater access to an expert source of information about judicial proceedings, each party's legal rights and remedies, and the parties' chances of success in court. The unrepresented party has no comparable source of information when a "neutral" mediator facilitates an agreement. One scholar described the potential harm for unrepresented litigants in court-sponsored mediation programs:

> From an unrepresented litigant's point of view, however, the effect of the [mediation] rules can be devastating. The pressure exerted by courts to send cases to mediation and the lack of explanation of the mediation process raise serious questions about the "voluntary" nature of the decision to mediate. Once in mediation, the pressures on mediators to obtain settlements are immense. With a large number of unrepresented litigants, this pressure guarantees that mediators will rarely, if ever, exercise the

option to terminate the mediation due to the incapacity of an unrepresented litigant to participate. . . . In theory, judges could provide a check on the dangers identified above in mediation, because mediated agreements are usually sent to them for approval. In reality, judges typically rubber-stamp agreements reached in mediation.[72]

Calculating the risks presented by mediation and other informal processes is particularly complex when there are power imbalances between the parties to the dispute. Such imbalances may exist where only one party is represented by an attorney, or they may result from differences in economic power, gender, class, sexual orientation, or cultural differences.[73] Some commentators argue that mediation is more appropriate than litigation for relationships marked by power imbalances, particularly gender. They argue that the hierarchical, "winner takes all" approach of a still white, male-dominated adversary system further disempowers and silences the less powerful party. Mediation, by contrast, with its emphasis on listening, relationships, and problem-solving has greater potential to "heal" and "hear" all voices. Further, mediation's focus on permitting participants to express emotions and articulate needs may be better suited to women than to men. But other scholars have concluded that the risk of loss of rights in mediation is heightened when one party is less powerful than the other.[74] The lack of formal procedures; the confidential, private setting; the focus on the parties' "needs" rather than "rights" under substantive family law; and the virtual lack of review of both the process and the outcome of mediation create a setting where the more powerful may dominate, and bias and prejudice go unchecked.[75]

Domestic violence can create a particularly disabling power imbalance in mediation. Where intimate violence has occurred, there has already been a severe abuse of power, and the consequent imbalance can make mediation impossible. While there is a broad range of views about the appropriateness of mediation for couples who have experienced domestic violence, a consensus has emerged that such cases require special treatment. This consensus is reflected in standards for mediators[76] and mediation statutes and rules.[77] Despite this consensus and the substantial research that supports it, there is evidence that many family courts still order couples who have experienced domestic violence to mediate parenting disputes with little or no particularized examination of the couples' circumstances.[78] The courts' lack of success in screening for these cases places burdens on court-based mediators and increases the risk that this particular power imbalance will go unchecked.

The court system's increased reliance on nonlegal players to make or influence decisions also poses risks to parties. With respect to parenting disputes, Martha Fineman was one of the early scholars to caution against "turn[ing] over the decision-making task to another professional group."[79] Fineman argued forcefully that mental health professionals have a bias in favor of joint custody, regardless of the parties' circumstances.[80] Judicial deference to the opinions of these experts thus poses risks to primary caregiver parents—still mostly women—and their children. To combat these risks, Fineman argued for a return to a legal model that protects and recognizes the role of the parent who assumes care for the child, and she proposed a "primary parent" rule to implement this goal.[81]

Other, more recent critiques raise concerns about the bases for the "expert" opinions of nonlegal personnel in child custody cases. Tippins and Wittmann, a family law attorney and a psychologist, argue that while forensic psychological assessments are often "pivotal documents" that form the basis of judicial determinations of a child's best interests, these assessments fail to meet ethical and scientific standards of both psychology and law:

> Indeed, there is probably no forensic question on which overreaching by mental health professionals has been so common and so egregious. Besides lacking scientific validity, such opinions have often been based on clinical data that are, on their face, irrelevant to the legal questions in dispute. . . . Indeed, whatever position one might take on the ultimate issue rule with respect to other species of expert testimony, such opinions by mental health witnesses on the ultimate question of a child's best interest ought not to be allowed. . . . The best interests standard is a legal and socio-moral construct, not a psychological construct. There is no empirically supportable method or principle by which an evaluator can come to a conclusion with respect to best interests entirely by resort to the knowledge base of the mental health profession.[82]

Others have noted that this critique can also be applied, perhaps more forcefully, to the range of nonlegal court personnel who conduct custody investigations and assist courts in reaching custody decisions: "Custody evaluators are more likely to make inferences and recommendations from unsubstantiated theory, personal values and experiences, and cultural and personal biases. Our own observations and reviews of evaluations over several decades lead us to the same conclusion. Common examples include unexamined strong beliefs in the primacy of mothers (or essentiality of fathers) regardless of the circumstances, biased perception of their clients derived from their own negative marital and divorce experiences, or a conviction that joint physical custody benefits (or harms) all children."[83]

Most recently, a researcher and practitioner reflected on the challenges of integrating attachment theory and knowledge in child access decision-making, noting that such research "deserves a place in the family court's deliberations and planning for children but, to date, that place remains ill-defined. Inconsistencies and misunderstandings, conundrums and complexities of applying attachment knowledge to divorce and separation matters are evident throughout the field."[84]

Another danger of increased reliance on nonjudicial personnel stems from the often-unclear ethical standards that govern the behavior of these actors. For example, while some states require mediator confidentiality and prohibit ex parte contacts with judges about mediation sessions, not all states have such rules. Indeed, some state statutes authorize mediators to make recommendations to the court if mediation fails.[85] Moreover, while a consensus is emerging about the appropriate standards for ethics, training, and qualifications of some of the more established new players, such as mediators, the regulatory structure to monitor compliance with these standards is largely nonexistent. Many mediators are ill equipped or poorly trained.[86] Bad mediators can do great harm—especially to vulnerable parties—when the "empowering" promise of mediation instead becomes an exercise in coercion and arm-twisting.[87]

The ethical obligations of newer court-connected personnel, such as "custody evaluators" or "parenting coordinators," are even less clear. Despite the efforts of professional organizations and some courts to develop ethical standards and clarify the roles of such staff, problems remain. Commentators have raised concerns about the practices of evaluators and coordinators in both obtaining information about parties and sharing such information with judges and others.[88] These concerns exist when parties are represented by counsel and court personnel do not appropriately consult with counsel before giving "advice" to parties or seeking information from them.[89] The concerns are even more acute when parties are unrepresented and have little understanding of the relative authority of various players in the family court system.[90]

Of course, any critique of the new paradigm requires consideration of whether the traditional adversary system poses similar or comparable risks. Judges, too, make bad decisions that may result in the loss of rights. But the impact of such inadequate judging is mitigated by the availability of appellate review, a public record, and established grievance procedures. Few, if any, similar protections exist against bad mediating, custody evaluating, or parent coordinating.

A particularly troubling aspect of the new paradigm is the loss of family privacy and autonomy that results from the family court's expanded role. When family disputes are viewed as opportunities for therapeutic and holistic interventions,[91] increased state interference in family life is disconcertingly easy to justify. The risk of due process violations and privacy losses increase as the goals of court involvement become more ambitious and the roles of both judges and non-judicial personnel expand.

A principal goal of the unified family court movement is having one judge hear all matters involving a single family.[92] This may produce more informed and more efficient decision-making.[93] But it may also result in judges having access to information about a family that would be inadmissible in traditional adversarial proceedings. As a result, judges may reach decisions in one proceeding based on legally irrelevant or highly prejudicial information.[94] In addition, a judge's role in the new "problem-solving" family court has shifted from the narrow job of resolving disputes to the less defined, and potentially broader, role of using the court's authority "to motivate individuals to accept needed services and to monitor [the parties'] compliance and progress."[95] This expanded role creates a greater risk of unwarranted intervention in traditionally private spheres of family life, particularly for parties who lack the protection of legal representation.

These risks are magnified by the multiplicity of court-sponsored actors and services in today's family courts. Given the courts' expanded mission and the emphasis on therapeutic intervention, parties seeking remedies such as divorce or child support may be required to comply with orders or referrals for parenting classes,[96] substance abuse or mental health evaluations,[97] custody evaluations,[98] family mediation,[99] and other similar "services."

For those with resources, the impact of the new paradigm may be mitigated by their ability to limit court involvement in family breakup. When a court orders mediation, represented parties may be able to bypass court-sponsored programs. Their attorneys can object to mediation, negotiate directly with opposing counsel, or hire a private mediator.[100] Similarly, when parties can afford private custody evaluations, courts will often allow them to substitute their own experts for the court's staff.[101] Further, parties represented by attorneys are often able to negotiate out-of-court agreements and can present them at the first court proceeding. In this way, they avoid referrals for services and remain "under the court's radar." By contrast, for families who enter the system without lawyers and without resources for "outside" experts or services, involvement in the web of court-based interventions is almost impossible to avoid if they seek legal remedies such as custody orders or child support.

Low-income families, particularly mothers, have long been at risk of unjustified or inappropriate state intrusion through the child welfare system.[102] But the new regime is raising similar concerns for low-income families seeking divorce, child support, or parenting remedies. Many commentators and practitioners have described bias in the legal system against the poor, particularly in their roles as parents.[103] This bias may trigger greater scrutiny and intrusion of the kind embraced by the new regime—required attendance at parenting education or mental health evaluations, and continuing oversight by parenting coordinators, custody evaluators, and other newly created players in the family justice system. The expanded vision of the family court thus risks creating a "process gap" between rich and poor family disputants that exacerbates the two-tiered system of substantive family law that other scholars have described.

The requirement that family members participate in services may even extend to victims of domestic violence seeking protective remedies in family court. To avoid "losing sight of the victim," many of these courts include the battered parent in orders for counseling and other services.[104] "Services" in these contexts require significant disclosure of personal information by family members, with few rules or procedures to protect the scope of the information sought or, in some instances, the limits of its dissemination. Such orders may undermine the goals of family safety by allowing a batterer to continue control over the victim by bringing contempt actions or otherwise using court orders for victim services as a way to manipulate the victim.[105] For all these reasons, court-ordered participation in these programs burdens families' privacy and encroaches on their autonomy.

Finally, in addition to the risks for individuals and families, the new paradigm's expanded vision and de-emphasis of legal norms may have unintended systemic consequences. Asking the judicial system to shift from legal decision-making to treatment and service provision challenges the capacity of courts. Although families may benefit from the capacity-building and problem-solving approaches embraced in the new paradigm, most courts are not equipped to provide these services. Court-based procedures have historically been designed to determine facts and enforce norms. Courts, with their "limited remedial imaginations," may not be the best institutional settings for resolving the nonlegal issues the new paradigm places within their authority.[106] Asking a court system to take on these tasks may also detract from its fundamental role as a forum for fair and authoritative dispute resolution.[107] Scarce resources must be spread even more thinly, and some courts may have difficulty meeting both basic conflict resolution functions and the broader and more ambitious goals of the new paradigm.[108]

The devaluation of legal norms and the displacement of adjudication as a means of resolving parenting disputes may also have negative consequences for the development of family law and policy. First, this displacement may compromise the refinement and improvement of law that comes from regular appellate review of trial court decisions. To be sure, appellate review of family cases has always been somewhat limited. Prevailing standards in child custody and access cases have afforded trial judges broad discretion, making appellate reconsideration less likely than in other areas of law. The absence of lawyers in many family law cases also limits the number of appeals. But when a substantial majority of cases are resolved through mediation or other non-adjudicative processes, the opportunities to fine-tune doctrine through appellate review shrink dramatically.[109] This risks freezing family law doctrine and may stifle important law reform efforts. In a related context, Owen Fiss has argued that advocates of alternative dispute resolution often err in reducing the social function of the lawsuit to one of resolving private disputes.[110] Proponents of the new paradigm may commit a similar error by conceptualizing family conflict as affecting only those individuals immediately involved in a family dispute. But "family law has historically been one of the most powerful ways that we, as a society, have defined our values and have articulated our aspirations for personal relationships, particularly relationships between adults and children and between women and men."[111] Eschewing adjudication and ignoring legal norms risks short-circuits this important, value-defining process.

A related concern about ad hoc private decision-making is its impact on the authority of legislatures to craft sound family law policy. A legislatively enacted child custody statute, for example, embodies a democratically endorsed statement about how children should be cared for and how parenting disputes should be resolved. Citizens respect and instantiate this democratic statement by using it to govern the resolution of future disputes. If disputing parties do not consider themselves bound by established legal norms, then there has been a power shift from society as a whole (as represented by the legislature) to private disputants and the facilitators charged with processing their disputes. To the extent that society has a legitimate role in determining how parenting disputes are resolved, the reliance on private, nonlegal decision-making may not be entirely a good thing. This is a particular concern when vulnerable parties waive important financial or safety protections in private processes such as mediation.

Conclusion

The paradigm shift in family dispute resolution combines an expanded vision of family courts with a recharacterization of parenting disputes as primarily nonlegal events. The result is a family dispute resolution system that is less constrained by legal norms and more reliant on nonlegal personnel than its more traditional predecessors. In this sense, the current family court regime exhibits many of the features that undermined the nineteenth-century juvenile court movement. Thus, while the delegalization of family dispute resolution offers a number of potential benefits, it also poses substantial risks, both to the families and children whose lives are affected by family conflict and to the larger legal system.

4

The New Vision Meets the New Family

The composition and structure of the families who appear in family court has changed dramatically in recent decades. As one commentator describes it, "a turnover in our intimate partnerships is creating complex families on a scale we've not seen before."[1] In addition to resolving conflicts between divorcing parents, family courts now deal routinely with child-related disputes involving unmarried parents, stepfamilies, gay and lesbian families, and third-party caregivers. Moreover, both the number and the percentage of family litigants who lack legal representation have skyrocketed. In this chapter, we explore these changes in family structure and circumstances, and analyze their implications for the new dispute resolution paradigm. Our analysis suggests a troubling mismatch between the complex realities of today's families and many of the assumptions underlying the new paradigm.

Twenty-First-Century American Families

The Decoupling of Marriage and Parenthood

Perhaps the most significant changes in family structure over the last half century have been the decline of marriage and the resulting decoupling of marriage and parenthood. In 1960, more than two-thirds of all Americans in their twenties were married. By 2008, that figure had dropped to 26 percent.[2] While many of these young adults will eventually marry as they reach their thirties or forties, a substantial percentage will not. According to a recent Pew Research Center study, barely half of all adults in the United States were married in 2011—a record low—compared to nearly three-quarters in 1960.[3] And families composed of minor children living with their married mothers and fathers now make up only about 21 percent of all American households, down from 30.9 percent in 1980.[4] As a result, family life in the United States "no longer centers on married couples and their children."[5] Rather, marriage has become "just one of several permissible choices for individuals who wish to pursue an intimate relationship within the framework of the law."[6]

Although marriage has declined, parenthood has not.[7] The result has been a dramatic increase in the percentage of children born to and living with unmarried parents. Today, more than 40 percent of all births in the United States are to unmarried women, compared to approximately 6 percent in 1960 and less than 20 percent in 1980.[8] This sharp increase in nonmarital births, coupled with continuing high rates of divorce, has had a dramatic impact on the living arrangements of children and the adults who care for them. In 1971, 83 percent of children under the age of eighteen lived with two married parents, while in 2010 only 66 percent did so.[9] The absolute numbers are also significant. According to the 2010 census, there were more than 7.6 million unmarried-couple households in the United States.[10] Close to half of these households include children.[11]

These overall statistics also mask some striking differences by age and socioeconomic status. More than half of all women under thirty who give birth in the United States today are unmarried, as are more than 60 percent of new mothers with a high school education or less. By contrast, among college-educated women, less than 10 percent of today's births occur outside marriage, a rate that is virtually unchanged from a generation ago.[12] This "marriage gap" also has a racial dimension. Marriage rates for African Americans have fallen sharply over the last two decades,[13] with the sharpest drop occurring among African Americans in the lowest education and income brackets.[14] As a result, marriage has effectively disappeared in some low-income communities of color.[15]

Divorce rates show a similar socioeconomic gap. While divorce rates for both college and noncollege graduates increased during the early days of no-fault divorce, by 2004 the divorce rate for those with college degrees had fallen back to the levels of the mid-1960s—before the sexual revolution and no-fault reforms—while for everyone else divorce rates have continued to rise.[16] These differences have led some commentators to suggest that marriage has become a luxury good, and that the intact, two-parent family is "emerging as a marker of class."[17] For purposes of family dispute resolution, the more important implication is that the profile of families with parenting disputes is likely to vary significantly by age and class. For older, college-educated parents, most child-related disputes are likely to stem from the dissolution of a marriage, while for younger, less-educated parents, those disputes are likely to follow shorter and more informal cohabitation relationships, in which the partners may have had little commitment to each other and minimal experience parenting together. Parents with less education are also more likely to have had children with more than one partner, further complicating parenting relationships and disputes.[18] A one-size-fits-all dispute resolution model is unlikely to work effectively in this variegated context.

Cohabitation relationships are also more fluid and less stable than marriage, perhaps in part because of the lack of legal recognition and protection accorded to them.[19] In the United States, unmarried cohabitants are more than twice as likely as spouses to dissolve their unions. Thus, while a significant percentage of unmarried parents are cohabiting at the time a child is born, they are not likely to stay together for the duration of the child's minority.[20] In a recent summary of research, two University of Michigan demographers reported that two-thirds of unmarried couples living together at the time a child is born split up by the time the child turns ten.[21] Another study found that between 25 and 30 percent of children born to cohabiting partners would experience three or more parental relationship transitions by age three.[22] An increasing percentage of the caseload in many family courts consists of child-related disputes arising out of the dissolution of these nonmarital relationships.[23]

Recent changes in federal and state child support policy have increased the likelihood that nonmarital families will seek judicial remedies for parenting disputes. Until recently, child support proceedings initiated by state agencies addressed only paternity and support issues. Parents involved in these proceedings who sought to address custody or visitation matters were required to do so in separate, often costly domestic relations proceedings, generally without the benefit of legal representation.[24] As a result, many unmarried support obligors failed to pursue custody or visitation orders. In the past several years, however, the mission of child support agencies has expanded to include the establishment of "parenting time" arrangements that promote the involvement of noncustodial parents (generally fathers) in their children's lives.[25] For example, the Obama administration now encourages state child support agencies to address parenting responsibilities at the time an initial support order is entered, and has proposed a mandate that agencies include "parenting time" provisions in all new child support orders, beginning in 2019.[26] Congress has also considered legislation that would require state child support enforcement agencies to assist parents with establishing parenting time arrangements on a voluntary basis. Because of these developments, parents involved in state-initiated paternity and child support proceedings—a majority of whom have never married— are increasingly likely to seek judicial resolution of parenting disputes.

But if marriage has declined as a predominant family form, it has retained its place as an American ideal. In a 2006 Gallup poll, 91 percent of respondents reported that they were either married or intended to marry someday.[27] Only 4 percent had ruled out marriage.[28] Thus, "[t]he ideal of marriage still serves as the pedestal for intimate partnerships."[29] As sociologist Andrew Cherlin has explained, the United States is unique among nations in its strong support for marriage, on the one hand, and its postmodern penchant for self-expression and personal growth on the other. As a result of these twin commitments, "Americans step on and off the carousel of intimate partnerships" far more often than their counterparts in other Western countries.[30] "Whether an American parent is married or cohabiting or raising children without a partner, she or he is more likely to change living arrangements in the near future than are parents in the rest of the Western world."[31] With each change of living arrangement comes the potential for conflict over adult relationships with children and the resulting specter of court involvement.

The Prevalence of Stepfamilies

The rise in cohabitation and the decoupling of marriage and parenthood has also led to a significant increase in the prevalence of stepfamilies. According to some scholars, stepfamilies have become America's fastest growing family form.[32] A recent Pew Center study found that more than four in ten American adults have at least one step-relative in their family—either a stepparent, a step- or half-sibling, or a stepchild.[33] In past decades, stepfamilies were typically created by the remarriage of a custodial parent after divorce. Today, they are more likely to arise outside of marriage, when a single mother cohabits with a man who is not the biological father of her children.[34] Researchers estimate that one-third of U.S. children will live in a remarried or cohabiting stepfamily before reaching adulthood.[35] More than half of all coresidential step-parents also have biological children residing in another household.[36]

Relationships between stepparents and children present challenges for the legal system, particularly after the adult partnership ends. Traditional family law doctrine generally refused to recognize any ongoing legal ties between a child and a current or former stepparent. Thus, a stepparent who wished to maintain a relationship with a child that the stepparent had helped raise was dependent on the goodwill of the child's biological (or legal) parent. Today, by contrast, courts are increasingly likely to evaluate claims by current and former stepparents based on their caretaking activities and the quality of their relationship with the child in question. For example, for purposes of allocating custodial and decision-making responsibility, the American Law Institute's *Principles of the Law of Family Dissolution* includes in its definition of a parent any individual who has lived with the child for at least two years and, with the consent of the child's legal parent(s), has assumed a significant share of caretaking functions.[37] The comments to this definition make clear that marriage is not essential to the creation of parental status under this provision, but that a court should recognize an individual as a parent only when doing so would serve the child's best interests.[38]

As a result of these changes, "[s]tate laws on stepparent rights and obligations vary so widely that, stitched together they would resemble a patchwork quilt of disparate rules and interpretations."[39] Moreover, while adoption of a more functional approach to legal parenthood arguably serves the best interests of the particular children involved in these disputes, it risks undermining the certainty and predictability that families and family law have traditionally valued.[40] Conferring enforceable parental rights on former live-in partners over the objection of a child's legal parent also increases the number and types of families subject to ongoing judicial oversight. The fluidity of many stepparent relationships, particularly those formed by cohabitation, further exacerbates these risks.[41]

Multi-generational Families and Third-Party Caretakers

Stepfamilies are not the only family form in which adults who have not traditionally been recognized as legal parents are raising children. An increasing number of children now live in households where grandparents and other relatives have assumed significant child-rearing responsibilities. A 2010 Pew Research study found that approximately one in every ten children in the United States lives with a grandparent, a share that has increased steadily since 2000 and spiked sharply during the recession that began in 2007.[42] Close to half the children who live with a grandparent are being raised primarily by that grandparent. In a majority of these grandparent-headed households, one or both parents are also present, while for about four in ten of these children there is no parent in the household.[43]

Grandparent-headed families face both economic and legal challenges. Most grandparent caregivers have very limited financial resources. The Pew study reported that nearly one in five were living below the poverty line, while 47 percent had household incomes that fell between one and three times the poverty line.[44] An earlier study by the Urban Institute concluded that 37 percent of the grandparents raising grandchildren had incomes below the national poverty level.[45] Moreover, since many grandparent caregivers lack formal custody of the children they are raising, they may have difficulty obtaining health care for the children or enrolling them in a local school.

Shifting and uncertain legal standards confound the status of grandparent caregivers and complicate the resolution of child-related disputes between grandparents and parents. In 2000, the United States Supreme Court held that the U.S. Constitution prohibits state courts from applying a pure best interests standard to award visitation to nonresident grandparents over the objection of a child's parent who had not been found unfit.[46] But the Court refused to specify what legal standard would satisfy constitutional requirements or to indicate whether its opinion applied to grandparents who reside with a child or serve as a child's primary caregiver. As a result, state courts and legislatures have interpreted the Supreme Court's decision in different ways. Some courts have treated grandparent caregivers as functional parents and have accorded them the same legal status as parents; others have that held that grandparents cannot contest a parent's decision to deny access to a child unless they can show that the parent is unfit or that exceptional circumstances exist—standards that remain undefined in many jurisdictions. This uncertainty complicates efforts to design a dispute resolution system that will work for grandparent-headed families.

Gay and Lesbian Families

Another important change in the composition of American families is the increase in the reported number and visibility of gay and lesbian parents, many of whom are raising children together. According to U.S. Census Bureau figures, the number of same-sex-couple households increased by more than 80 percent between 2000 and 2010, from approximately 358,000 reported households in 2000 to more than 646,000 in 2010.[47] This rate of increase was much faster than the increase observed for all households, as well as the increases for married and unmarried heterosexual-couple households.[48] Additionally, a higher percentage of same-sex-couple households than opposite-sex-couple households were either interracial or interethnic.

A significant percentage of same-sex partners are raising children together. Data collected in 2009 indicated that more than 16 percent of unmarried same-sex-couple households included children under age eighteen, up from approximately 12 percent in 2000.[49] Among same-sex couples who identified as spouses, more than 30 percent were raising children.[50] A recent report on the status of gay and lesbian families confirms that between 2.0 and 2.8 million children are being raised by LGBT parents, a number that is expected to grow rapidly in the coming years.[51] Geographically, same-sex couples are most likely to be raising children in many of the most socially conservative parts of the country, including the Deep South.[52] Child-rearing among same-sex couples is also more common among partners with less than a high school education, a pattern that does not occur among opposite-sex couples.[53] Thus, same-sex families who appear in court are likely to face economic and cultural stresses beyond those experienced by their opposite-sex counterparts.

Parenting by same-sex couples raises challenges for family law. Often, the children in these households lack a biological or formal legal connection to one member of the couple. If the adult relationship ends, the nonbiological "parent" may have difficulty maintaining a relationship with the child, particularly if the biological parent objects. Increasingly, these parentage disputes are ending up in family court, and increasingly judges are using their equitable powers to grant parent-like rights and obligations to individuals who have assumed a parental role but who have not traditionally been recognized as parents. Court rulings are inconsistent, however, and often rest on detailed case-by-case examination of the intentions of the ex-partners and the strength of the bonds between the child and the adult seeking parental status. While access to marriage for same-sex couples may simplify some of these disputes, particularly for children born during the marriage, recognition as a same-sex spouse does not automatically confer recognition as a parent.

The Impact of Reproductive Technology

The development and widespread acceptance of assisted reproductive technology (ART) has also increased the diversity and complexity of family forms. A recent article in the American Medical Association's online ethics journal indicates that family formation through ART accounts for three out of every one hundred children born in the United States today—far exceeding the number of parent–child relationships formed through adoption.[54] While the majority of ART usage involves couples undergoing in vitro fertilization using their own gametes, a growing percentage of ART use involves third-party gamete contributors who assist in an individual's or couple's reproductive plan. Such collaborative reproduction creates the potential for uncertainty about legal parentage, particularly if it takes place outside conventional medical settings.

As reproductive science has advanced, both public attitudes and legal treatment of ART have shifted dramatically. Prior to 1970, for example, donor insemination efforts were "viewed with such horror that bills were introduced in state legislatures to ban the procedure."[55] Today, by contrast, more than three-quarters of the states have laws that facilitate artificial insemination by declaring the consenting husband of the sperm recipient to be the legal father of the resulting child.[56] Increasingly, these presumptions of legal parenthood are being extended to consenting partners outside of marriage.[57] Similarly, the development of in vitro fertilization in the 1970s was initially greeted with outrage and skepticism, but is now both widespread and legally acknowledged.[58] Indeed, at least one million families have been created over the past half century through the use of donor sperm or eggs.[59]

ART has greatly complicated traditional understandings of parenthood. A child created through ART may have a multiplicity of potential parents: a genetic mother, a genetic father, a gestational mother, and any number of social or intended parents. Increasingly, family courts are called on to mediate among these competing claimants. Many gay and lesbian couples, as well as many single parents, have taken advantage of ART to create families that supersede the traditional boundaries of marriage, biology, and adoption. At the same time, the increasing prevalence of gestational surrogacy, in which a woman gestates and bears a child who is not genetically related to her, "has created another generation of familial and legal dilemmas for our society."[60] As the Colorado Supreme Court observed in a case involving conflicting claims of legal fatherhood, "Parenthood in our complex society comprises much more than biological ties, and litigants increasingly are asking courts to address issues that involve delicate balances between traditional expectations and current realities."[61]

Although many commentators have suggested that the legal system has lagged behind these technological and demographic developments, "major changes are stirring."[62] In particular, in sympathetic fact situations and with the approval of a majority of family law scholars, the legal system has begun to shift away from traditional definitions of parenthood based on marriage or biology to functional norms that focus on the lived experiences of individual children and their caretakers. As one leading family law scholar put it, "nurture has dislodged nature as the primary determinant in the resolution of legal disputes within these new family forms. Adults who lack a genetic tie to children with whom they have established a parent–child bond are scoring victories in court battles over biological parents who seek to exclude these functional parents from the families they helped construct. Increasingly the central issue is whether the adult has functioned as a parent in the child's life."[63] Recognition of functional parenthood increases both the number and variety of parenting disputes that family courts will be called on to resolve.

Pro Se Litigants

Not only have disputing families become more complicated and diverse, but the way those families interact with the legal system has also changed. In particular, the number of self-represented litigants in family court has skyrocketed. Although comprehensive nationwide statistics do not exist, studies have indicated that between 55 and 90 percent of family cases involve at least one self-represented party.[64] In many large urban jurisdictions, a substantial majority of family law cases proceed entirely without lawyers.[65] Thus, far from being exceptional, *pro se* litigants are now the norm in family courts across the country. Indeed, experts have called the rise in unrepresented litigants the single most important issue facing family courts today.[66]

There are a number of reasons why parties in family cases represent themselves. Some disputants believe their cases are simple and they can handle the issues on their own.[67] The widespread availability of legal information on the Internet has encouraged some consumers to bypass lawyers and other professionals.[68] Others distrust lawyers, worrying they will exacerbate conflict or create unnecessary issues in order to enhance their fees.[69] But most individuals, particularly those with low or modest incomes, cannot afford legal representation.[70] And even where parties' incomes are low enough to be eligible for free legal assistance, existing legal aid and legal services offices can only meet a fraction of the need.[71]

Pro se litigants challenge courts, under both adversary and nonadversary models. They are often unfamiliar with legal doctrine and have difficulty navigating the complex procedures that govern the processing of legal disputes. Some courts have established programs to support *pro se* litigants; indeed, recent Supreme Court precedent suggests courts have an obligation, where parties are without counsel, to provide "alternative procedures that assure a fundamentally fair determination."[72] But limited advice, education, and form pleadings do not adequately prepare most parties for the complexity of court proceedings. As a result, the presence of large numbers of unrepresented parties in family court proceedings distorts the traditional roles of judges, court clerks, and other court personnel as well as the court system itself.

The presence of substantial numbers of unrepresented parties challenges court clerks and other court personnel in their traditional roles as neutral administrators who are expected to interact primarily with judges and lawyers. When *pro se* parties seek assistance and advice as they attempt to initiate and pursue their cases, court personnel risk losing their impartiality and may violate rules against unauthorized practice of law. These risks may be particularly salient in the new paradigm, where nonjudicial court personnel are regarded as part of a multi-disciplinary dispute resolution team. The challenges posed by unrepresented litigants are also heightened as family courts increasingly adopt triage systems that depend on judgments by nonjudicial personnel regarding which dispute resolution processes and services are appropriate for which individual cases.[73]

The need to assist and educate *pro se* parties also challenges the traditional conception of a judge's role as a passive umpire and impartial finder of fact and law.[74] Indeed, a growing number of advocates, as well as judges from state and federal courts, have recognized that the judge's role may have to be expanded to meet the court's obligation to *pro se* litigants.[75] As one civil trial judge's bench book describes this tension:

> A challenge for judges in seeking justice in their courts increasingly involves the issue of how to interact with self-represented litigants. There is a growing and accepted school of thought that a judge must be pro-active in seeking and adopting policies and procedures that are friendly to all parties, including those represented by counsel and those representing themselves. Many authorities now recognize . . . for a judge to do nothing to address the needs or problems faced by self-represented litigants actually advances injustice and contributes to the loss of respect for the judicial system by a substantial portion of the public.[76]

Pro se parties pose particular challenges to non-adversarial dispute resolution processes such as mediation. Like judges and court staff, mediators, as neutral facilitators of communication and negotiation, are supposed to be "impartial third parties."[77] This neutrality is viewed as both central to the legitimacy and effectiveness of mediation,[78] and critical for maintaining ethical standards for mediators.[79] As a result, even mediators with legal expertise are generally constrained from opining about the merits of either party's positions or predicting a likely outcome were the disputed matters litigated.[80] Yet mediators who work with unrepresented parties are often put in the position of providing information about legal standards (which may sound very much like legal advice to the layperson). If a mediator declines to provide such information, she risks having uninformed parties reach agreements that the parties may not understand or are contrary to their interests.[81]

The concerns about uninformed decision-making are particularly acute when the mediation is court-ordered, as it is in many child access cases. By contrast, if a mediator provides legal information related to the disputants' situation, she risks crossing the line from facilitation to evaluation—a move that many mediators reject.

While many have recognized this conflict for mediators, few agree on the appropriate response. Some believe that providing traditional legal representation to parties participating in mediation would address the concerns and improve the process, but they recognize that state budget constraints make this solution unlikely.[82] Others argue for responses that would fundamentally change mediation—building in more formality to the process,[83] or reconceiving the mediator's role to include providing legal education when mediating cases with unrepresented parties, particularly in a court-based setting.[84] Others have discussed the importance of simply "providing clearer guidance for mediators working with self-represented parties, considering the special needs of parties without attorneys."[85] These changes will require rethinking some of the rules and standards governing mediator and lawyer conduct as well as rules governing unauthorized practice.

Finally, the rapidly increasing numbers of unrepresented parties in family courts may threaten the ability of these courts to fulfill their core function—to provide for the peaceful resolution of family disputes by ensuring timely access to legal processes and remedies. Because the absence of lawyers decreases the likelihood that cases will resolve without a judicial hearing, court systems with a high percentage of unrepresented parties face expanding dockets of litigated cases.[86] This has resulted in substantial delays at all stages of the proceedings. These delays translate to deferred divorces that prevent remarriage, loss of needed financial support for children and their caretakers, and disrupted relationships between parents and children who lack custody or visitation arrangements. To afford timely access to critical legal remedies and processes, today's dispute resolution regime must respond to the realities of today's families.

Lagging Assumptions of the New Paradigm

These changes in family structure have significantly increased both the number and complexity of parenting disputes that end up before the courts. They have also expanded the variety of personal relationships that give rise to parenting and other family disputes. The new dispute resolution paradigm has failed to account fully for these changes. Indeed, although the new paradigm purports to offer a new vision for the resolution of family conflict, it leaves largely unexamined the models of family and intimate relationships on which the traditional, adversary model was based. As a result, the new paradigm assumes a family structure that is both more static and more homogeneous than today's reality. In this section, we explore the assumptions about families and family relationships embodied in the new paradigm, and contrast these assumptions with the more complex demographic and economic realities discussed above.

The Assumption That Disputants Have Established Relationships with Each Other and Children

A key assumption of the new paradigm is that family disputants have established relationships with one another and with any children involved in the dispute. For example, child access mediation emphasizes the restructuring of *existing* parental and family relationships. Similarly, collaborative practitioners often seek consensus by asking estranged partners to recall times in their past when they were able successfully to resolve disputes together. And most parenting plans are designed to create a structure within which former spouses or partners will continue to parent their children together. More generally, advocates of the new paradigm emphasize the importance of *preserving* family relationships and the need to facilitate a transition from a nuclear to a binuclear household.[87] These formulations assume a shared family past and a set of relationships that precede the family's appearance in court.

While the assumption of a shared past may be accurate for some disputing families, particularly spouses undergoing divorce, it is much less likely to hold for others. Unmarried parents, in particular, often have little experience raising children together. Indeed, studies estimate that less than half of all unmarried mothers are living with the child's father at the time a child is born.[88] These never-married couples face the daunting task of initiating their role as parents at the same time as they are attempting to define their own relationship. Unmarried parents are also likely to be younger and less educated than the divorcing parents for whom the new paradigm was designed. Even some strong advocates of shared parenting acknowledge that where parents are not living together at the time of a child's birth or separate soon after birth, "the prognosis for a long-term co-parenting relationship that is meaningful and important to the child is not good."[89]

The decoupling of marriage and parenthood discussed above, and the federal government's emphasis on establishing paternity and child support obligations based on biology alone, increases the likelihood that the parents who appear in family court will have only a tenuous connection to each other. While some family courts have developed innovative programs directed at this group of previously unconnected parents,[90] most court-based interventions continue to assume that all disputing parents have a shared family past that justifies a shared future.

A related assumption of the new paradigm is that disputing family members have a history of communication and cooperation on which they can draw in restructuring their relationship and building a viable parenting partnership. Indeed, one leading family mediation text asserts that, "[i]n simple terms, therefore, mediation is about getting the parties to talk to one another again."[91] The author justifies this characterization by explaining that, before the breakup, the family made its own decisions on important matters and settled disputes in its own way. Although conflict and distress may have interrupted the capacity to communicate, the autonomy of this "self-contained disputing arena" should not be questioned, and reestablishing communication should be of paramount importance.[92]

Like the assumption of a shared past, the assumption of prior successful communication and decision-making is tenuous for many disputing parents, particularly those whose relationships have been marked by violence or prolonged conflict, as well as those who have never established a household together. The new paradigm's emphasis on these assumptions suggests that it is built around the experiences of divorcing parents, who account for a shrinking percentage of family disputants. The diversity of twenty-first-century families requires a rethinking of these assumptions.

The Assumption of Adequate Personal and Financial Resources

In addition to an established relationship and a history of communication, the new paradigm assumes parties with sufficient personal and financial resources to support effective participation in consensual dispute resolution processes. Indeed, a commitment to party self-determination is at the core of the new dispute resolution regime.[93] Explanations of the mediation process highlight this commitment. In sharp contrast to traditional adversary procedures, mediation is described "as a disputant-centered, disputant-dominated process. It relie[s] on the disputants' active and direct participation in the mediation process and in decision-making."[94] Mediation thus offers disputants "a means to wrest control over both the dispute resolution *process* and the dispute resolution *outcome* from legal and counseling professionals."[95] Consistent with this emphasis, ethical codes for mediators consistently describe party self-determination as the fundamental principle of mediation.[96]

Collaborative practice emphasizes similar norms of party self-determination and active engagement. In a collaborative representation, all significant negotiations are conducted in meetings where both clients are present. "In these meetings and throughout the collaborative process, the lawyers climb down from their pedestals and encourage the clients to control the agenda and the outcome."[97] While the lawyers are responsible for managing the process and for creating "a safe environment for client-centered dialogue," the parties themselves are in charge of all decisions.[98]

Collaborative practice thus imposes high expectations on disputants. While the adversarial paradigm assumed that family members in conflict often lacked the capacity to make decisions, "[Collaborative Family Law] assumes that most people in conflict can, with proper support, make decisions for themselves. They do not need either their lawyers or a judge to decide matters of importance for them."[99] Collaborative practitioners also "expect active client participation in all stages of work."[100] Such active participation assumes a high level of emotional maturity. To participate effectively in the collaborative process, clients "must demonstrate an acceptance of the fact of their separation, the willingness to manage or to learn to manage their emotions, an interest in the well-being of the other side, and a commitment to an honourable divorce process."[101] While some family disputants possess these qualities, many others may not.

More generally, the new paradigm's emphasis on resolving disputes through private agreements, and the limited role of courts in scrutinizing those agreements, assumes parties with both the desire and the capacity to understand the issues raised by their situation, appreciate the other party's perspective, and generate fair and workable solutions. At the same time, the new paradigm deemphasizes the role of legal norms in generating and evaluating those options. The new paradigm thus places disputing family members at the center of both the work of norm creation and the process of using those norms to resolve their disputes and rebuild their lives.

While this is an admirable aspiration, it may be unrealistic for many of today's family disputants, particularly those who lack access to legal information and advice. As one of the "founding fathers" of divorce mediation has acknowledged, "participating in mediation can actually be more emotionally draining and even traumatizing than court action and certainly than lawyer-conducted negotiations."[102] Participation in other alternative dispute resolution processes may be similarly demanding.

The new paradigm also rests on the assumption that parties will have the necessary financial resources to participate meaningfully in the many court-based proceedings and programs associated with parenting disputes in the new paradigm. Most facilitative and transformative mediation models are built on the assumption that participants will have independent legal advice about any agreements developed in the process. Indeed, most mediation standards and ethical rules governing lawyer–mediators prohibit mediators from drafting agreements and require or encourage them to advise participants to have lawyers draft the agreements reached in mediation.[103] But this advice is of little use to the majority of participants in most court-based mediation programs, who lack access to free legal representation and cannot afford to hire lawyers for traditional representation. As a result, these participants may lack the information they need to make informed choices about parenting arrangements and obligations. Other processes, such as collaborative law, require the participation of lawyers and are largely unavailable to lower-income families.

Moreover, the emphasis on private norm creation and application may leave parties vulnerable to power imbalances. Family mediation has long been subject to critique on these grounds, particularly by feminists and others concerned about the impact of domestic violence.[104] More recently, scholars have raised similar concerns about other settlement-oriented practices, particularly informal practices engaged in by judges and other court personnel.[105] Advocates of the new paradigm have been slow to address these concerns, perhaps because of their assumptions about the availability of legal representation as a means of ameliorating power imbalances. However, pervasiveness of unrepresented parties in today's family courts undermines this assumption.

The court's commitment to provide "coordinated holistic services . . . to address the physical and mental needs of the family"[106] in the new paradigm also requires that participants devote significant time to dispute resolution. In addition to formal court proceedings, parties may be required to attend parent education, custody evaluations, mediation sessions, and other "services" depending on their circumstances and perceived needs. Most courts are located in commercial districts of towns and cities, are open only during normal working hours, and do not have child care. As a result, a dispute resolution system that requires the presence of parents on multiple days can impose a financial burden that many lower income families find difficult to absorb.

The Assumption of Equal and Established Parental Status

The new paradigm also assumes parents (generally two) of equal and established status. For example, the co-parenting norms that underlie mediation and other non-adversary dispute resolution processes assume that the disputants stand on an equal footing with respect to their recognition as parents. Similarly, court-connected parent education classes, now offered or mandated in many jurisdictions, focus on the transition from parenting in an intact, two-parent household to parenting in a binuclear, post-divorce family.[107] While there is some variation in curricula and program goals, divorcing couples are the primary audience for which these are designed.[108] Despite this focus on post-divorce parenting, most parties seeking any child-related order, including, in some states, paternity orders, are required to attend these education programs. As other scholars have noted, such a "one-size-fits-all" approach to parenting education fails to address the needs of many families with child-related issues.[109]

Parenting plans, which are in use in at least half the states, reflect a similar assumption of two (and only two) established parents.[110] These plans eschew the allocation of "custody" or "visitation," and urge "divorcing parents develop and implement an individualized plan to carry out their ongoing parenting responsibilities."[111] The widespread use of parenting plans is designed to encourage "continued participation of both parents in their children's lives through shared parenting."[112] Like parenting classes, these plans assume that disputants stand on an equal footing and have a history of shared parenting.

The assumption of equal and established parental status likely holds true for parenting disputes that arise out of a divorce or long-term cohabitation relationship where paternity has been acknowledged. It is considerably more problematic as applied to putative fathers whose status has not been legally recognized, or to disputes involving grandparents, stepparents, or non–biologically related adults who have functioned as parents to the children in question. As two noted family law scholars recently commented, while child support calculations have become a matter of routine, "the parentage determinations on which they rest, have not."[113] The same is true in the context of custody and child access—while the principle of shared post-separation parenting is widely endorsed, the criteria for determining who qualifies as a parent are deeply contested. The diminished role of legal norms in a system that eschews adjudication leaves the new paradigm poorly equipped to resolve disputes about parental status or to develop appropriate ground rules for allocating responsibility between and among adults with different legal relationships to children.

The Assumption of a Static Post-Separation Family

The new paradigm also assumes an enduring, binuclear family after parental separation or divorce. This concept was first popularized by Constance Ahrons, who asserted that the child's post-divorce family should be regarded as being "binuclear," with membership in two households rather than one.[114] In her book *The Good Divorce*, Ahrons characterized the binuclear family as a form of limited partnership established for the purpose of co-parenting children across two households.[115] This concept of the binuclear family underlies the central tenet of the new paradigm that divorce and parental separation do not signal the end of a family, but rather its reorganization into two connected households. A core purpose of both mediation and parenting plans is to coordinate the decision-making and activities of these two households in order to a create a consistent and viable parenting partnership.[116]

The assumption of an enduring binuclear household fits uneasily with the realities of today's families. In particular, the assumption fails to account for the introduction of new partners and parental figures that often follow an initial divorce or parental separation. Such multiple transitions are particularly salient for unmarried parents. In their study of fragile families and child well-being, Sarah McLanahan and her colleagues found that almost 30 percent of mothers who were unmarried at the time of their child's birth were either living with a new partner or had had a new cohabiting or marital relationship by the time the child was five.[117] If long-term dating relationships are included, the prevalence of new intimate partnerships within five years rises to more than 50 percent.[118] And many families experience multiple transitions; almost 20 percent of unmarried mothers have had two new partners by the time a child is five, and 10 percent have had three or more new partners.[119]

Moreover, unmarried parents are also likely to have children by multiple partners. According to the fragile families study, one-fifth of all unmarried mothers—and one-third of mothers who had not lived with the child's father—have had a child with a new partner by the time their first child is five.[120] Unmarried fathers are even more likely to re-partner and to have had children with multiple partners. These transitions and multi-partner families complicate child-rearing and co-parenting relationships in ways that the new paradigm largely fails to acknowledge.

Many divorced parents also fail to conform to the model of a static binuclear family. More than half of all divorced parents remarry, most within a few years after the divorce.[121] Close to half of all remarried households include the biological children of one or both partners; as a result, stepfamilies account for a large and growing percentage of all U.S households.[122] But divorce rates are higher for remarriages than for first unions, and the presence of children increases the already higher risk that a second marriage will end in divorce.[123] Indeed, Andrew Cherlin has identified "sheer movement, frequent transitions [and] shorter relationships" as the most distinctive characteristics of American family life.[124] By assuming a stable, binuclear family after parental divorce or separation, the new paradigm skirts these realities and risks disserving the interests of this growing group of families.

The sharp increase in the number and complexity of parental reloca-tion disputes also highlights the problematic nature of assuming a stable, binuclear family.[125] As Theresa Glennon has written, relocation disputes highlight the tension between two competing models of divorce—the economic clean-break model, under which ex-spouses and cohabitants who part ways are entirely separate individuals, unencumbered by ongo-ing legal or financial relationships, and the co-parenting model, which requires divorced and separated individuals to continue to be closely enmeshed in each other's lives.[126] Parental relocation is common in the aftermath of divorce or separation; indeed, for many separated parents, particularly mothers with primary child-care responsibilities, such relocation is an economic necessity.[127] Yet, many co-parenting agree-ments limit the ability of a child's primary residential parent to change residence. Similarly, statutes and court rules in many states require a divorced or separated parent who seeks to change a child's principal residence first to notify the other parent.[128] If the nonresidential parent does not consent to the move, the residential parent must obtain judicial permission to relocate. Often that permission is not forthcoming or is conditioned on the requesting parent relinquishing primary residential custody.[129] Significantly, while judges are increasingly likely to restrict a residential parent's ability to relocate, they rarely restrict the mobility of a nonresidential parent—even one with joint legal custody, and even though the effect on a child of such a parental move may be just as dra-matic and just as negative. Nor do most courts consider the possibility of a nonresidential parent following a residential parent to a new locale when evaluating the residential parent's request to relocate.[130] While the new paradigm's emphasis on planning and preventive law offers parents the opportunity to anticipate and adjust for these transitions, the com-mitment to a static binuclear family constrains parents' ability to do so effectively.

The Separation of Parenting Disputes from Other Legal Issues

Finally, the new paradigm assumes that disputes about children can be separated from other legal matters. Most court-connected mediation programs address only issues related to post-separation parenting. Even programs that address a broader range of issues generally focus only on issues that arise out of the parties' relationships with each other, as opposed to their relationships with the state or other third parties. And few family court systems partner with community programs or are designed to help families access resources outside the judicial branch.

This emphasis on resolving intra-family disputes is consistent with the long-standing divide between the public and the private aspects of family law. But that divide has blurred in recent years as families have become more fragmented and more diverse. This blurring formed part of the impetus for the unified family court movement, whose advocates hoped to spread the model of a single court that would hear all cases involving children and families, regardless of whether the state was directly involved.[131] But most court systems continue to hear child welfare cases initiated by state authorities in separate courts from those hearing divorce and parenting disputes arising out of relationships among family members. This continued divide creates often intractable burdens for family members who must appear in both courts in order to resolve closely related matters, often without the benefit of legal assistance. For example, a grandparent who appears as a party or witness in a state-initiated child welfare action often ends up as the caretaker for the child who is the subject of the proceeding. In order to enroll the child in school or to access financial resources, the grandparent may need a custody or support order, which is not available in the child welfare proceeding but must be obtained separately from the court that hears intra-family matters. This current fragmented court structure fails to recognize the interrelated nature of many family conflicts that implicate both public and private family law.

Moreover, the legal needs of many low-income and nonmarital families are often broader than the family members' relationships with one another, and involve access to public programs and benefits.[132] For example, working parents may need reliable and affordable child care in order to make a co-parenting arrangement work. Similarly, both residential and nonresidential parents may need access to job training or housing subsidies in order to live and work in proximity to each other. And children, as well as parents, may need ongoing counseling or therapy to adjust to changes in family structure. The new paradigm downplays these interconnections. As one commentator has noted, "Identifying parental conduct as the sole source of problems for children of divorce, legislators ignore the structural causes of inter-parental conflict inherent to divorce, and the harsh price divorce exacts on parents, most crucially on mothers. Financial strain and the lack of representation in legal procedures, to name two examples, are influential stress factors that accompany divorce."[133] Unmarried parents are at least as vulnerable to such structural impediments and stress factors.

A family dispute resolution system that focuses exclusively on intrafamily relationships is not sufficient to support or strengthen the most vulnerable families and children. In her recent book *Failure to Flourish: How Law Undermines Family Relationships*, legal scholar Clare Huntington demonstrates the many ways in which the state influences and structures family life.[134] In particular, she shows how state subsidies and economic policies often favor middle- and upper-income families and compromise the ability of lower-income parents to maintain the stable and committed relationships that are optimal for raising children. Huntington thus exposes as inaccurate and debilitating the myth that successful families operate apart from the state, and that families who seek or accept state support should be pathologized as dependent. As Huntington's analysis makes clear, an effective family dispute resolution regime must attend to the economic and structural barriers that affect family relationships and inhibit the ability of many separated and divorced families to parent their children effectively. The new paradigm's isolation of parenting disputes from broader family needs undermines its ability to achieve these goals.

Conclusion

The mismatches we describe between the assumptions underlying the new paradigm and the complex realities of today's families are not unique to the current dispute resolution regime. Indeed, the traditional adversary system was also built around a series of unrealistic assumptions about families.[135] But the adversary regime developed at a time when the range of legally cognizable family disputes was less expansive and the families entitled to legal remedies less diverse. Just as the adversary system's assumption that "divorce ends a family as well as a marriage" failed to serve the interests of many children and families, so, too, may the new paradigm's emphasis on co-parenting within a binuclear household fails to capture the realities of many of the families it affects.

Moreover, the new paradigm's emphasis on private ordering and party autonomy demands considerably more of family members than did its court-centric and lawyer-driven predecessor. Given these increased demands, it seems particularly important that today's family dispute resolution regime rest on a complete and accurate picture of the families whose lives it so deeply influences. The new paradigm also promises more to families and children than did the traditional adversary regime. As chapter 3 explained, the new paradigm seeks not merely to resolve a family's immediate legal disputes, but to enhance the material and psychological well-being of individuals and families in conflict. To fulfill this more expansive and ambitious mission, today's dispute resolution regime must confront the realities of today's families, rather than assume an outdated or idealized version.

5

From Gladiators and Umpires to Problem-Solvers and Managers

The shifts in family dispute resolution described in the preceding chapters have important implications for lawyers and judges. In particular, these changes challenge the traditional understanding of lawyers as zealous client advocates and the traditional role of judges as passive and impartial umpires. While lawyers continue to represent clients in the new paradigm, they are called on to do so in different or expanded ways. In addition, the current regime invites lawyers to assume new roles as facilitators and dispute resolution neutrals. Similarly, while judges continue to adjudicate the small percentage of family cases that go to trial, they have also taken on expanded roles as team leaders, managers, and therapeutic agents. These changes reduce the distinctions between judging and lawyering, and blur the roles of judges and attorneys; they also challenge existing ethical norms for both lawyers and judges. This chapter discusses these new and expanded roles and explores their implications for families and family dispute resolution.

Traditional Roles of Lawyers and Judges: The Zealous Advocate and the Neutral Umpire

The adversary system in the United States is built on the assumption that legal disputes are best resolved in a setting where an advocate for each party presents evidence and arguments to an impartial decision-maker, most often a judge. The adversarial paradigm rests on the belief that "out of the sharp clash of proofs presented by adversaries in a highly structured forensic setting is most likely to come the information from which a neutral and passive decision-maker can resolve a litigated dispute in a manner that is acceptable both to the parties and to society."[1] The paramount duty of a lawyer in this system is to advocate "zealously"[2] for the client's cause. Moreover, the dominance of rights-based solutions to legal disputes means that "the primary responsibility of the lawyer is the furtherance of her clients' goals framed as legal ends."[3] To function effectively within such a rights-based system, the advocate "must focus her energies and talents on convincing decision makers—real or imagined—that she has the stronger rights-based arguments."[4]

The judge in the adversary system strives to be passive and impartial, finding facts and interpreting the law in an objective and unbiased manner. The primary goal of judging is to resolve the immediate dispute, based on legally relevant evidence.[5] The judge does not intervene substantively during a trial, but instead withholds judgment until all the evidence and arguments are submitted. In reaching a decision, the judge relies only on evidence admitted under governing rules and, while she may consult with other judges and law clerks, the judge acts largely alone. As one commentator described it, "Orderly procedure presumes that a judge is able to be objective, to look dispassionately at the whole case . . . Socrates said four things belong to a judge: to hear courteously, to answer wisely, to consider soberly, and to decide impartially."[6]

This view of the adversary system, and the roles of lawyers and judges in it, has always been somewhat of a caricature, particularly in family law. The characterization of lawyers as "gladiators" has elided the reality that rules of procedure, evidence, and ethics limit the lawyer's "zealousness" by prohibiting behavior designed to foster delay or harass opponents.[7] These rules also seek to instill an ethic of civility and reflect the multiple roles that lawyers assume, both within and outside the courtroom.[8] The behavior of practicing family lawyers also belies strict adherence to the adversary paradigm. In a landmark 1995 study of two thousand divorce lawyers, researchers found that lawyers are generally less adversarial than their clients and often seek to persuade clients to accept "reasonable" settlements in light of existing law.[9] These findings were confirmed in a more recent empirical study of family lawyers in New England.[10]

The view that family lawyers should temper zealous advocacy, particularly when children are involved, is reflected in ethical norms for family lawyers developed by the American Academy of Matrimonial Lawyers (AAML) to supplement existing ethical rules: "The traditional view of the matrimonial lawyer (a view still held by many practitioners) is of the 'zealous advocate' whose only job is to win. However, the emphasis on zealous representation of individual clients in criminal and some civil cases is not always appropriate in family law matters. Public opinion (both within and outside the AAML) has increasingly supported other models of lawyering and goals of conflict resolution in appropriate cases."[11]

Despite these caveats about zealous advocacy, many family lawyers continue to practice within the win/lose framework of the adversarial model.[12] Moreover, current ethical rules that govern lawyers' conduct have constrained departures from adversarial practice. While the traditional role of zealous advocate will remain appropriate for some family cases, the shifts in family dispute resolution have created lasting and fundamental changes in the functions of lawyers and their relationships with clients and other professionals working in the family justice system.

The description of the judicial role as passive, objective, and detached is also somewhat of out of sync with the way judges have always functioned. For example, when one or both parties are unrepresented, or represented by inexperienced or incompetent counsel, judges have often taken on a more active role to educate parties or their attorneys on legal doctrine and procedures. And while a judge's traditional role as decision-maker is a solitary one, judges in courts with substantial dockets take on administrative roles and manage court personnel. Further, many court-watchers have observed that, despite an ethical obligation to be neutral and fair, judges in family cases tend to draw on their own experiences, values, and, in some cases, biases in reaching decisions.[13] But these departures from the judge's traditional role have been limited and viewed as exceptional. The shifts in family dispute resolution and the expanded goals of today's family courts represent a more radical challenge to the goals and ethical norms of judging, as well as the day-to-day work of judges.

New Roles for Family Lawyers

The changing role of lawyers in the new paradigm includes both a revised understanding of their responsibilities as client representatives, as well as the addition of a variety of entirely new functions.

Representing Clients in a Settlement Culture

Although lawyers continue to represent clients in the new paradigm, they do so within a changed dispute resolution framework.[14] Instead of assuming that disputes will be resolved by an argument over rights before a third-party decision-maker, the new paradigm assumes that resolution will generally occur through problem-solving and negotiation in which parties play an active role. Moreover, although these negotiations take place in the shadow of the law, neither legal rules nor rights dictate outcomes.[15] This shift from third-party adjudication to party-directed negotiation has significant implications for the role of lawyers as client representatives.

THE LAWYER AS COUNSELOR: REDEFINING CLIENT GOALS, NEEDS, AND INTERCONNECTED INTERESTS

The new paradigm has changed the obligations of attorneys as client representatives, redefining the meaning of competence and requiring a broader understanding of different ways to resolve disputes. Traditionally, a lawyer's role as counselor in family law and most other areas was viewed quite narrowly. The client would communicate his or her goals and the lawyer would help the client "succeed" by achieving those goals. The lawyer viewed the client in isolation, with interests largely antagonistic to those of other family disputants. In translating the client's goals to a legal remedy, the traditional family lawyer viewed the legal aspects of the dispute as easily severable from nonlegal issues, and attended only to the legal issues. When deciding about dispute resolution options, the lawyer viewed litigation as the obvious choice, with settlement negotiation between lawyers as a stage in the litigation process. Under this traditional model, the lawyer generally deferred to the client in framing goals but was the primary decision-maker and actor in achieving those goals.[16]

Under the new regime, the family lawyer plays a more active role in refining the client's goals and reorienting the client from a short-term to a long-term perspective. For example, a divorce client might initially articulate her goals to the lawyer as a "clean break" from her ex-spouse and sole custody of the children. Rather than simply asserting sole custody as the client's legal position, the lawyer might probe for the client's underlying interests and explore with the client the impact of her immediate goals on her children. As a result of this discussion, the client's short-term position might be adjusted to support her longer-term interest in preserving the children's relationship with both parents and thereby fostering the well-being of the children.[17] This attention to long-term interests is an outgrowth of the lawyer's reconception of the client as a part of a family system with interests that overlap with those of other family members, including the client's purported adversary. It also reflects the primacy of settlement in the new paradigm and thus the need to work toward solutions that meet the interests of both parties, as well as the needs of their children.

The new lawyer also takes a more active role in counseling the client about dispute resolution options, encouraging participation in those processes that promote settlement and client self-determination. While the lawyer would include litigation and traditional negotiation as options, she would also discuss the benefits of alternatives to litigation, including a wide range of mediation approaches, early neutral evaluation, and collaborative or cooperative practice. This discussion requires that the lawyer understand the way these processes work, the roles of the various players, and the benefits and risks of these alternatives. By acquiring and communicating this knowledge to the client, the lawyer acts as a "dispute resolution manager."[18]

The lawyer's role as a dispute resolution manager also requires that lawyers act as "gatekeepers." Not every client or dispute is appropriate for every dispute resolution process. For example, mediation may be counter-indicated for couples that have experienced domestic violence.[19] Moreover, different issues may lend themselves to resolution by different process options.[20] Thus, divorcing parties increasingly turn to mediation for child access issues while relying on arbitration or traditional negotiation for complicated property matters. Lawyers also help clients consider the financial and other costs associated with various dispute resolution options. Among the considerations is whether the client is willing and able to assume the substantial self-determination and self-advocacy required by many alternative dispute resolution processes.[21] Finally, depending on what dispute resolution option the client chooses, the lawyer may work with the client to select an appropriate neutral, assuming the choice is not mandated by the court.

All of these expanded counseling functions require the lawyer to develop a much more active and collaborative relationship with her client early in the representation process. Indeed, Canadian scholar Julie MacFarlane identifies the lawyer's relationship with her client as one of the three core dimensions that distinguish the new lawyer from her more traditional counterpart. Macfarlane explains that the new family lawyer "considers her client a partner in problem solving, at least to the extent that it is feasible and desirable (for the client) in any one case."[22] Similarly, collaborative practice views clients as co-participants in the dispute resolution process and gives them the ability and the responsibility to control the outcome. This partnership entails more client participation in both the choice of dispute resolution process and in the conduct of negotiations with the other side.

Macfarlane identifies two other dimensions that characterize the new lawyer. The first is the elevation of negotiation and problem-solving skills. Macfarlane acknowledges that lawyers have always negotiated on behalf of their clients, but notes that they have done so in a model that favors arm's-length communication between agents and positional bargaining in the shadow of the courtroom. "The old tools of positional bargaining, which are often a ritual bluff and bluster represented by a terse exchange of offers," do not serve the new lawyer or her client in the consensus-building that is at the heart of the new paradigm.[23] As a result, these techniques "are being replaced by greater reliance on problem-solving strategies and more effort to directly include the client in face-to-face negotiation."[24]

The other core dimension is an enhanced focus on interpersonal communication, not for the purpose of courtroom advocacy, but rather as the primary vehicle for the resolution of conflict, whether via negotiation, mediation, or another settlement process. Macfarlane notes that effective interpersonal communication includes "so-called emotional, as well as legal, intelligence, including attributes, such as empathy, self-awareness, optimism, and impulse control, which are important qualities for an effective negotiator."[25] Communicating persuasively in a settlement culture also means paying greater attention to what the other side in a dispute needs and wants, since successful resolution depends on obtaining the assent of both parties.

THE LAWYERS AS DISPUTE RESOLUTION ADVOCATE:
SUPPORTING CLIENT SELF-DETERMINATION

In a traditional adversarial model, the family lawyer plays the central role in the "advocacy" stage of the proceeding, either in pretrial negotiation or, less often, in court.[26] Clients are consulted about terms of settlement but generally are not present during settlement negotiations. Indeed, studies of negotiation practice, including among family lawyers, suggest that lawyers control both the process and the outcome of negotiation in an adversary regime.[27] If a case goes to court, the lawyer tells the client's "story," while the client plays a relatively minor role as witness. The client's participation is limited to answering the lawyer's questions on direct or cross-examination.

In the new regime, clients play a much more active role in the dispute resolution process. For example, client self-determination and party empowerment are at the core of both mediation and collaborative law. In the mediation context, this client role usually translates to active participation in the mediation, with the parties, rather than their lawyers, directly expressing their needs and interests. It also means that parties are the primary decision-makers not only about the terms of the ultimate agreement, but also about how their interests will be expressed and framed. This enhanced party "voice" is "associated with parties feeling that the mediation process and outcome are fair and legitimate."[28] To the extent that clients need help in navigating the process, mediators, rather than lawyers, are charged with the task of "structuring the mediation process and asking questions in order to improve communication between the parties."[29]

Collaborative law similarly emphasizes the centrality of the client's role. Indeed, leading collaborative authorities stress that responsibility for resolving a dispute "rests firmly on the shoulders of the client."[30] To achieve a comprehensive and durable agreement, collaborative practitioners insist that clients, rather than their lawyers, assume responsibility for considering, weighing, and deciding among the available options. As one commentator colorfully described the clients' role, "Whereas in traditional negotiation, clients, like traditional fathers at the birth of their children, sit in a waiting room—actually separate waiting rooms—while the lawyers work out some of the most important details of the clients' future lives; in [collaborative practice] the clients shape and take ownership of their futures."[31]

Lawyers play a more limited role in most of the settlement-focused dispute resolution settings. In the early days of family mediation,[32] for example, many lawyers viewed themselves as peripheral when clients participated in mediation. Seeing themselves as bystanders to the process, lawyers frequently suggested that clients attend mediation sessions without lawyers and consult with the attorney only if an agreement was reached.[33] Some proponents of mediation actively discouraged the participation of lawyers.[34] While this narrow view of the lawyer's role in mediation has changed, lawyers continue to play a supporting, rather than a primary, role when cases move to the mediation table. Lawyers help prepare clients to articulate their needs and interests in mediation through the counseling process described above. Once parties reach mediation, the lawyer may or may not be present. If present, the lawyer is expected to defer to the party's voice, but may provide some "coaching" about the legal implications of the client's interests and potential agreements. The lawyer might also monitor the client's disclosure of information during mediation, with an eye toward the potential impact of such disclosures if the case moves to litigation. The lawyer's principal role during mediation, however, is to review, and in some cases draft, agreements reached by their clients. Research suggests that the more experience lawyers have as counsel in mediation, the more likely they are to promote "client involvement, and adopt a less adversarial and more problem-solving approach during the session."[35]

While lawyers assume a more active role in collaborative practice than in mediation, collaborative lawyers share both agenda-setting and decision-making authority with their clients. For example, all significant collaborative negotiations are conducted in meetings at which both lawyers and clients are present. Moreover, clients assume a primary role during these four-way meetings, both in articulating their goals and needs and in generating and evaluating options to meet those needs.

Collaborative lawyers and their clients also share responsibility for generating the governing norms and standards by which to evaluate settlement options. Legal norms are relevant, but are only one reference point among many. The parties' standard of fairness is equally important, "and part of the collaborative process is the joint search for, and the adoption of, the parties' particular standard."[36] Thus, collaborative lawyers work in partnership with their clients, both with respect to generating outcomes and in managing the dispute resolution process.

Another way that lawyers share responsibility with clients in the new paradigm is by providing "unbundled" legal services or limited task representation rather than full representation.[37] When clients retain lawyers for unbundled services, the "attorney performs some, but not all, of the tasks contained in the traditional full-service model. The lawyer may represent the client on the complex issues and coach the client on the simpler aspects of the matter (the most common pattern)."[38] These services may be related to traditional litigation—conducting legal research, drafting or reviewing pleadings, accomplishing service of process, or preparing clients for or attending court appearances. Discrete task representation can also support clients in the newer dispute resolution alternatives. A client may engage a lawyer to discuss dispute resolution options, to prepare for mediation, to coach or "script" the client's role in the negotiation process, to attend a mediation or negotiation session, or to review or draft an agreement reached during mediation or direct negotiation with the other party. Engaging a collaborative lawyer for a non-litigated resolution is also a form of limited representation.

The availability of unbundled legal services responds, in large part, to the vast number of parties in family cases who cannot afford full representation, but need assistance with specific legal tasks or aspects of their dispute.[39] Some clients may also see limited task representation as a way to retain more control over the resolution of their dispute. When a client retains a lawyer for limited representation, "the client and lawyer decide together which tasks would be most appropriate for the lawyer to perform, and which the client will handle."[40] In this way, clients "retain control over the process and . . . call upon the attorney for discrete, specific tasks."[41]

Unbundled legal representation has been embraced by the American Bar Association, state bar associations, and judges throughout the country.[42] Lawyers are increasingly making these services available to build their own practices and to respond to client wishes, particularly in family law, where the demand for limited scope representation has been the highest. Experts expect that limited representation will continue to grow as fears of malpractice exposure prove unfounded and ethical rules are modified to accommodate this new role for lawyers.

THE LAWYER AS PLANNER: PREVENTING CONFLICT AND HARM

The lawyer–client relationship in family law traditionally began after a serious dispute between family members had occurred. The client would consult a lawyer when her husband or live-in partner moved out or, more likely, when she wanted to commence a legal action or was served with court papers. The lawyer and client would then engage in what has been called "legal triage for acute legal problems."[43]

In the new regime, by contrast, family lawyers increasingly play a role before a conflict occurs. This pre-dispute consultation emphasizes the lawyer's roles as a planner and "peacemaker." Lawyers in this role help clients by proposing a plan for the careful private ordering of affairs as a method of avoiding the high costs of litigation and ensuring desired outcomes and opportunities.[44] While the concept of preventive law has been around for decades, it has gained new currency with the changed focus in family dispute resolution.[45] Familiar examples of the family lawyer's role as planner include drafting and advising about prenuptial and domestic partnership agreements, which are now widely accepted and enforced by courts.[46] But today's preventive lawyer goes further in counseling individuals to use legal mechanisms to anticipate and plan for family transitions.[47] This kind of planning is particularly helpful to clients such as nonmarital partners or de facto parents, who may be unprotected by the law in the absence of an agreement. Lawyers can engage in interdisciplinary partnerships to anticipate and resolve issues, ranging from establishing or limiting parentage to delineating post-separation obligations. Family lawyers also advise clients to designate dispute resolution methods in advance of conflicts, urging the use of mediation or other alternatives to litigation. In this way, lawyers help clients anticipate and prepare for family transitions, thus reducing the possibility of conflict or mitigating the harm from it.

THE LAWYER AS HEALER: RESTORING AND IMPROVING
FAMILY RELATIONSHIPS

Family lawyers who represent clients in the new paradigm may also seek to expand their role from advocacy to "healing." For decades, prominent lawyers and academics, including Harvard Law School dean Erwin Griswold and former Chief Justice Warren Burger, have urged lawyers to use their skills as problem-solvers to reduce conflict and help clients to heal rather than fight.[48] More recently, an overarching framework for the lawyer as "healer" has emerged in the "comprehensive law movement." This movement takes "an explicitly . . . integrated, humanistic, interdisciplinary, restorative, and often therapeutic approach to law and lawyering. It is the result of a synthesis of a number of new disciplines within law and legal practice . . . collaborative law, creative problem solving, holistic justice, preventive law, problem solving courts, procedural justice, restorative justice, therapeutic jurisprudence, and transformative mediation."[49]

Echoing the ambitious goals of the new family court system, the lawyer as healer moves beyond resolving disputes and seeks to improve the legal, emotional, and psychological well-being of her clients and their families. As a leading proponent of collaborative law, Pauline Tesler, has explained, "A successful collaborative representation not only resolves the legal issues associated with divorce, it can also help the clients aspire to and achieve transition through an extremely difficult life passage with dignity and a sense of recovered competency and wholeness."[50] The goals for both attorneys and judges who approach the law from this perspective are to "improve or repair" family relationships and help family members find "a greater sense of resolution, closure, and respect for each other and the justice system."[51]

Lawyers practice "healing" when they work with clients—often in partnership with other professionals—to frame goals and make dispute resolution choices that "maximize the emotional, psychological, and relational well-being of the individuals and communities involved."[52] Lawyers also help families heal from conflict and (re)build a parenting partnership when they encourage non-adversarial dispute resolution options such as mediation and collaborative practice. Similarly, a lawyer who assumes the role of a neutral may choose a process that focuses on healing over dispute resolution or other goals. Transformative mediation, for example, is an approach to mediation that measures success "not by settlement *per se* but by party shifts toward personal strength, interpersonal responsiveness, and constructive interaction."[53] Under this model, the mediator's focus is on transforming the parties' interactions with one another from "destructive to constructive," on the assumption that this, rather than the settlement of a single dispute, will contribute more to healing the relationship.[54]

In addition to viewing law as a way to "heal" clients, the new paradigm holds out the promise of "healing" lawyers as well. Much has been written about lawyers' dissatisfaction with traditional law practice, particularly in family law.[55] Family lawyers see clients "under extreme stress, whether grieving, angry, or fearful, or in a state of significant, though transient, diminished capacity."[56] As a result, family lawyers deal with angry and unhappy clients on a regular basis. Even clients who "win" in court are often dissatisfied at the end of the case, having experienced the emotional trauma of the family conflict and often "want[ing] results courts are wholly unable to provide."[57] For these reasons, family lawyers are particularly vulnerable to the high incidence of stress, substance abuse, and "burnout" experienced by the legal profession.

Lawyers who have shifted their role from advocate to healer often report more rewarding relationships with clients and more satisfaction with their work. For example, a leading advocate of collaborative law has written, "Not least of the benefits of collaborative practice is that it seems to evoke in those lawyers who embrace it a rekindled joy in the practice of law."[58] By seeking to heal their clients' relationships and to increase their clients' well-being, lawyers improve their own well-being and career satisfaction.[59]

Lawyers as Dispute Resolution Neutrals

In addition to transforming the role of the family lawyer when representing clients, the new regime offers enhanced opportunities for lawyers to serve as neutrals who facilitate agreements, evaluate competing claims, or, in some instances, resolve disputes. To be sure, family lawyers have always moved in small numbers from practicing law to serving as judges or other hearing officers. But the new regime allows lawyers to combine client representation with work as a dispute resolution neutral, and to shift back and forth between these roles.

Although many lawyers now serve as mediators, lawyers were largely absent in the early days of the family mediation movement. In the early 1980s, nearly 80 percent of the family mediators in the private sector, and more than 90 percent in the public sector were mental health professionals.[60] Few lawyers were mediators, and many lawyers and legal organizations actively opposed mediation. This started to shift in the 1990s with the rise of mandatory mediation and the development by the Family Law Section of the ABA of model standards aimed specifically at lawyer–mediators. A primary goal of the ABA standards was to permit lawyers to serve as mediators without violating the ethical ban on representing both husband and wife in a divorce.[61] The standards were successful in achieving this goal. By 1996, lawyers made up nearly 40 percent of the membership of the Academy of Family Mediators.[62] As mediation pioneer Bernard Mayer has colorfully put it, "the law profession at first resisted mediation and then co-opted it."[63] Under the new dispute resolution regime, opportunities continue to increase for lawyers to serve as private or court-based mediators, either in full-time positions or as part of a more general law practice.

The new paradigm also offers lawyers other opportunities to serve as neutrals. For example, some lawyers have assumed the role of parenting coordinators who serve as a "combination educator, mediator, and limited purpose arbitrator in parenting disputes."[64] Judges may appoint parenting coordinators in ongoing cases or private parties may retain them to manage recurring child custody and visitation issues. While such coordinators generally are not empowered to decide or change court orders establishing primary or joint custody, they are often authorized to resolve minor conflicts about children's schedules, activities, child-care arrangements, or other day-to-day matters.[65]

Lawyers have also assumed the role of "early neutral evaluator" (ENE), most often in court-based or court-supported programs. Drawing on elements of mediation, arbitration, and case management, a number of family courts now require or permit parties to participate in a process in which an ENE evaluates child access or financial issues.[66] Depending on the nature of the dispute, ENEs can be nonlegal court staff, accountants, or lawyers. The goal of these programs is to provide an evaluation of the merits of the case early in the process so that parties, particularly *pro se* litigants, can make more informed decisions about whether to pursue litigation. To this end, the ENE meets with the parties, analyzes relevant information, and provides a report about the likely resolution of the issues were the case to proceed to trial. If the parties settle, the ENE will draft the agreement. Many of these programs follow expedited schedules, often resulting in a report within two or three months of the filing of a complaint.[67] The expectation is that this process will encourage parties to settle and will resolve disputes more quickly and less expensively than litigation or other processes.

Finally, family lawyers can serve as neutrals for parties with resources, who retain them as arbitrators[68] or private judges.[69] In both instances, the lawyers derive their authority to serve as neutrals from the agreement of the parties. Unlike a mediator, an arbitrator or private judge makes a decision for the parties, and the agreements typically provide that the neutral's decision will be binding and final.[70] This form of "private adjudication" permits parties to control both the process and choice of "judge" and to preserve privacy.

Lawyers who serve as third-party neutrals occupy a middle ground between client representatives and judges. They act as facilitators, evaluators, or decision-makers, depending on the process used. These roles require many of the same skills as lawyers use to represent clients in the new paradigm. At the same time, these roles have much in common with functions that judges have traditionally performed. Lawyers who serve as neutrals may develop the rules governing the process that, despite often being quite informal, determine what is said and what is excluded from the discussion. Similarly, if the process is evaluative or binding by the parties' agreement, lawyer neutrals render decisions that share the characteristics of judicial judgments. Despite these similarities to judging, lawyer neutrals are still bound by ethical rules that conceive of lawyers as client representatives.

New Roles for Judges

The paradigm shift in family dispute resolution has generated new roles for judges as well as lawyers. The traditional goal of judging, in family and other civil matters, has been to adjudicate disputes. As a result, the judge's principal role was to preside over trials, hear from competing sides, and declare a "winner." As discussed in chapter 3, the new family court has expanded its goals beyond dispute resolution to include problem-solving, healing, and proactive management of family conflict. To accomplish these ambitious goals, many courts are now designed to "provide coordinated holistic services . . . to address the physical and mental needs of the family."[71] To accomplish this expanded mission, judges have assumed a range of new roles. Adjudicating legal rights may now be secondary to the therapeutic goals of diagnosing and treating family dysfunction and managing family reorganization. Moreover, as family dockets and court personnel expand, judges have assumed substantial administrative and managerial duties, particularly in large urban jurisdictions.

Judges as Problem-Solvers and Interdisciplinary Team Members

In many family courts, judges work closely with lawyers, mental health professionals, and court personnel to address a wide range of family needs. While the matters that bring a family to court are initially framed as legal issues, problem-solving courts and judges approach the family "holistically."[72] Judges involve a wide range of stakeholders and consider a host of interconnected issues in an attempt to create a lasting solution to the family's conflicts and dysfunctions. In addition to the disputants themselves, these problem-solving teams might include other family members, social workers, psychologists, substance abuse specialists, mediators, and evaluators who work together to develop plans to address the family's long-term needs.

The judge's role in this process is characterized by "hands-on judicial involvement."[73] As one National Center for State Courts report described it, "Problem-solving courts require judges to be personally engaged with each [party], and this personal involvement creates a tension with the traditional role of the judge as a detached, neutral arbiter."[74] Depending on the extent of that involvement, the problem-solving judge has been variously described as "coach,"[75] "social worker,"[76] "cheerleader,"[77] or "therapist."[78]

While some family court judges have expressed concern over these new roles,[79] many judges have found enhanced satisfaction in going from "detached neutral arbiter to the central figure in the team."[80] A recent survey of 355 judges compared the level of judicial satisfaction experienced by judges in problem-solving courts (drug courts and unified family courts) with judges in traditional courts hearing family and criminal cases. The authors found "that the problem-solving model that is developing in the movement toward family court reform has potential to increase judicial satisfaction for family court judges."[81] Earlier studies of problem-solving drug treatment courts revealed similar positive therapeutic outcomes for judges. "As two judges write, 'judging in this non-traditional form becomes an invigorating self-actualizing and rewarding exercise.'"[82]

Judges as Settlement Advocates

Propelled by rising family law dockets and a commitment to non-adjudicative dispute resolution for families, judges have become settlement advocates in their courts. While judges have long presided over settlement conferences in family law cases, "'settlement seeking' has now become a 'core activity' for family court judges in parenting disputes."[83]

Drawing on interviews with family court judges and practitioners in Canada and New York, researcher Noel Semple recently explored the ways in which judges "prioritize the pursuit of voluntary settlement."[84] While judges draw on a variety of approaches in doing this work, the predominate model was one in which the judge conducts some evaluation of the legal issues in the case and shares it with the parties in an effort to encourage settlement. Judges and practitioners distinguished the active role judges play in settlement conferences from the more facilitative and passive role of a mediator.

Encouraging judges to act as settlement advocates raises concerns about judicial neutrality. For example, parties may assume that a judge's comments during settlement discussions will govern the judge's decisions if that judge hears the case on the merits.[85] As a result, when judges conducting settlement conferences make predictions or comments about the law, parties, especially when unrepresented, may believe that their settlement options are limited. This concern about prejudgment is particularly pronounced, Semple concludes, where the governing legal standard is highly discretionary—as it is in custody and child access cases. In response to these concerns, some court systems use a model in which the "settlement seeking" judge hands off the case to another judge should the parties proceed to trial. Even under this model, however, settlement judges may have implied authority or "moral suasion."[86]

Prejudgment concerns are especially salient in "one-judge" models, in which the same judge who conducts the settlement discussions will hear the case if no settlement is reached. Judges and lawyers in Semple's study reported that judges were particularly "effective" in reaching settlement when the parties knew the case would be heard by the same judge.[87] Judges also opined that the "one judge" system was a more efficient use of judicial resources, in that judges who engaged in settlement discussions were more familiar with the cases at trial than a new judge would be.[88]

Judges in the new paradigm also delegate settlement duties to others. This delegation may involve custody evaluators, parenting coordinators, early neutral evaluators, volunteer practitioners, retired judges, or court-based family mediation programs.[89] As part of this delegation process, judges work with parties and, when present, their lawyers, to decide whether a particular dispute resolution option is appropriate and to identify the best point in time for the process to occur.[90]

Judges have also developed new systems designed to encourage and support lawyers seeking to resolve cases outside of court. Some courts have created local rules or practices that stay court proceedings and deadlines while parties attempt to resolve a case through mediation or collaborative practice. The Uniform Collaborative Law Act, adopted by a number of jurisdictions, requires that litigants notify courts when they sign a collaborative participation agreement and treats that notification as an application for a stay of judicial proceedings.[91] In one jurisdiction, a family court judge has created a "Collaborative Law Department," designating "a single courtroom where collaborative lawyers . . . could bring any problems that might arise in their cases. . . . [W]ith the establishment of this department, collaborative law cases would be put on a special track once they were filed, where they could be nurtured and where the collaborative law agreement would be enforced."[92]

Judges as Case Managers

Family cases in the traditional adversary system followed a predictable and fairly consistent track once brought to court. The case began with the filing of a complaint and answer, and then proceeded to trial if the case did not settle, with a possible scheduling or settlement conference along the way. Unless one or both parties filed pretrial motions, courts generally did not initiate any further activity in the case until immediately before trial.

Managing cases in today's family courts is a much more proactive and complex task. As a result, case management has become more central than adjudication to the judge's role, particularly in large urban jurisdictions.[93] Where parties are unrepresented, this case management role may require a judge to assume some of the functions traditionally allocated to lawyers. While judges have always been more active in hearings that proceed without lawyers, this transfer of roles in the new regime goes well beyond the courtroom setting. Judges work with parties early in cases to manage and educate about dispute resolution options. Through management and referral to programs such as parent education, judges also serve a counseling and supportive role traditionally reserved for lawyers.

Over a decade ago, Andrew Schepard described the initial phase of this redefinition of the judicial role as one that transformed the family court judge from "fault finder" to "conflict manager."[94] Schepard argued that to fully realize the goal of improved outcomes for families in court, judges needed to complete a third phase of judicial transformation:

> Phase III custody courts need to establish differential case management plans (DCM) for high conflict cases. These plans should develop criteria to "triage" these particularly difficult cases early in their judicial life cycle without burdening the great percentage of reasonably cooperative divorcing parents with unduly intrusive state intervention . . . Mental health and child protection systems must be integrated into the DCM plan. DCM plans also must create an expedited, actively managed dispute resolution plan for the chaotic and conflicted families involved in high conflict cases to insure that someone in authority monitors the behavior of parents and the welfare of their children.[95]

In the decade since Schepard made his predictions, many family courts and judges have moved into this phase of more sophisticated and complex case management. Judges have adopted a variety of approaches to accomplish these management tasks. In what has been called a "tiered service" model, judges begin child access cases by referring parties to educational programs to prepare them for post-separation parenting and to provide basic information about the legal system's approach to these cases.[96] Under this tiered system, most cases then proceed to mediation as the preferred dispute resolution process. If mediation is unsuccessful, other court personnel, including volunteer attorneys and judges, may engage parties in further settlement efforts as a prerequisite to a court hearing.

Other court systems have developed different tracks for cases depending on, among other factors, the level of conflict and the services needed by families. Under this "triage" model, judges and other court personnel devote substantial time and attention to determining which dispute resolution process and educational, therapeutic, or assessment programs are appropriate for a given case.[97] In addition to mediation, cases are screened for a variety of other processes, including "conflict resolution conferences; non-confidential dispute resolution and assessment, personal communication; early neutral evaluations special programs for high-conflict and chronically litigating families; collaborative law; cooperative negotiation agreements; and parenting coordination."[98] In this sense, many of today's family courts are approaching Frank Sander's vision of becoming not just "a courthouse but a Dispute Resolution Center, where the grievant would first be channeled through a screening clerk who would then direct him to the process (or sequence of processes) most appropriate to his type of case."[99]

Judicial responsibility for triaging cases further complicates the judicial role. However, many advocates of the new paradigm argue that it will "provide the most appropriate services, resulting in more efficient use of resources and reducing the burden on families."[100] At the same time, scholars have cautioned that the combination of expanded dispute resolution options and the large numbers of unrepresented parties pose significant challenges for family courts attempting to make informed triaging decisions. Nancy Ver Steegh and others have questioned whether court-based "triage professionals" can make these decisions in ways that insure the "substantive and procedural safeguards necessary to preserve confidentiality, protect litigants' due process rights, and provide accountability," particularly with respect to families experiencing domestic violence.[101]

Judges in the new paradigm also engage in ongoing monitoring of family cases through review and status hearings, requiring continuing court involvement even after the entry of a final order. The increased prevalence of joint legal custody and other shared parenting arrangements has expanded opportunities for such ongoing judicial involvement. All of these functions require judges in the new family courts to spend substantial time on administration and management. They also enhance the similarities between child access disputes between parents and more public child welfare cases, where judges and other court personnel have traditionally exercised an ongoing family oversight role.

Implications of New Roles for Lawyers and Judges

The expanded roles of lawyers and judges in the new paradigm hold significant promise for families. For example, clients who are advised about the range of dispute resolution options are better able to choose the option that will work best for them. Collaborative lawyers who involve clients in settlement negotiations and who share decision-making authority should create more satisfying lawyer–client relationships, as well as more durable parenting agreements. Unbundling and discrete task representation should increase the availability and reduce the costs of legal representation. And in those cases that reach the court system, families may benefit from judicial flexibility and more active case management, as well as from the ability to choose among court-based dispute resolution options. Court-based education and conflict resolution services should also strengthen families and reduce the likelihood of future litigation.

But these transformed roles also present challenges for lawyers, judges and family disputants that have not been fully explored or addressed. First, the majority of today's family litigants have no lawyers and, therefore, will not realize the benefits of working with the "new" family lawyer. Moreover, these unrepresented parties may be particularly vulnerable in a court system made more powerful and complex by the new judicial roles. As one commentator noted when analyzing the changing nature of family law practice:

> So long as the trends toward increasing social and economic polarization of the country continue, it seems likely that there will be more than ever two worlds of family law practice. In one world, those who can afford marriage and divorce will be able to order their family affairs with relative privacy and with access to complex multidisciplinary services, managed by highly specialized family law attorneys. The other world will be one in which those who cannot afford private legal representation will have their families managed by government entities in which lawyers will play a far more limited role and routine legal services will be delivered in the least expensive manner possible, often by paraprofessionals with specialized training only in their particular family law field.[102]

The changed roles of both lawyers and judges have also blended the previously distinctive functions of each of these critical legal players. While the resulting flexibility creates new opportunities to respond to families in conflict, this blurring of roles may have unintended consequences that could harm rather than help families. Lawyers and judges in the new regime have many overlapping functions. These blurred roles may occur in a single case. For example, the lawyer, who once focused primarily on the client's interests, and the judge, formerly focused on adjudicating the dispute, are now engaged in the common task of "problem-solving." This involves both the lawyer and judge seeking services and solutions for the family that may go beyond resolving the dispute. In this process, judges and lawyers may also serve as part of a team that includes a number of nonlegal professionals. In these settings, where team members are aligned in supporting a plan that minimizes the relevance of legal norms, judges, lawyers, and other team members may all play very similar roles.

These blurred roles raise challenges in preserving the integrity and fairness of the family dispute resolution system. Accountability may be diminished in a system where lawyers and judges share roles. It may be unclear who has made decisions and what standards apply to those decisions. When a client is unhappy with decisions reached as a result of team "problem-solving," who is responsible? Similarly, when lawyers act as facilitators or decision-makers in mediation, arbitration, or private judging, questions may arise about the respective responsibilities of the lawyer neutrals and the judge overseeing the case should the parties seek court approval of decisions reached privately or return to court for post-judgment matters. When judges act to promote settlement, the parties' perception of the judge's traditional decision-making role may compromise the voluntariness of the parties' decision to settle.[103] Having the same judge serve as both settlement seeker and adjudicator may also raise due process concerns, given the difficulty of ignoring inadmissible information revealed during unsuccessful settlement discussions.[104]

These new roles also challenge the ethical norms that have traditionally governed the conduct of judges and lawyers. For example, while the scope of representation may be limited, attorneys providing discrete services form an attorney–client relationship and are bound by the ethics rules governing the practice of law.

Lawyers' ethical rules, however, generally assume the full representation model. As a result, discrete task representation may challenge notions of competency,[105] loyalty to client,[106] and the lawyer's obligations to the administration of justice.[107] On a more practical level, providing unbundled legal services, particularly in a high-volume, court-based setting, may result in inadvertent violations of rules governing actual, potential, or imputed conflicts of interest among clients.[108] Opposing counsel in cases where the other party has engaged a lawyer for limited representation may also risk violating ethical rules that prevent a lawyer from communicating directly with clients who are represented by counsel.[109] When limited representation involves court appearances or drafting documents, there may be uncertainty about the lawyer's obligation to disclose his or her assistance[110] or withdraw from the case after the end of his or her involvement.[111]

The practice of collaborative family law has also posed challenges to traditional notions of professional responsibility. For example, the disqualification requirement at the heart of collaborative practice was initially challenged as contrary to traditional ethical standards that limit attorney withdrawals that prejudice clients.[112] This concern is particularly acute for low-income clients who may not have other options for representation if a collaborative lawyer withdraws because settlement efforts have failed. Opponents of collaborative practice have also argued that a lawyer who signs a four-way collaborative participation agreement may assume duties to another party to the agreement, whose interests may conflict with those of the lawyer's client—a situation that could raise ethics concerns.[113]

The interdisciplinary nature of collaborative practice also poses ethical challenges. While it has long been common for family litigants to retain mental health or financial professionals at the same time as they retain lawyers, the collaborative model requires these professionals to work as a team and coordinate their client services.[114] This involvement of lawyers in team problem-solving with a systemic perspective challenges ethical norms related to undivided client loyalty and the duty to keep client communications confidential.[115] These interdisciplinary partnerships may also be at odds with rules prohibiting fee sharing between lawyers and non-lawyers, as well as the rules limiting the lawyer's ability to advise a client on nonlegal matters.[116]

Lawyers who serve as mediators may also confront ethical challenges. In particular, a lawyer acting as a mediator or other neutral may run afoul of conflict of interest rules if the mediator's discussion of legal information constitutes the practice of law and amounts to dual representation of the two family members.[117] Similar concerns arise when the lawyer mediator drafts or memorializes an agreement of the parties following mediation, particularly when the parties are unrepresented.[118]

The new roles assumed by judges are also in tension with the ethical guidelines and norms that continue to apply to judges in most jurisdictions. The judge's obligation to be impartial may be challenged when he leads or participates on a team working toward the improved health or well-being of a family member, particularly where the judge is urged to act as a "cheerleader" for particular parties in these proceedings.[119] For example, one of the founders of the therapeutic jurisprudence movement applauds the "the ability of a domestic-violence court judge to be more than 'merely adjudicatory,'" and argues that judges in problem-solving courts "can function as an advocate for victims."[120] But such advocacy seems inconsistent with the conception of a judge as a neutral umpire. This kind of teamwork may also result in judges having contacts with parties or lawyers that are arguably prohibited by the rules forbidding most ex parte contact by judges with parties before the court.[121] The ability of community groups to provide assistance to courts, a promising idea in family dispute resolution in some contexts, might also interfere with the ethical requirement that a judge "uphold the integrity and independence of the judiciary."[122]

The judge's role as settlement advocate may also be at odds with the existing ethical framework. While the judicial conduct code gives judges the right to pursue settlement,[123] the pressure to settle cases in today's large family courts may result in judges going beyond the role envisioned by the code. When judges lead settlement conferences in today's family courts, the majority of parties are unrepresented. Typical codes of judicial conduct assume the presence of counsel in settlement conferences, treating "parties unrepresented by counsel" as exceptional circumstances that warrant special consideration when a judge decides on an "appropriate settlement practice for a case."[124]

These tensions and disconnects between existing ethical norms and the new roles of lawyers and judges should not lead to rejection of these roles. Rather, it suggests that more work is needed both to modify existing rules to accommodate the new roles and to tailor the new roles to conform to ethical norms that are worth retaining. Some of this work has already started. As a result of the ABA's Ethics 2000 Amendments to the Model Rules of Professional Conduct, ABA Model Rule 1.2(c) has been adopted in most states to clarify lawyers' ability to provide limited scope representation, as long as it "is reasonable under the circumstances" and the lawyer obtains the client's informed, preferably written, consent.[125] The Ethics 2000 Amendments also included amendments to ABA Model Rule 6.5 that eliminate the lawyer's affirmative duty to check for potential client conflicts as well as the attribution of one lawyer's conflicts to other lawyers in the same organization as long as the lawyers are from legal services organizations serving low-income families.[126] While these amended rules begin the process of adapting the ethical framework to accommodate limited representation, much more is needed to encourage widespread availability of unbundled services.

A number of commentators have analyzed the rules and have suggested additional measures to address specific aspects of limited scope representation.[127] In 2014, the ABA issued a report examining efforts in various jurisdictions to facilitate limited representation and recommending modifications in ethical and procedural rules to better address the needs of *pro se* litigants and to accommodate lawyers' ability to provide unbundled legal services.[128] These commentators recommend more widespread adoption of specific rules to allow lawyers to withdraw from representation when they have completed the promised, limited representation, after giving the client notice and the opportunity to be heard if the client objects.[129]

There is also a need to clarify the scope of a lawyer's ability to provide "behind the scenes" assistance to *pro se* litigants, such as ghostwriting pleadings under the client's name or coaching a client for a hearing, without the lawyer entering an appearance with the court.[130] These changes will add greater protection to both clients and lawyers as limited scope representation expands throughout the country.

The ABA and a number of jurisdictions have also made changes in ethical codes to encourage the lawyer's role as "dispute resolution neutral."[131] In 2000, the ABA considered some of the ethical issues raised by the increasing numbers of lawyers acting as mediators. The group focused primarily on the lawyer–mediator's obligation to make clear to participants that he or she is not representing either of the parties. In doing so, the rule defines the nature of a lawyer who is acting as a "third-party neutral," stating that it may include "service as an arbitrator, a mediator, or in such other capacity as will enable the lawyer to assist the parties to resolve the matter."[132] As one commentator noted, "It is significant that for the first time the Rules refer to lawyers acting on behalf of individuals in a strictly non-representational capacity by explicitly stating that a third-party neutral 'assists two or more persons who are not clients.'"[133] The 2000 Amendments to the Model Rules of Professional Conduct also extended the application of Rule 1.12 beyond "judges and arbitrators" to include "mediator[s] or other third-party neutral[s]."[134] While these rules place limits on the conduct of attorney mediators, they provide needed guidance to lawyers assuming these new roles as dispute resolution neutrals.

Scholars and practitioners have also engaged in substantial efforts to address the ethical challenges presented by collaborative practice. In 2007, the ABA issued a formal ethics opinion finding that collaborative practice—including the attorney's obligation to withdraw if a matter goes to trial—represents a permissible limited scope representation under the ABA Model Rules, so long as the client gives informed consent. In particular, the lawyer must assure that the client understands that if the collaborative process does not result in settlement of the dispute, the collaborative lawyer must withdraw and the parties must retain new attorneys to litigate the case. The opinion also found that the disqualification provision and associated four-way agreement at the heart of collaborative practice did not create a non-waivable conflict of interest under the ABA rules. The ABA reasoned that when a client has given informed consent to a representation limited to collaborative settlement efforts, the lawyer's agreement to withdraw if the collaboration fails does not impair the lawyer's ability to represent the client, but rather is consistent with the client's limited goals for the representation. The ABA opinion accords with a number of state bar ethics opinions, which have concluded that collaborative law is generally consistent with the Model Rules of Professional Conduct and the obligations of lawyers to clients.[135]

The Uniform Collaborative Law Act (UCLA), approved in 2007 and enacted in a handful of states, also seeks to harmonize collaborative practice with the traditional ethical obligations of lawyers. The UCLA "mandates essential elements of a process of disclosure and discussion between prospective collaborative lawyers and prospective parties to better insure that parties who sign participation agreements do so with informed consent."[136] The UCLA also obligates collaborative lawyers to screen clients for domestic violence and, if such violence is present, to proceed with a collaborative process only if the victim consents and the attorney reasonably believes that the victim is safe. In addition, the UCLA creates an evidentiary privilege, held by the parties, for communications made during the course of the collaborative law process.[137]

The UCLA also provides a mechanism to respond to concerns about the impact of lawyer disqualification on low-income clients. Advocates for low-income clients had expressed concern that vulnerable clients would be left without legal representation if a collaborative process fails, due to the imputed conflict rules that would disqualify entire legal aid offices if the collaborative lawyer had to withdraw from the case.[138] The UCLA provides for an exemption from the imputed conflict rule when the collaborative client is a low-income client, and appropriate precautions are in place to avoid disclosure of information to the litigation attorney in the legal aid or legal services office.[139]

Scholars and practitioners have paid less attention to the changes in the judicial role and to whether those changes necessitate modification of existing norms for judicial conduct. The National Drug Court Institute (NDCI) has begun this task for problem-solving courts, focusing on the role of judges in drug courts.[140] The NDCI's work in this area provides a good model for evaluating and analyzing judicial ethics in other problem-solving courts, including family courts.

Conclusion

The new paradigm has expanded and transformed the roles of lawyers and judges. Lawyers have moved beyond their traditional role as zealous advocates for individual clients to become planners, healers, and dispute resolution advocates. Even when lawyers continue to act as client representatives, the new paradigm invites more active client participation and a more equal sharing of decision-making authority. Many family lawyers have also become dispute resolution neutrals, and have taken on some of the functions traditionally associated with judges. At the same time, the role of family court judges has also changed. Judges are no longer just "neutral umpires"; instead, they have become active managers of cases and dockets, as well as leaders or members of interdisciplinary teams. They have also become settlement advocates and have taken on functions traditionally associated with lawyering. This reconfiguring and blurring of attorney and judicial roles challenges existing ethical rules, as well as the concepts of lawyering and judging on which these ethical norms are based. While scholars and practitioners have begun to rethink these ethical rules, much work remains to be done.

6

The Influence of Comparative and International Family Law

The United States is not the only country to have experienced a "velvet revolution" in family dispute resolution.[1] Similar changes have taken place in countries throughout the industrialized world, particularly in western Europe and the British Commonwealth. Moreover, the growing importance of international law norms regarding children's participation in legal proceedings has influenced the shape of family court reform in a number of jurisdictions outside the United States. American judges, court reformers, and academics have been exposed to these developments through collegial exchanges, journal articles, and professional and scholarly conferences.[2] In this chapter, we describe these international and comparative law developments, explain how they have influenced reform efforts in the United States, and suggest how they might serve as models for further innovation.

Out of the Court System and into the Community

The focus of family dispute resolution reform in the United States has been on court-based processes and services, with the court situated at the center of a problem-solving dispute resolution regime. In Australia, by contrast, recent reform efforts have shifted family dispute resolution away from the court system and into the community. The central feature of this move from court- to community-based processes and services has been the development of a nationwide network of Family Relationship Centres (FRCs).

FRCs are community-based institutions, funded by the Australian government, that provide dispute resolution and support services to families experiencing child-related conflict, in particular parents who have separated from each other or who are contemplating separation.[3] The Centres provide education, advice, referrals, and mediation to individuals and families at little or no cost. A key purpose of the FRCs "is as an early intervention initiative to help parents work out post-separation parenting arrangements and manage the transition from parenting together to parenting apart."[4] The Centres are designed to act both as an initial response service and as the triage unit for family breakdown.

In addition to providing services, the FRCs have a broader, philosophical purpose. "One of the aims of the FRCs is to achieve a long-term cultural change in the pathways people take to resolve disputes about parenting arrangements after separation."[5] The concept is that parents who are in conflict about their children have a relationship problem, but not necessarily a legal one. The centrality of the FRCs in the family law system was designed to signal that most post-separation parenting disputes are primarily relationship problems that are best resolved through relationship-focused services. The FRCs thus seek to "reframe parental conflicts arising from divorce and separation from a legal problem with relationship conflicts to a community public health problem with legal elements."[6] As two leading American commentators explain, "The FRCs were created to change the Australian national culture of separation and divorce by creating a social norm that parents and children should plan their own futures rather than going to court to resolve their disputes. They are designed to replace the court system or a lawyer's office as the first port of call for divorcing and separating families in Australia."[7]

Unlike the court-centric approach of the United States, the Australian reforms "locate responsibility for the design and implementation of mediation and education services for divorcing and separating families in a national community-based system of service providers, rather than the court system."[8] Consistent with this community orientation, the FRCs are not located in or near courthouses, but rather in highly visible shopping centers and malls, and they are operated not by the government, but by community-based organizations, experienced in counseling and mediation.[9] Moreover, although the FRCs operate under national guidelines, individual Centres have considerable autonomy to tailor their services and approaches to the particular needs and characteristics of the communities they serve. These design characteristics reinforce the message that "separating and divorcing families, with all of their impacts on the parent and child mental health, the workplace, the court system, and the future of the society, are the communities' responsibility, not the legal system's alone."[10]

Although the FRCs are designed to help parents resolve disputes related to separation and divorce, they also provide more comprehensive family services. In particular, the Centres seek to provide information and support to parents going through relationship difficulties. They do this primarily by referring such parents to relationship counseling, or to services to address more specific problems such as gambling, alcohol addiction, financial problems, or anger management.[11] The FRCs are also meant to play a role in strengthening intact family relationships "by offering an accessible source for information and referral on relationship and parenting issues, and providing a gateway to other government and nongovernment services to support families."[12] Indeed, "the potential for a supportive and preventive role in strengthening family life and in helping people whose relationships are experiencing significant difficulties was a key rationale for the development of the FRCs."[13]

In addition to serving parents, the FRCs are intended to address the needs of other family members affected by parental conflict. "In particular, they offer a way of addressing grandparents' desire to remain involved in the grandchildren's lives when involvement has become problematic, as a consequence of parental separation."[14] In addition, the Centres support couples contemplating marriage by providing information about premarriage education.

The Australian government has made an extensive financial and political commitment to the FRCs. Indeed, the government has described the FRC initiative as "the biggest investment in Australian family law ever."[15] During the initial three-year rollout period from 2006 to 2009, the government spent nearly $400 million (AUD) and established sixty-five FRCs across the country.[16] Each FRC serves about three hundred thousand people. In order to ensure that there were sufficient services to which the FRCs could refer clients, the government also expanded the range of post-separation services available to families, including additional contact centers to provide safe transfer arrangements between parents having difficulty managing parenting time transitions, and an intensive therapeutic program for high-conflict families.[17] The government also launched a major advertising campaign to ensure public awareness and to educate people about the Centres.[18] The personal involvement of the prime minister was a major factor in approving and funding these new initiatives.[19]

Although the FRCs represented a major new initiative, they built on prior reforms in family law and dispute resolution in Australia. Those efforts included a strong nonprofit relationship counseling sector, thirty years of experience with a court-based conciliation service in the Family Court of Australia, and the gradual development, since the mid-1980s, of a range of community-based mediation services to assist separated parents.[20] Moreover, the FRC initiative grew out of forces similar to those that produced the new paradigm in the United States. The FRCs were created during a time of ferment about the role of law, courts, and lawyers in family disputes. As in the United States, empirical research provided increasingly persuasive evidence that children of separating and divorcing parents were at enhanced risk for emotional, educational, and economic difficulties as a result of their parents' conflict. In the face of this evidence, several Australian commissions and studies raised questions about whether courts were too adversarial a forum to resolve separation and divorce-related parenting issues.[21] The FRCs were a direct response to these concerns.

The FRCs were also a response to political pressure by interest groups, particularly fathers' rights organizations. "Fathers' groups, in particular, put great pressure on the Australian national government to redress what they perceived of as gender bias in parenting determinations by enacting a presumption of joint parenting."[22] In response to this pressure, the government, in 2003, initiated a parliamentary inquiry to explore the option of a rebuttable presumption of joint custody, understood as equal parenting time, for separating and divorcing parents. Although the Commission did not recommend a presumption in favor of equal time, it did recommend a presumption of equal parental responsibility, as well as measures to encourage greater levels of shared parenting time.[23] The government incorporated these recommendations into the Shared Parental Responsibilities Act of 2006, which requires courts, in contested cases, to "consider" orders for the child to spend equal time with each parent and, if such an equal time arrangement is not practical, to consider an arrangement for the child to spend "substantial and significant time with each parent," including both weekday and weekend time, so that both parents can be involved in the child's daily routine.[24]

Although FRCs are community-based, they remain connected to the court system. Indeed, part of the package of reforms that accompanied the creation of FRCs was a requirement that, with certain exceptions for abusive or violent situations, parents must participate in mediation with a certified professional before they can file an application for a parenting order in court.[25] Most certified professionals are affiliated with a Family Relationship Centre; thus, most required mediation is now provided through the FRCs.[26] The FRCs also provide services to many low- and moderate-income parents who do not qualify for legal aid and thus would be unlikely to access the court system, but may still need help in resolving parenting disputes.[27]

The FRCs' relationship to lawyers and the legal profession has evolved since their inception. The Centres were originally conceptualized as a distinct alternative to legal intervention. Indeed, as part of the FRCs' original operational framework, legal practitioners were excluded from accompanying their clients to FRC-provided services, including mandatory mediation.[28] However, this framework has since been modified, and many FRCs have formed partnerships with locally based legal services organizations. The role of lawyers within the FRC framework has increased largely because dispute resolution without legal support proved ineffective for certain families—specifically those affected by domestic violence or child maltreatment.[29]

Within these partnerships, the FRCs "encourage lawyers to work with separating and divorcing families as part of a holistic interdisciplinary team that addresses a family's needs, not just legal issues."[30] The purpose of these partnerships is to "assist separated or separating families by providing access to early and targeted legal information and advice when attending Family Relationship Centres."[31] The services provided by these legal organizations are primarily offered at the FRCs with which they partner, although about one third of the organizations provide services both at the FRCs and at their own offices.[32] Most commonly, the legal services organizations provide individual legal advice, advice on family violence issues, and group legal information sessions.[33] Initial evaluations suggest that that these partnerships are viewed positively by FRC staff and by participating attorneys, and that FRC clients value the services provided by the participating attorneys.[34]

The FRC initiative was accompanied by other reforms directed at the handling of family cases. In particular, legislation passed in 2006 authorizes judges hearing family cases to conduct "less adversarial trials" and to adopt a more proactive approach to case management. For example, the judge is empowered to intervene at the beginning of a hearing and to ask each litigant to state directly "what sort of parent they now wish to be, what sort of parent they wish their former partner to be and how they plan to cooperate around achieving this goal."[35] According to a leading Australian researcher, "This is a profoundly different process to that of the traditional adversarial trial in which each side seeks to win by maximizing their own advantages, minimizing their own disadvantages, and doing the opposite with respect to the other parent."[36] Initial feedback suggests that litigants who experienced the less adversarial procedures were substantially more satisfied with the court process than litigants whose cases were resolved through traditional adversary trials.[37] Parents who experienced the less adversary process also reported lower levels of conflict and less psychological acrimony with their ex-partner four months after the close of court proceedings than did their adversarial counterparts.[38]

Although the FRC initiative focused primarily on the process by which family disputes are resolved, it was also designed to affect the substantive outcome of those disputes. In particular, the initiative responded to the desires expressed by fathers' groups for more parenting time, and the primary architects of the initiative viewed enhancing non-resident father involvement with children as an important goal. "One of the most important measures of the FRCs' success in relation to parenting after separation will be in the extent to which non-resident parents (mostly fathers) are able to maintain involvement with their children."[39] Early studies indicate that the FRCs have been only partially successful in this regard. In a survey of parents who reached agreement through the required mediation, only 8 percent of fathers, compared to 73 percent of mothers, reported that the agreement provided for the child to live mostly with them.[40] With respect to equally shared parenting, fathers were considerably more likely than mothers to report that the agreement specified that the child was to live about the same amount of time with each parent (33 percent compared to 18 percent, respectively).[41] This raises the possibility that mothers and fathers have different understandings of what constitutes an equal sharing of parenting time.

It is still too early to assess the success of the FRCs in any comprehensive way. However, initial studies suggest that the Centres are achieving at least some of their goals. Since the introduction of the FRCs, there has been a substantial reduction in applications for court orders in cases involving children.[42] Simultaneously, public use of mediation and counseling services has increased. A comparison of separated parents before and after the establishment of FRCs found that higher proportions of parents in the pre-reform than the post-reform cohort had contacted or used the services of lawyers, legal services, or courts, while a higher percentage of the parents in the post-reform cohort had contacted or used counseling, mediation, or dispute resolution services.[43] Thus, "consistent with their mission, FRCs have become the first point of entry into the family law system for the majority of separated parents in disputes over their children."[44]

Early evidence also indicates that parents are generally satisfied with the mandatory dispute resolution services provided largely through the FRCs. Over half of all clients who participated in mandatory dispute resolution reached full or partial agreement, and more than 70 percent agreed that the process took the children's needs into account.[45] More than half of all participants also reported that the process worked for them, although fathers were more likely to report this than were mothers.[46] By contrast, only 44 percent of all parents believed that the parenting agreement would help them and their ex-partner make decisions together about their children into the future.[47]

The FRCs have been less successful in serving intact families. Surveys indicate that the bulk of the work of the FRCs has been in helping parents resolve post-separation disputes over parenting, and that the FRCs were being used by a relatively small percentage of intact families.[48] A 2010 Auditor General's Report confirmed that the FRCs "do not appear to be a major source of assistance for intact family members who are seeking assistance for their relationships."[49] The report also noted that some FRC staff had interpreted the FRC mission of "strengthening family relationships" to refer only to post-separation relationships.[50] At the same time, the report noted that, consistent with the terms of the FRC Operation Framework, some Centres were investing a considerable part of their resources into community engagement, as opposed to individual client services, and that many of these community engagement activities "transcend the 'intact/separated' distinction."[51]

The FRCs have also been criticized for their handling of intimate partner violence. "There is some evidence that issues of family violence and fear linked to ongoing family arrangements are not always seen to be adequately dealt with by the FRCs."[52] "Safe and fair resolution of cases involving violence continues to be the most difficult challenge for all parts of the family law system, including courts and FRCs."[53] This is an important critique since studies indicate that a significant percentage of the families who interact with the FRCs experience such violence. For example, in a survey of FRC staff, 62 percent reported that more than half of the families they saw experienced violence or abuse.[54] Similarly, a recent government audit noted that "most FRC managers and other stakeholders reported . . . that complex cases (involving issues such as domestic violence, drug and alcohol abuse, and mental health) represented the bulk of the work of most FRCs."[55] In response to these concerns, the Australian government in 2011 passed a Family Violence Act designed to "provide better protection for children and families at risk of violence and abuse . . . [and] ensure [abuse] is reported and responded to more effectively."[56] The act emphasizes the importance of considering abuse or violence when determining the best interests of children, requires that lawyers, counselors, and other collaborative professionals advise families to prioritize the safety of their children, and improves abuse and violence reporting practices.[57]

Other, more tempered, criticism of FRCs focuses on the cultural appropriateness of the Centres. Australia has significant Iraqi, Lebanese, and Turkish populations, and one report concerning cultural appropriateness centered on these cultures.[58] The report concluded that while language barriers are not a major concern, cultural norms, including "face-saving and preserving the integrity of the collective," may run counter to the collaborative dispute resolution utilized by FRCs.[59] Moreover, people from these cultures often prefer to seek advice from sources within their communities, rather than from government entities.[60] Cultural differences regarding the nature and sources of family conflict also decrease the chances that these families will seek help from FRCs.[61]

Although Australia represents the most comprehensive attempt to shift family dispute resolution from the courts to the community, a number of other countries have also sought to minimize court involvement in parenting disputes arising out of family dissolution. In Japan, if parents divorce by mutual consent and agree on matters concerning their children, their divorce may be registered with the local authority without any judicial or administrative intervention.[62] Similarly, in China, separating spouses who believe that they can reach an agreement often choose an administrative divorce procedure, which includes access to mediation assistance from a nonjudicial government body, as opposed to divorcing through the People's Court.[63] In a related development, advocates for women in India have developed community-based alternatives to formal court processes for addressing issues related to domestic violence, designed both to ensure accountability and to change prevailing social norms.[64]

Denmark has gone a step further and made divorce an administrative procedure for the vast majority of couples. Over 90 percent of Danish divorces are granted by a county official whose role is to guide couples toward agreement on parenting issues, as well as financial support and property settlement.[65] To assist couples in resolving these issues, the official can draw on the services of child psychologists and other experts. According to one observer, "the overall approach is one of 'joint problem solving' with the assistance of an interdisciplinary staff, as needed. The context is a 'divorce office,' not a court of law and not an office for dispute resolution."[66]

Other countries have shifted responsibility away from courts by disconnecting child-related issues from the divorce action itself. For example, in England and Wales, neither divorce nor parental separation automatically affects the allocation of parental responsibility, and courts are not required to issue custody or residence orders unless a parent specifically requests one.[67] This "nonintervention principle" is codified in the first section of the Children's Act of 1989, which directs courts not to make orders with respect to a child "unless it considers that doing so would be better for the child than making no order at all."[68] A key aim of this provision was to redirect parenting issues away from courts and "to stop orders being routinely made following a divorce."[69] Consistent with this aim, the great majority of separating and divorcing parents make caretaking arrangements for their children without seeking court orders.[70] Similarly, in Germany, a parental divorce no longer requires a court ruling on custody, and custody orders are issued only if a parent specifically requests court involvement.[71] In France, as well, the allocation of parental authority is a "separate issue from the dissolution of the marriage," and parents are encouraged to reach their own agreements, which can be approved by a court independently of the divorce proceedings.[72]

Although the specifics of these developments vary by country, they share a common aim—to move the resolution of parenting issues arising out of family reorganization away from the judicial system and into administrative or community venues that emphasize non-adversary decision-making by the parties themselves.

Hearing Children's Voices: The Influence of International Legal Norms

International legal norms relating to children have also influenced developments in family dispute resolution in countries around the world. One of the most important sources of these international norms is the United Nations Convention on the Rights of the Child (Convention, or CRC). The CRC is the most widely adopted treaty in human rights history, and has been ratified by all but two of the world's UN member states. Although the United States participated actively in drafting the Convention and is a signatory, it is one of the two states that have not ratified the Convention.[73]

The Convention offers a vision of children both as rights-holding individuals and as members of families and communities, whose unique capabilities and vulnerabilities call for special attention and protection.[74] In addition to articulating independent rights for children and imposing obligations on both state institutions and families to protect children's interests, the CRC affords children the right to participate in legal decision-making that affects them. In particular, Article 12(2) requires that a child "be provided the opportunity to be heard in any judicial and administrative proceedings affecting the child, either directly or through a representative or an appropriate body, in a manner consistent with the procedural rules of national law."[75] Article 12 also specifies that the views of the child must be "given due weight in accordance with the age and maturity of the child."[76]

The right of children to be heard and taken seriously is "one of the fundamental values of the Convention."[77] Indeed, the Committee on the Rights of the Child, the body established to oversee implementation of the Convention, has identified Article 12's participation mandate as one of the four general principles of the Convention.[78] The Committee has also emphasized that a child's right to be heard applies to all judicial and administrative proceedings that affect children, including divorce and parental separation.[79] Moreover, the Commission has recognized that this participation mandate applies not only to formal judicial proceedings, but also to "alternative dispute resolution mechanisms such as mediation and arbitration."[80] For this reason, the Committee has specified that "all legislation on separation and divorce has to include the right of the child to be heard by decision makers and in mediation processes."[81] Moreover, since the child's views must be given due weight, the decision-maker must "inform the child of the outcome of the process and explain how her or his views were considered."[82] A number of regional human rights conventions contain similar child-participation mandates that apply to divorce and custody proceedings, as well as state-initiated child welfare actions.[83]

In many of the countries that have ratified the CRC, Article 12 has been the impetus for a "significant cultural shift in which children are no longer simply seen as passive victims of family breakdown, but increasingly as participants and actors in the family justice system."[84] As a result of this cultural shift, policy-makers in a number of countries have implemented reforms designed to enhance children's participation in the legal processes that govern parental divorce and separation.[85] To date, most of these reform efforts have focused on children's participation in formal, judicial proceedings. Similarly, the available international literature on children's participation in family proceedings has tended to focus mainly on approaches occurring under the auspices of litigation.[86] Recent scholarship and reform efforts suggest, however, that the CRC's participation mandate has begun to influence family court reform efforts beyond the context of litigation.

In response to the CRC's participation mandate, a number of countries have passed legislation requiring that courts deciding custody and parenting matters ascertain and consider the views of the children involved.[87] A few countries have gone a step further and mandated that parents, as well as judicial decision-makers, consider children's views when negotiating a post-separation parenting arrangement.[88] Despite these legislative mandates, empirical research suggests that judges do not always solicit children's views, nor do they afford children an opportunity to be heard, even in contested cases.[89] Moreover most legislative mandates do not specify *how* decision-makers are to ascertain children's wishes, nor how much weight a judge must give to a child's views. Family law scholars in a number of countries have criticized these shortcomings and have invoked Article 12 of the CRC to advocate for reforms that would enhance the participation of children in both contested and consensual divorce and custody proceedings.[90]

As family courts in other countries have moved away from adversarial judicial proceedings toward mediation and other forms of alternative dispute resolution, they have begun to consider how best to incorporate children's voices into these alternative processes. To date, however, these efforts have been halting. For example, in England, parents who seek court intervention in custody disputes are routinely referred to conciliation, and children over the age of eight are generally expected to attend these court-connected conciliation sessions.[91] Outside the context of court-connected conciliation proceedings, however, a child has no right to be heard.[92] Moreover, while British parents who participate in mediation "are encouraged to ascertain their children's wishes and feelings, and to bear these in mind in mediation meetings, there has been little enthusiasm amongst mediators in the UK to involve children directly in the mediation process."[93] Similarly, ever since Sweden introduced mediation into its family court system more than thirty years ago, "attention was called to the importance of the child's participation in these talks and consideration of the child's preferences."[94] Despite the official emphasis on children's participation, however, Swedish mediators and court officials have shown "a clear ambivalence in regard to the participation of the children."[95] As a result, Swedish scholars have argued that while Swedish law stresses the importance of the child's preferences, "the current practice of resolving issues of custody, residence, and access provides insufficient opportunity for the child's wishes to be considered."[96]

Norway's experience demonstrates a similar gap between legislative prescription and practice. Norway has incorporated the CRC's participation mandate into its domestic law and has emphasized that it applies to both adversarial and non-adversarial family law proceedings.[97] In particular, Norwegian law requires both married and unmarried parents to participate in family mediation before they can obtain a divorce or apply for certain economic benefits available to never-married parents. As part of this process, mediators are required to inform parents that the child's interests are paramount and that the child has a right to be heard in the designing of post-separation parenting arrangements. More than 90 percent of parents come to an agreement either before or during family mediation. However, despite this emphasis on incorporating the children's views, research on family mediation in Norway shows "that children's participation in family mediation is still rare and when it does occur, it takes place in an unsystematic way."[98]

In the United States, as well, most discussion of children's participation in divorce and custody proceedings has focused on litigated cases. These discussions have been controversial and have produced widely divergent practices. For example, judges in most states have discretion to determine whether and how to consider a child's views in deciding custody and parenting matters.[99] In some jurisdictions, judges exercise this discretion by routinely interviewing children in chambers, while other jurisdictions discourage such informal judicial interviews.[100] States also differ with respect to whether judicial interviews with children must be recorded and whether the parents' counsel must be permitted to attend.

Similar variation and controversy exist regarding the representation of children in divorce and custody matters.[101] In most states, judges have the authority to appoint counsel for a child who is the subject of a custody dispute if the judge determines that such an appointment would be in the child's best interest.[102] In general, such appointments are made only in highly contested cases and only after settlement attempts have failed. Moreover, courts and commentators disagree about the appropriate role of a child's attorney—in particular, whether the attorney should function as a traditional client-directed lawyer or should represent the child's best interests. Both the American Bar Association and the American Academy of Matrimonial Lawyers have issued standards of practice for lawyers representing children in custody and visitation proceedings.[103] However, both sets of standards focus on legal representation within an adversary paradigm, and neither addresses in any detail the role of counsel for children in non-adversarial proceedings.[104]

Architects of the new paradigm have paid little attention to the participation of children in non-adversary family dispute resolution. Most court-connected mediation programs are reluctant to involve children directly in the mediation process.[105] For example, a 1996 study of California family courts found that less that 16 percent of court-connected mediators interviewed the children.[106] More recent evidence confirms this reluctance. For example, the Model Standards of Practice for Family and Divorce Mediation provide that "[e]xcept in extraordinary circumstances, the children should not participate in the process without the consent of both parents and the children's court-appointed representative."[107] The use of the phrase "extraordinary circumstances" sets a deliberately high barrier, and in scenarios where one parent supports a child's inclusion and the other parent objects, the objecting parent can terminate the mediation rather than be required to involve the child.[108]

Moreover, there is a divergence of views among mediators regarding the value of children's participation. While some mediators favor the inclusion of children at mediation sessions, others maintain that a child need not be physically present to have his or her voice heard.[109] Still others oppose the involvement of children at any point in the mediation process, citing concerns about creating loyalty conflicts, as well as undermining parental autonomy or compromising mediator neutrality.[110] Mediators who are trained as lawyers are less likely than those from a mental health background to favor the involvement of children in mediation.[111]

Child-Informed Mediation and the CRC's Participation Mandate

In contrast to the prevailing wisdom in the United States, reformers in other countries have developed mediation models that emphasize the inclusion and perspective of children. First pioneered in Australia, these models "evolved as a strategic enactment of United Nations principles around enabling children to present their wishes in family law proceedings about them."[112] As originally designed, the Australian version had two variants, both intended to encourage parents to consider the perspective of their children during the mediation process.[113] In child-focused mediation (CF), the mediator responsible for mediating the dispute gave parents general information about the effects of divorce and parental conflict on children, and helped parents consider how the information applied to their particular children. In child-inclusive mediation (CI), a separate mental health professional, designated as a child consultant, interviewed the parties' children and shared information from that interview with the parents prior to the first mediation session; the child consultant also provided general information about the effects of divorce and parental conflict. Subsequent research has referred to both variants as forms of child-informed mediation.

Evaluation of child-informed mediation has yielded promising results. A study conducted one year after intervention found that parents who participated in both variants of child-informed mediation experienced improvement in family functioning, including lower inter-parental conflict.[114] Families in the CI group, who received specific feedback from their children's interview, experienced additional benefits, including better mother–child relationships, higher levels of child-reported closeness to fathers, and greater parental satisfaction with post-separation arrangements.[115] A four-year follow-up study found that many of these benefits endured over time.[116] Parents in both groups reported lowered levels of acrimony and conflict, as well as higher levels of satisfaction with parenting arrangements. Moreover, only 10 percent of families in the study reported no contact between the children and the nonresidential parent, a much lower percentage than Australia's national average of 28 percent.[117]

Some research in the United States has built on these studies. Researchers in Indiana conducted a randomized trial that compared these two "child-informed" mediation models with a more traditional mediation approach that did not focus explicitly on children's perspectives. Parents who agreed to participate in the study were randomly assigned to either a child-informed mediation model or mediation-as-usual model. The Indiana study used child consultants to provide feedback to parents in both child-informed variants, so as to avoid concerns about compromising mediator neutrality.[118] Moreover, unlike the original Australian research, the Indiana study did not "screen out" families based on the level of conflict or the perceived maturity of parents. Indeed, parents in the Indiana study were generally low income, high conflict, and often experiencing multiple stressful life circumstances—factors that "place families at particularly high risk of negative outcomes after divorce, and are a population most in need of services."[119]

The results of the Indiana study suggest that child-informed mediation models offer significant benefits to these families. Although parents in both traditional and child-informed mediation were highly likely to reach agreement, parents in the child-informed groups were more likely to report that they had learned something in mediation, and that the other parent had learned something as well. Mediators were also more satisfied with the child-informed models than with the more traditional approach and thought that the child-informed approaches worked best for their cases. Mediators also reported that parents continued to discuss the information provided by the child consultants during the negotiation phase of the mediation; furthermore, mediators expressed satisfaction that the child consultants could deliver messages to parents that mediators, as neutral parties, did not feel comfortable delivering.

The agreements reached in the child-informed models also differed in significant ways from those reached in the more traditional mediation process. Child-informed agreements were more likely to designate parents as joint legal custodians and to allocate more parenting time to the nonresidential parent than agreements reached during traditional mediation. Child-informed agreements were also more likely to address communications between parents and to include more aspirational language about that communication, as well as more child-related rationales for many of their provisions. Overall, researchers judged the agreements reached in the child-informed processes "as being more likely than [mediation-as-usual] agreements to facilitate positive child adjustment to divorce."[120]

These results are consistent with recent social science research suggesting that children's participation in family dispute resolution can have a beneficial effect on child well-being and on post-separation family functioning. For example, researchers have noted that children are often better able to cope with the changes that accompany family reorganization if they know and understand the reasons for those changes, and if they feel their views have played a role in the decision-making process.[121] Involving children in mediation and other non-adversary processes may also provide them with some sense of input into a process that otherwise feels totally out of their control. Older children who participate in crafting a parenting plan may also be more inclined to comply with the arrangements reached as a result of that process.[122] Including children in family dispute resolution processes may also help to keep parents focused on the children's interests and away from their other marital disputes.

Studies also suggest that, when given the opportunity to participate in mediation, children are generally enthusiastic about speaking with a mediator.[123] This is consistent with more general research indicating that children whose parents are separating want to be informed and consulted about the reorganization of their family and their future living arrangements.[124] While most children do not want the responsibility of deciding where they should live, they do want to express their views and to have a say in the arrangements that affect their day-to-day lives.[125]

Empirical studies also indicate that the tradition of not listening to children's voices in divorce and custody disputes has had unintended negative consequences for children and families.[126] In particular, research with children has revealed that keeping children in the dark often contributes to the pain and confusion associated with family transitions. Children who are excluded from decision-making processes "complain about feeling isolated and lonely during the divorce process, and many older children express anger and frustration about being left out."[127] Moreover, children who lack information and involvement in the separation process are "more likely to suffer from symptoms such as anxiety, depression and conduct disorder, to exhibit distress, and to blame themselves for their parents' separation."[128] By contrast, children who are well-informed about their parents' decision-making process seem better able to buffer the impact of post-separation changes, to maintain self-esteem, and to regain cognitive control over events.[129] These findings suggest that reformers concerned about improving outcomes for children affected by divorce and parental separation should focus not only on reducing parental conflict but also on enhancing the participation of children in non-adversary dispute resolution processes.

Conclusion

These international and comparative law developments confirm that family law reform in the United States does not take place in a geographic vacuum, and that legal systems around the world are experimenting with alternatives to traditional, adversary procedures for the resolution of family disputes. Continued exchange and cross-fertilization is likely to benefit reform efforts both in this country and abroad. More specifically, the experience of Australia and several other countries suggests that courts may not be the only—or the most appropriate—venue for many non-adversarial processes. Moreover, the success of child-inclusive mediation challenges the traditional reluctance of U.S. reformers to prioritize children's participation in family law decision-making; it suggests instead that children and families may benefit from dispute resolution models that allow children to participate more directly in the processes of family reorganization that accompany divorce and parental separation.

7

Creating a Twenty-First-Century Family Dispute Resolution System

The late twentieth-century paradigm shift that we have analyzed was designed primarily to address the shortcomings of the adversary system as a means of resolving divorce-related parenting disputes. As such, it focused primarily on developing court-based processes and services designed to reduce parental conflict and to promote positive co-parenting relationships between partners who had raised children together. Courts also saw dissatisfaction with adversary justice as an opportunity to develop dispute resolution alternatives that could move cases more quickly and inexpensively through the judicial system. While these remain worthy goals, they are not sufficient to create a just and effective twenty-first-century family dispute resolution system. Such a regime must respond to the challenges described in this book and must address the needs of today's families in all their variety and complexity. In this chapter, we offer a series of recommendations to advance these goals.

First, while courts will continue to play a role in resolving family disputes, our analysis suggests that relying primarily on the judicial system to provide non-adversary dispute resolution may itself be problematic. Moreover, attempting to turn family courts into multi-door dispute resolution centers may detract from their essential role as adjudicators of last resort and forums for the creation and enforcement of important societal norms. Hence, we recommend that twenty-first-century reformers consider moving some of the non-adversary processes and services that characterize the new paradigm out of the court system and into the community.

Second, while twentieth-century reformers were correct to focus on children's needs and interests, subsequent developments both domestically and internationally emphasize that children have voices as well as needs. And current social science research suggests that children benefit when decision-makers incorporate their voices in the resolution of family disputes. Hence, we recommend that twenty-first-century reformers look for ways to enhance children's participation in the non-adversarial resolution of family disputes.

Third, twentieth-century reformers correctly recognized that the increased prevalence of divorce and the breakdown of gendered parenting roles required a rethinking of then-prevailing custody norms and an emphasis on family reorganization and post-divorce co-parenting. But the last few decades have brought further changes in family structure, including a sharp rise in unmarried parenthood and an increase in the importance of stepparents and other third-party caretakers. The current dispute resolution paradigm has not responded adequately to these changes. Thus, we recommend that today's reformers look beyond divorcing couples and adopt processes and services that better serve the needs of never-married parents and other family structures.

Twentieth-century family court reformers also argued convincingly that disputing families were not well served by existing models of lawyering. Their initial response was to minimize the role of legal norms and strive to eliminate lawyers from the system. But our analysis suggests that this strategy was misguided, particularly for families of limited means, for whom access to legal information and advice is often critical to just and effective dispute resolution. We therefore recommend that, rather than bypassing lawyers, reformers pursue alternative models of legal representation that can both enhance access to legal services and promote durable resolutions for families.

Our analysis also reveals that, in order to provide these new models of legal service, lawyers need skills and habits of mind that are different from those that legal education has traditionally emphasized. Hence, we recommend significant changes in the education and training of lawyers. These recommendations are consistent with other reforms that are currently taking place within legal education, but they have a particular salience in family law.

Finally, our analysis highlights the close connection between changes in legal doctrine and changes in dispute resolution processes. Indeed, the twentieth-century paradigm shift that we have analyzed was facilitated by important doctrinal changes, including the shift from fault to no-fault divorce and the widespread endorsement of joint custody. Further reform efforts should be mindful of the connection between legal process and legal doctrine. To this end, we recommend that twenty-first-century reformers pursue doctrinal changes that support the goals of both non-adversary dispute resolution and, when necessary, the adversary system, by enhancing both predictability and access to justice. We develop each of these recommendations below.

Shifting Families and Services from Courts to Communities

To date, architects of the new paradigm have focused largely on the court system as the setting for innovations in family dispute resolution. But courts may not be the best places for these alternative processes and services. To some extent, the reliance on court-based solutions to parenting issues is a relic of the fault-based divorce system, under which divorce and child custody were state-controlled remedies granted to one spouse against the other. But while the state's role in policing exit from marriage has diminished sharply, reformers have continued to rely on courts as the default arena for resolving parenting disputes. Reformers should rethink this continuing reliance and consider moving many of the dispute resolution processes and services associated with the new paradigm out of the court system and into the community.

Moving non-adversary family dispute resolution away from the courts and into the community offers a number of potential advantages. First, it reinforces the message that divorce and parental separation are not primarily legal events, but rather ongoing processes of family reorganization. Particularly where children are involved, a onetime judicial pronouncement is unlikely to accomplish this reorganization; rather, the transition is likely to require ongoing planning and collaboration by parents and other family members. Locating these planning efforts in the community, rather than the court system, helps to normalize this reorganization process—recharacterizing it as a life-cycle challenge, rather than a quasi-criminal event that requires the full machinery of the state. Shifting the resolution of parenting issues from the courts to the community may also reorient parents away from third-party adjudication and encourage them to take responsibility for resolving their current and future disputes.

Second, locating family dispute resolution services in the community should make it easier for individuals and families to access those services; this is especially important in a system where a substantial majority of disputants are not represented by counsel. Low-income families, in particular, may be more likely to take advantage of community-based services, as they may be wary of interacting with state bureaucracies, particularly courts. Allowing families to access services without resorting to court action may also encourage family members to take advantage of those services on a proactive or preventative basis, before positions harden and emotions escalate. Shifting services from courts to communities may also allow for better coordination of family dispute resolution with other community resources and programs, such as housing and child-care assistance. Community-based centers may also provide a mechanism for coordinating the remedies and services available to families involved in multiple legal proceedings. Finally, reliance on community-based resources should allow more sensitivity to diverse cultural norms.

Disaggregating some family services from the court system should also allow the court system to focus on what it does best and what it alone can do: authoritatively resolve high-conflict cases, protect vulnerable family members, and articulate norms for novel legal problems. Critics have warned that asking courts to act as problem-solvers of first resort for most families in transition may compromise courts' ability to perform these critical backstop functions.[1] Judges have voiced similar concerns, suggesting that the time and energy required to provide an even playing field for large numbers of *pro se* litigants may deplete resources that would be better spent on other, more traditional judicial tasks. Moving non-adjudicative dispute resolution processes and services away from the court system into the community may ameliorate these concerns and enable courts to more effectively carry out their core justice functions.

Recent evidence suggests, however, that reorienting some families away from court-based processes and services may be a challenging task. A recent British poll indicated that while more than half of British adults who are seeking divorce or legal separation believe that non-court-based solutions may be better for the well-being of children and/or couples, only half of them say they would consider trying a non-court-based solution instead of going court if they were to divorce in the future.[2] The poll also revealed "patchy understanding" and "ill-founded skepticism" about alternatives to litigation: just 23 percent of British adults believe that non-court-based methods of divorce and separation make the terms of the separation clear to both parties, and just one-quarter think that non-court-based methods of divorce protect the rights of both parties.[3] Moreover, the poll revealed that more than a third of British adults (36 percent) do not know what family mediation is.[4] Early experience with voluntary mediation programs in many communities in the United States revealed similar knowledge and participation gaps.[5] To counter this skepticism and lack of information, reformers should consider developing well-run pilot programs, in conjunction with university researchers, and making them available to families on a voluntary basis at minimal cost. As a condition of access, participants would agree to participate in a research study of the program. As an incentive, court systems might agree to provide expedited handling of consent agreements arising out of these community-based programs.

Several promising models for such community-based programs currently exist. The Australian Family Relationship Centres, described in chapter 6, provide a variety of family education and dispute resolution services previously available through the court system. Closer to home, the Resource Center for Separating and Divorcing Families (RCSDF), a new interdisciplinary center affiliated with the University of Denver, seeks to foster healthy family reorganization and out-of-court dispute resolution by providing comprehensive and affordable dispute resolution, counseling, educational, and financial planning services for transitioning parents and children.[6] Available dispute resolution services include mediation, early neutral evaluation, and legal education; RCSDF also offers both individual and group counseling, as well as assistance in developing parenting plans. Services are provided on a sliding scale by graduate students working side by side with licensed attorneys, psychologists, and social workers. In addition to providing separation-related services to families, the RCSDF will train law students, as well as other graduate students interested in working with divorcing and separating families. These and similar community-based programs provide useful templates for reform.[7]

Enhancing Children's Participation in Non-adjudicative Family Dispute Resolution

The paradigm shift that we explore in this book has been justified, in significant part, by the benefits it offers to children. Yet, reformers in the

United States have paid relatively little attention to children's involvement in the new family dispute resolution processes. To the extent that reformers have considered children's participation, they have emphasized the risks of involving children in their parents' conflict. While these concerns are not unfounded, recent social science evidence supports the greater inclusion of children's voices in decisions and processes relating to separation and divorce, particularly in a non-adversary context. This evidence demonstrates a positive correlation between children's participation in decisions related to family restructuring and children's post-separation well-being. As a recent comprehensive literature review concluded, "the research literature to date provides a resounding clarion call—children and their parents have better relationships and there is less parental conflict between the parents when children are part of the process."[8] Moreover, many of the concerns that have traditionally been raised about the risks of children's involvement in family disputes are specific to the adversary paradigm and apply less forcefully to children's participation in non-adversary dispute resolution processes. For example, the tension between parents' due process rights and informal judicial interviews of children evaporates when parents, rather than judges, are the relevant listeners and decision-makers. Similarly, concerns about divided loyalties are less salient when the focus of the dispute resolution regime is on developing a durable post-separation parenting plan, rather than identifying the better custodian or more deserving parent. Non-adversary processes should also minimize the incentive for parents to manipulate children or encourage them to take sides against the other parent.

In light of this evidence, reformers should focus on the inclusion of children in family dispute resolution processes and services. Promising models and pilot projects already exist, both in this country and abroad. These include various types of child-inclusive mediation, discussed at length in chapter 6 and currently practiced in Australia and by many private mediators in the United States and Canada. Another promising model is the use of a child specialist as part of an interdisciplinary collaborative team. This mental health professional is retained jointly by separating parents and is responsible for ascertaining the views of the children and communicating those views to parents as part of the collaborative decision-making process.[9] More generally, lawyers and mediators who work with divorcing and separating parents should urge their clients to explain the separation process to their children and to discuss contemplated parenting arrangements in an age-appropriate way. Research indicates that children who are well informed about their parents' decision-making process are better able to manage the transitions associated with separation and divorce. Evidence also indicates that parents are more likely to keep their children informed if their lawyers advise them to do so.[10]

Court-connected programs should also explore ways to provide information directly to children and to encourage children to express their views. For example, consistent with the new paradigm's emphasis on promoting child-focused decision-making by parents, court-based custody evaluators might redirect some of their efforts away from assessments of parenting capacity designed to assist judges, and toward a more facilitative model designed to improve parental decision-making by ascertaining and amplifying children's voices. Courts should also consider expanding existing parent education programs by incorporating sessions for children. Again, promising examples of such programs exist, both in this country and abroad. For example, Kids' Turn is a California nonprofit organization started more than twenty-five years ago by family law attorneys, judges, and mental health professionals that provides educational programs and resources for children of all ages experiencing separation or divorce, in tandem with programs for parents. An evaluation found that school-aged children who participated in the six-week program showed significant improvement in their adjustment to divorce based on a variety of behavioral criteria.[11] Similarly, Seasons for Growth, an Australian program that uses a strengths-based approach to address issues of change, loss, and grief, has been accessed by over sixty thousand Australian children affected by parental divorce or separation.[12] Finally, courts and community-based programs should increase the availability of written, visual, and web-based materials designed especially for children who are experiencing family transitions.

Providing Processes and Services Responsive to the Needs of All Families

A core focus of the new paradigm has been conflict reduction for divorcing families. But divorcing families make up a shrinking percentage of the caseload in most family courts.[13] There are several reasons for this. Divorce rates, which rose as high as 50 percent by the mid-1990s, have dropped to 40 percent today,[14] leading to fewer divorcing couples in family courts. And many of these divorcing couples, who are generally more affluent than their nonmarital counterparts, are able to bypass court-based programs by engaging lawyers, private mediators, and other non-court-connected experts. At the same time, changes in federal and state law have brought increasing numbers of nonmarital families into the family court system, many of whom have limited means and lack legal representation. These changes include statutes that facilitate paternity establishment, encourage or require custodial parents and state authorities to establish child support orders, create enhanced child support enforcement tools, and establish new remedies for family members experiencing domestic violence.[15] Moreover, although child support and child access remain legally distinct, federal and state child support programs increasingly encourage, and in some cases require, unmarried parents to address custody and visitation issues at the time a child support order is entered.[16] The parents affected by these legal changes have varying levels of commitment to and communication with one another. Their needs are different and more varied than those of most divorcing parents.

Despite this diversity among families, most family courts retain a tiered service model designed around the needs of divorcing nuclear families.[17] These services often begin with parent education programs that focus primarily on the detrimental impact of divorce-related conflict and the importance of post-divorce co-parenting. Armed with this knowledge and perspective, parents are referred to court-connected mediation, the goal of which is to help them develop a formal parenting plan that will ensure the continued involvement of both parents in the children's post-divorce lives.

To make these services more responsive to the needs of today's families, reformers should first rethink their goals and structure. With respect to parent education classes, research demonstrating that divorcing parents and their children benefit from education about post-divorce parenting is, at best, thin.[18] If a family's need for a legal remedy justifies mandatory education, that education should focus on the actual needs of families at this difficult time. While information about co-parenting after divorce is useful for some families, many under economic stress would benefit more from concrete financial and legal information relevant to their situations.

Parent education programs should also be more responsive to the range of family types in court. While a small number of existing programs focus on never-married parents, these programs capture only part of the complexity of child-rearing within the varied compositions of today's families. Programs should address the particular challenges of raising children where the disputing caregivers include a grandparent or other de facto parent, or where parents share child-care responsibilities with other family members who are not before the court. Parent educators should also consider whether a curriculum designed to facilitate the transition to a binuclear household is appropriate for unmarried parents who have never cohabited or parented together.

Moreover, given shrinking court budgets, it is worth asking whether parent education programs constitute the most effective use of limited family services funds. In particular, courts should consider reallocating a portion of their parent education budgets to programs more directly related to strengthening families. These would include the creation or expansion of *pro se* advice centers or other legal services. Experience suggests that making legal advice available early in the litigation process results in fewer high-conflict, protracted cases. Expanding access to legal services would also facilitate informed agreements and provide support for parties in cases that need to be adjudicated. Other programs that could be expanded include court- or community-based supervised visitation centers, jobs and employment skills programs for low-income child support obligors, and counseling programs for batterers.

Finally, it may be time to move beyond the "heart" of the tiered service model—facilitative and, to a lesser extent, transformative mediation—as the preferred alternative to adjudication.[19] These approaches to mediation, which emphasize party autonomy and self-determination, may work well for some divorcing and separating parents.[20] But these models do not work for all disputing families. Parents and other caregivers vary in both their capacity and interest in self-determination.[21] Moreover, the lack of free or affordable legal representation makes it difficult for many to participate meaningfully in mediation. Developing new models of legal representation, discussed below, may ameliorate some of these concerns. But reformers should also consider endorsing new models of mediation in which mediators play an expanded role educating parties and evaluating alternatives, so that unrepresented parties can experience the benefits of mediation without substantial risk.

Court- and community-based programs should also explore other models of dispute resolution to respond to the wider range of needs presented by today's families. These include more use of evaluative mediation, in which the "mediator makes a judgment about a dispute at hand, and expresses that judgment to the parties."[22] Evaluative mediation can be helpful to unrepresented parties as long as it is not accompanied by pressure to settle. Other options include hybrid models that combine mediation with evaluative processes such as parenting coordination and early neutral evaluation.[23] These combinations "meld opportunities for self-determination, such as education and the provision of information, with other process components that tend to be more directive, such as recommendations and reporting, that combined may help to influence the parties' decisions and help them to arrive at an agreement that is best for them."[24]

Other forms of dispute resolution that should be available to a wider range of families include family group conferencing and collaborative practice. Family group conferencing involves the "practice of convening family members, community members, and other individuals or institutions involved with a family to develop a plan to ensure the care and protection of a child."[25] This dispute resolution process has generally been limited to child welfare cases initiated by state authorities—cases typically heard in separate juvenile courts. But such a multiparty process, when combined with access to legal information and advice, might also work well for parents who share significant caregiving with extended family members. The stark divisions that have resulted in mediation for "private" intra-family disputes and family group conferencing when the state is a participant may no longer make sense given the common issues in both kinds of cases.

Similarly, reformers should work to make collaborative practice available to more families, particularly those with limited means. In particular, attorneys who provide legal services to low-income families should be trained in collaborative practice and techniques. Combining such training with the modifications to ethical rules described below should make this dispute resolution process available to a broader cross-section of disputing families.

As the range of dispute resolution options expands, courts and community-based programs will need to carefully screen and direct participants to the appropriate services, including access to legal support or representation. A number of commentators have offered proposals for moving from the tiered "one size fits all" approach in today's courts to a more sophisticated and careful triaging of parties and cases.[26] Although triage could be accomplished in a variety of ways, three scholars have identified the essential elements: "(1) identifying issues, such as high conflict level, difficulty communicating, intimate partner violence, child abuse, mental illness, or substance abuse, early in the . . . process; (2) routing families to dispute resolution processes deemed most likely to be safe, appropriate, and effective; and (3) making referrals or connections to appropriate community services and resources. In addition to making choices regarding dispute resolution alternatives, triage may trigger more in-depth assessments, if available."[27] While this kind of approach will require substantially enhanced resources at the screening stage, it should result in more efficient use of resources, including fewer failed mediations.

Any proposal that vests significant discretion in court personnel to obtain information from parties and make judgments about the routing of cases presents risks, particularly to the majority of disputants who lack lawyers. Courts can minimize these risks by providing early access to individualized legal counseling on dispute resolution alternatives and ensuring accountability of triage professionals. Analyzing these risks in the context of intimate partner violence, Nancy Ver Steegh and her coauthors offer a number of other suggestions which are designed to "maximize the ability of parties to make informed decisions about participation in dispute resolution processes."[28] These include giving "the parties, rather than a triage professional," the ultimate choice "with respect to participation in a dispute resolution process," with judges deciding in cases where parties disagree, and including the option to fast track cases to a judge, preferably with appointed counsel."[29]

Similar cautions should apply to programs that seek to integrate parenting time orders with paternity and child support determinations. Arguably, such programs respond to the problem of courts addressing parenting issues in isolation from related legal matters. However, mandating the adoption of parenting plans in government-initiated child support proceedings poses risks for some parents. As two commentators have noted, a program that requires adjudication of child access in exchange for public benefits or assistance in enforcing child support orders "threatens to undermine the due process rights of *both* parents, impose an unjust burden on low income families, and immerse the federal government and state agencies in decisions that are more appropriately left to parental discretion and impartial adjudicators."[30] Instead, parents involved in child support agency proceedings should be offered the option and support necessary to develop parenting plans at the time child support is established, modified, or enforced. To do this, child support agencies should partner with "non-profits and legal services providers that have the trust of the low income community to develop voluntary programs for integrating support and visitation for families in need of such services."[31] In this way, the predominately low-income and nonmarital families currently involved in state-initiated child support proceedings will have the opportunity to address parenting time issues in an integrated way that respects their privacy and decision-making autonomy.

By expanding the range of services available and by matching parties to appropriate services, while respecting a family's choice of dispute resolution options, today's family courts can move beyond divorce and better meet the diverse needs of all the families who seek to reorganize and resolve disputes about children.

Expanding Access to Legal Services through New Lawyering Models

Whether dispute resolution takes place in a court, an agency, or a community-based resource, access to legal information and advice is critical to ensuring that the interests of all family members are protected during the process. The problem of lack of access to legal advice currently pervades the family justice system in both traditional and problem-solving courts. Contrary to the views of some early reformers, the shift from adversary to non-adversary dispute resolution has not eliminated the need for lawyers, nor diminished the importance of legal advice. It has, however, changed the roles and responsibilities of lawyers. The new lawyering models described in this section should improve the ability of lawyers to operate within the new paradigm and should enhance the ability of the system to address the unmet legal needs of so many disputing families.

Although a majority of disputants in today's family courts proceed without legal representation, both courts and court reformers have been slow to respond to the needs of unrepresented parties.[32] Initially, some judges discouraged any such reform efforts, reasoning that making court more accessible would encourage parties to dispense with lawyers even where parties could afford legal assistance. But more recently, courts have realized that most unrepresented parties are not appearing without lawyers by choice and are here to stay. Courts have responded with some limited supports for unrepresented parties. These include standardized family law pleadings available online or in court clerks' offices, court-based *pro se* offices that provide legal information to unrepresented parties, telephone hotlines, and educational websites.[33] All of these services can be expanded and made more widely available to orient family disputants about the array of community- and court-based resources available in a particular jurisdiction. Such services can also inform parties about the range of legal rights that might be relevant in some cases.

Technology can play a role in expanding access to legal information and advice through court and legal aid websites that have effective systems for updating content, as well as offering videos, podcasts, and interactive quizzes.[34] Effective web portals can answer questions about individual eligibility for legal services, provide brief advice, and help with document assembly. Video conferencing, Skype, and similar technologies can also make information and advice available to those in rural and other remote areas. Thus, both traditional and technologically supported *pro se* assistance can be an important first step in supporting family members in conflict or transition.

Some family courts have also made efforts to simplify court-connected dispute resolution processes to make them more accessible to unrepresented parties. Consistent with the focus of the new family courts, these processes are focused primarily on the resolution of child access disputes. More recently, a few courts have experimented with streamlining divorce proceedings with "one-day divorce" programs for people without lawyers.[35] If a litigant has successfully prepared a complaint and served it on the other party and there are no contested issues, the court will provide limited legal assistance and judicial support to complete the divorce in one day. While these programs are a welcome support to unrepresented parties whose cases get stalled because of difficulty meeting court procedural requirements, they are limited to parties seeking uncontested divorces.

But for many families, neither this limited *pro se* support nor simplified processes are enough. Many parties in complex or high-conflict disputes need individualized assistance from a lawyer. Moreover, when lawyers get involved in early stages, as planners or problem-solvers, conflicts can be avoided or reduced, thus decreasing the numbers of cases where full representation is needed. As discussed in chapter 5, the availability of unbundled legal services—when clients engage lawyers for discrete tasks—can expand family members' access to affordable legal services at critical points. For example, family lawyers may provide discrete task representation designed to minimize the possibility of future conflict by drafting agreements for nonmarital parents, advising about the consequences of paternity establishment, and planning for child rearing for de facto parents. Where parties are already in dispute, limited task representation might include assisting parties in choosing a dispute resolution option, ghostwriting legal documents, preparing parties for mediation, attending a mediation or settlement conference, reviewing agreements, or representing a client for purposes of settlement only.

While some forms of unbundled services have been available for decades, particularly for transactional cases, they are not as widely available in family law. Bar associations and legal service providers have recognized the need for discrete task representation by endorsing the practice, modifying ethical rules, and providing public funding for *pro se* advice clinics in courthouses. But more comprehensive change is needed to fully establish discrete task representation in family practice. These changes include standardizing retainer agreements that conform to ethical rules permitting limited representation, modifying ethical rules to address permissible communication with clients receiving limited representation, and clarifying the extent of disclosure required for ghostwritten pleadings. Courts should also adopt rules that facilitate withdrawal for lawyers who agree to make limited appearances in court.

Standardizing practices and clarifying ethical rules should encourage more lawyers to offer unbundled services in family cases.

The legal profession should also develop structures to make limited task representation more accessible and more affordable. Government-funded legal service providers should consider redirecting legal services budgets, now used almost exclusively for either brief advice and referral or full representation, to expand limited task representation, particularly in court houses and other locations designed to bring legal services to the people who need it. Unbundled services should include representation before, during, and after court- or community-based mediation. Community- and court-based advice clinics should also serve the large influx of low-income parents in court as a result of the changes in paternity and child support policy discussed elsewhere in this chapter.

There is also a role for the private bar in making unbundled legal services more affordable and widely available. Supported by organizations such as the American Medical Association, the medical profession has expanded its delivery model to provide more affordable care by moving people from hospital emergency rooms to outpatient "urgent care centers and retail clinics" for minor or routine treatment.[36] Building on this model, the bar could encourage similar movement in the legal field. Freestanding legal advice clinics offering moderately priced, limited task representation have begun to appear in a few places in the United States.[37] Legal advice clinics might also be established alongside the "minute clinics" in Target and CVS that provide "immediate" help in "non–life threatening" medical situations.[38] This model is being tried in Canada, where an onsite law office at a Toronto Wal-Mart offers inexpensive, basic legal services seven days a week.[39]

This kind of legal service model may not afford the same level of service and protection as full representation. But for many family members, the alternative is either obtaining advice and forms from wholly unregulated Internet sources with no obligation to follow ethical norms, or foregoing assistance of any kind. In addition to filling a gaping need, these service models offer employment opportunities for new lawyers, who continue to face a discouraging job market.[40]

Policy-makers should also consider allowing attorneys to serve as "lawyers for the family" in limited situations involving divorce or parental separation. The legal profession has traditionally frowned on joint representation in the context of divorce, with many authorities viewing it as presenting a non-waivable conflict of interest.[41] But such a view seems anachronistic in an era of no-fault divorce, when voluntary agreement is encouraged and many couples are able to resolve the financial and parenting consequences of their dissolution without resort to litigation. Moreover, the paradigm shift described in the preceding chapters challenges the assumption that the interests of divorcing or separating parents are necessarily adverse, particularly with respect to the well-being of their children. Rather than seeing divorce and parental separation as presenting an inevitable battle between opposing interests, it may be more accurate to analogize many of these proceedings to the reorganization of an ongoing parenting partnership, in which the partners are substituting one type of family entity for another—a transaction for which joint legal representation may be both practicable and ethically permissible, provided both clients have sufficient information for informed consent.[42] Moreover, the increased acceptance of unbundled legal representation makes it possible for a lawyer to agree to represent both spouses for purposes of negotiating a parenting plan or settlement agreement, but not for purposes of litigation should negotiations break down.

In her recent article titled "Counsel for the Divorce," law professor Rebecca Aviel challenges the profession's traditional refusal to "unbundle partisan advocacy from legal representation"—a refusal that she deems particularly inapt for family lawyering.[43] Aviel explains that many divorcing parents both want and seek joint counsel, understanding that they have shared interests in minimizing transaction costs, maximizing the value of the marital estate, and reducing the hostility and animosity that harms their children. She argues persuasively that these couples are poorly served by the profession's insistence that they each retain their own lawyer or forego legal representation altogether. Moreover, Aviel notes that while most family law attorneys are reluctant to represent both parties explicitly, many endorse a form of de facto joint representation under which the attorney formally represents one of the parties, with the understanding that the other party will be unrepresented. She correctly characterizes these arrangements as "the worst of all worlds in advancing the values the rules purportedly protect."[44] Aviel concedes that joint representation would not be appropriate or ethically permissible in all situations—for example, where domestic violence exists, or where the parties have markedly different interests or earning capacities at the time of the divorce. She also emphasizes the challenges involved in obtaining informed client consent, and the importance of providing full disclosure of the risks and implications of joint representation. But she argues persuasively that "[p]articularly in domestic relations matters, where the adversarial paradigm is rapidly losing relevance for most families, it is time to consider whether lawyers can serve as 'counsel for the divorce', bringing to bear their skills as advisors, mediators, drafters, problem-solvers, and process managers."[45]

Finally, these new lawyering models can help fulfill the goals of the Civil *Gideon* movement—to ensure that parties have adequate legal representation in legal proceedings in which fundamental rights such as child custody are at stake.[46] Some who argue for a right to counsel in these cases assume that lawyers would be appointed in all contested custody proceedings and would take on a traditional adversarial role.[47] Others recognize that the goal of creating a fair and just system that protects basic rights can also be advanced by a combination of "expanding the roles of the court system's key players," including judges and mediators, and providing limited scope legal representation.[48] If the full range of services and legal support described in this chapter are implemented, the appointment of a lawyer to provide representation in "full dress adversary proceedings with robust and technical rules, where lawyers truly are necessary to fair and effective participation," should be limited to the relatively small subset of cases where the parties cannot or should not engage in cooperative negotiation.[49] For the majority of parenting disputes, the goals of Civil *Gideon* should be achievable by ensuring that parties have access to lawyers and other professionals to perform the more focused tasks and provide the range of dispute resolution services discussed in this book.

Training Lawyers for the New Dispute Resolution System

To practice effectively in the new paradigm, lawyers must master skills and develop competencies beyond those emphasized in the traditional law school curriculum. While a lawyer's ability to analyze cases and to construct persuasive legal arguments remains important, other skills and bodies of knowledge are equally critical to twenty-first-century family practice. These include communicating with clients and partnering effectively with other professionals, understanding clients' legal and nonlegal interests, engaging in interest-based negotiation, and helping clients choose the most appropriate dispute resolution process. In addition, to the extent that children begin to participate more directly in family dispute resolution, family lawyers must be knowledgeable about child development and must have the skills and motivation to communicate effectively with children.

The traditional law school curriculum is not well suited to teaching these skills. Despite recent curricular reforms, "it remains true that typical American law students earn most of their credits from classes in which they focus primarily on analyzing appellate cases, doing little writing, gathering no facts, and paying little attention to the realities of the clients' underlying interests."[50] Indeed, an analysis of a 2010 ABA curriculum study revealed that that about 80 to 85 percent of the first-year curriculum, and almost all required courses, focus on doctrinal instruction, and most of this instruction takes place through the study of appellate cases.[51] In addition, only a small percentage of the elective curriculum deals with legal skills, and law students generally have limited clinical and externship course opportunities.[52] Moreover, to the extent that law schools have integrated skills instruction into their curriculum, they have tended to emphasize the skills associated with adversarial litigation, such as trial practice and appellate advocacy, as opposed to the broader range of skills associated with problem-solving and conflict resolution. These curricular choices send the misleading message that most legal disputes are resolved by judges and that a lawyer's core function is to win in court, regardless of the financial and emotional costs and with little attention to a client's underlying interests.

The narrow focus of American legal education has been the subject of intense study and critique over the past two decades. In 2007, two widely publicized reports urged law schools to rethink their emphasis on legal doctrine and analysis, and to focus more directly on preparing students for practice. In "Educating Lawyers: Preparation for the Profession of Law," the Carnegie Foundation noted that most law schools do an impressive job of teaching students to "think like a lawyer" but "give only casual attention to teaching students how to use legal thinking in the complexity of actual law practice."[53] The report thus recommended that law schools integrate the study of legal doctrine and analysis with instruction in a range of lawyering skills and the inculcation of professional values from the beginning of law school.[54] Similarly, the Clinical Legal Education Association's 2007 report on "Best Practices for Legal Education" urged that schools reorganize their curriculum "to develop knowledge, skills, and values progressively; integrate the teaching of theory, doctrine, and practice; and teach professionalism pervasively throughout all three years of law school."[55] Articles by a number of legal educators have advocated similar reforms. One theme that emerges from these critiques is that the reliance on a single teaching method—case analysis and dialogue—does not prepare lawyers for the complexity and diversity of twenty-first-century practice. Another common insight is the need to train lawyers for an expanded and "reframed" definition of legal work that includes not only litigation, but also mediation, consensus-building, and conflict management.[56]

Family law and dispute resolution scholars have issued calls for more specific curricular reforms that would better train students to undertake the expanded roles associated with the new dispute resolution paradigm. The Family Law Education Reform Project, an initiative designed to recommend improvements in the education of family lawyers, concluded in 2006:

> Today's family lawyers need a thorough understanding of many issues and practices that traditional family law courses rarely touch upon. These include the appropriate—and inappropriate—uses of dispute resolution processes, new case management techniques in the family courts, the key roles played by professionals from other disciplines in the court system, and current research on such issues as the effects of conflict and loss of parental contact on children. Yet the materials from which most family law professors teach contain nary a word on most of these topics or on the skills necessary for effective family law practice.[57]

Law schools have instituted some curricular changes designed to address these concerns. A 2010 ABA survey on law school curricula "reveal[s] a renewed commitment by law schools to review and revise their curricula to produce practice-ready professionals."[58] The curricular changes include a substantial increase in all aspects of skills instruction, including law school clinics, simulation courses, and externship opportunities. A number of law schools have also enhanced their focus on non-adversary dispute resolution skills. Almost all law schools now offer a course or courses on dispute resolution, and at least seventeen law schools require all students to have some dispute resolution instruction.[59] A number of schools have also created programs or centers that focus explicitly on dispute resolution. But law schools need to do more. In order to fulfill the obligation to counsel clients about dispute resolution options, all lawyers need to be familiar with mediation and other alternatives to litigation, and law school curricula and advising should be designed to prepare students for that obligation.

Recent innovations in family law pedagogy show a similar emphasis on non-adversary dispute resolution skills. For example, current editions of most major family law texts now include materials on mediation and collaborative practice, as well as materials that focus on the interdisciplinary nature of family practice and the history and current role of family courts. Many family law courses now incorporate some skills training. A 2010 survey of nine law schools in New York concluded that these schools "are making substantial attempts to provide family law education to address the changing landscape of family law" by offering a range of survey courses, seminars, clinics, and externships.[60] But the report went on to conclude that schools need to "[c]ontinue to enhance family law curriculums by revamping existing courses consistent with the exigencies of the current family law landscape and by adding courses as necessary to address gaps in pedagogy."[61] It recommended "increased curricular focus on legal issues related to domestic violence and child maltreatment, the impact of increasing numbers of *pro se* clients, and practice issues including basic financial counseling, the structure and function of the current family law system, interdisciplinary practice, and cultural competency."[62]

Law schools should heed these recommendations and offer instruction in the full range of lawyering models and skills demanded by the new paradigm. All students should graduate from law school with an understanding of different methods of dispute resolution and an ability to discern which dispute resolution processes are likely to be most appropriate for which kinds of disputes and disputants. In addition to legal

research, writing, and analysis, students should master basic communication skills, as well as negotiation, mediation, and problem-solving
techniques. Wherever possible, students should have the opportunity to
practice these skills in clinical or externship settings.

Family law courses should also include instruction in communicating
and working with children. Social science research in both the United
States and England suggests that most family lawyers are uncomfortable
dealing directly with children and that most practitioners in the family justice system lack the necessary skill and understanding for effective face-to-face work with children.[63] Research with children confirms
these shortcomings. When asked about their experiences of talking with
family law professionals, young people in England, Australia, and New
Zealand reported that their discussions felt like interrogations, that the
lawyers and other professionals were judgmental, condescending, and
intrusive in their approach, and interventionist rather than supportive
in style.[64] To address these problems, family law educators should partner with child development professionals, as well as attorneys and mental health practitioners who specialize in working with children.

Doctrinal Changes to Support the New Dispute Resolution System

Designing processes that encourage family members to make informed,
safe, and voluntary choices about family reorganization is a central
theme of this chapter. However, as we have noted throughout this
book, process and doctrine are interconnected. Changes in substantive
family law doctrine can facilitate changes in family dispute resolution
processes. Conversely, changes in the way disputes are processed have
implications for the development and content of substantive legal norms.
As discussed in chapter 3, one characteristic of the current regime for
resolving parenting disputes is a significant devaluation of legal norms.
We find this development troubling and recommend renewed attention
to legal norms for a number of reasons.

First, legal norms are important because they play a vital role in the
functioning of the family justice system. Enhanced and improved alternatives to litigation should be the first option for all disputing families.
But courts, judges, and lawyers acting in their traditional roles serve

both as an incentive for parties reluctant to agree and as an indispens-able last resort for parents who cannot reach a cooperative resolution of their dispute, even with all the supports offered by the new paradigm. These are likely to include "high conflict" parties, and parties experiencing family violence or a substantial imbalance of economic power. And when parties find themselves in the adversary system, that system must be a robust one with clear substantive and procedural norms.

The devaluation of legal norms in resolving child access disputes in the current regime has also stifled debate about some of the most important issues facing family law today. These include questions about the legal definition and determinants of parenthood, and about the appropriateness and feasibility of joint parenting for couples who have never lived or parented together. While family law scholars have continued to discuss these issues, the new paradigm's retreat from adjudication minimizes the potential contributions of judicial voices and richly textured adjudicated cases.

Legal norms are also important because they influence the outcome and structure of out-of-court negotiations and other consensual dispute resolution processes. As Robert Mnookin and Lewis Kornhauser famously taught, parties to family law disputes bargain "in the shadow of the law."[65] Where that legal shadow is opaque or indeterminate, consensual resolution is more difficult. Indeterminate standards generate "high enforcement costs, inviting litigation and imposing substantial burdens on courts and parties."[66] By contrast, where the applicable legal norms are clear and widely known, parties are better able to evaluate options and proposals against potential outcomes in court. The content of the applicable legal norms also influences the disputants' perspectives of what resolutions are fair and equitable.

In addition, legal norms deserve attention because they continue to govern the outcome of disputes that cannot be settled and must be resolved by adjudication. Where high-conflict parties are unable to agree, the norms applied by third-party decision-makers are critical. While a dispute resolution system should not focus all its attention on the relatively small percentage of cases that will be resolved by judges, it cannot afford to ignore those cases. Legal norms also perform an important expressive function, particularly in family law.[67]

Moreover, the absence of explicit attention to legal norms is unlikely to prevent those norms from shifting or changing. Instead, the process may simply take place surreptitiously, without some of the safeguards that legal mechanisms provide. Martha Fineman has suggested that the legal system's initial embrace of presumptive joint custody developed as a result of just such a process, as judges ceded their authority over custody disputes to mental health professionals, who had a bias in favor of shared parenting.[68]

Legal norms thus matter, for both practical and prescriptive reasons. To function effectively, however, those norms should be clear, predictable, and easy to apply. These qualities are particularly important in a dispute resolution system where a substantial percentage of disputants are unrepresented and thus lack access to insider knowledge about how judges or other third-party decision-makers are likely to apply opaque or indeterminate norms.

The prevailing "best interests of the child" standard for resolving disputes between divorcing and separating parents fails to meet these objectives. Scholars have long criticized the standard for its vagueness and indeterminacy, qualities that "make outcomes uncertain and give judges broad discretion to consider almost any factor thought to be relevant to the custody decision."[69] Moreover, the best interests standard mistakenly assumes that judges have both the competence and the necessary information to determine what is best for any particular child. But courts are not well equipped to perform these tasks, and the mental health professionals on which many courts rely lack the expertise to advise judges about what post-separation parenting arrangements will best serve a particular child's interests.[70]

The best interests standard is also inconsistent with developments in other areas of family law, where vague, discretionary standards have given way to clearer, more determinant rules. For example, almost a generation ago, states replaced their highly discretionary child support standards with presumptive numerical guidelines. Similarly, many states have adopted statutory or de facto presumptions in favor of equal division of property to guide decision-makers in equitably apportioning marital assets. More recently, a number of jurisdictions have adopted or endorsed alimony guidelines designed to make awards of spousal support more consistent and predictable. In the face of these developments, the persistence of the highly discretionary best interests standard stands out as a "puzzling" anomaly.[71]

Over the past two decades, scholars and policy-makers have offered a number of proposals to replace the best interests standard with a more determinant rule or set of presumptions. An initial effort in this direction was a preference for the child's primary caretaker. This proposal directed judges to presume children's interests are best served by continuing to live with the parent who had been their primary caretaker before parental breakup.[72] Advocates of the primary caretaker preference argued that it advanced certainty and predictability while furthering the goal of stability for children. Critics objected to the proposal on the ground that it failed to account fully for children's needs and that it disadvantaged fathers, who were unlikely to have been primary caretakers. As a result, very few primary caretaker presumptions have found their way into law. A competing presumption in favor of joint physical custody has been advanced by some fathers' rights groups. But this proposal has encountered stiff opposition from judges and family lawyers, as well as advocates for mothers. These critics note that such a presumption focuses more on parents' rights than children's interests, and that it is likely to have its greatest impact in high-conflict cases that are least appropriate for joint custody.

More recently, the American Law Institute (ALI), as part of its "Principles of the Law of Family Dissolution," has developed a proposal that holds promise for today's families by combining a strong preference for parental decision-making with sensible default rules in cases where parents cannot agree. The approach is designed to "facilitate thoughtful planning by cooperative parents while minimizing the harm to children who are caught up in a cycle of conflict."[73] The cornerstone of the ALI approach is the parenting plan, which the Principles identify as "an individualized and customized set of custodial and decision-making arrangements for a child whose parents do not live together."[74] Parents who seek judicial intervention (including the termination of their marital status) must file, either jointly or separately, a proposed parenting plan that designates where a child will reside on given days of the year and that allocates decision-making responsibility for significant matters affecting the child. Consistent with the goals of the new paradigm, the parenting plan is not a recital of which parent gets custody and which has to settle for visitation. Rather, "the assumption of a parenting plan is that each parent ordinarily will play an important ongoing role in the child's life."[75] The ALI's terminology reflects this assumption. In lieu of references to custody and visitation, the ALI adopts the term "custodial responsibility" to refer to the time a child spends with each parent. Likewise, the ALI uses the term "decision-making responsibility" to "reframe the concept of legal custody to better connote a wide range of possible ways decision-making authority for a child can be divided, rather than a fixed template imposed by the state."[76] The ALI's approach thus shifts the focus from "who" will have custody of a child to "how" the parents will exercise their ongoing parenting responsibilities. The parenting plan must also contain a provision that addresses how the parties will resolve future disputes, thus minimizing the need and incentive for future court involvement.

If disputing parties are able to agree on a parenting plan—either on their own, or with the help of court-connected processes and services—no formal custody determination is required. Instead, "the Principles make clear that a court should defer to such privately negotiated arrangements except where the agreement is not voluntary or would be harmful to the child—a much higher degree of deference than formally exists in most traditional custody regimes."[77] Such deference recognizes that parents have greater expertise and access to information about their families than do judges or other court personnel. It also respects the range and complexity of parenting arrangements in today's families, both before and after parental separation.[78]

Where parents are unable to agree on a plan, the Principles offer a pair of sensible default rules. First, with respect to significant decision-making responsibility, the Principles establish a presumption in favor of joint decision-making responsibility if both parents have been exercising a reasonable share of parenting functions.[79] This presumption shifts the burden of proof with respect to joint decision-making to the parent who opposes it. The presumption can be overcome if there is a history of domestic violence or if the opposing parent shows that joint decision-making is not in a child's best interests.[80] A court may allocate significant decision-making responsibility as a whole, or separately for different categories of major decisions.

With respect to custodial responsibility, the ALI's "approximation standard" allocates residential time based on past caretaking patterns "so that the proportion of custodial time that the child spends with each parent approximates the proportion of time each parent spent performing caretaking functions for the child prior to the parents' separation or, if the parents never lived together, before the filing of the action."[81] By focusing on past caretaking, the approximation standard "anchors the determination of the child's best interests not in generalizations about what post-divorce arrangements work best for children, but in the individual history of each family."[82] Reliance on past caretaking is qualified to ensure that each parent receives an amount of residential time that will enable the parent to maintain a relationship with the child, even where that parent has not previously been involved in the child's caretaking. This qualification is particularly important for never-married families where the parents have not previously lived together. The approximation rule is also qualified to take account of the reasonable preferences of an older child and to avoid an allocation of custodial time that would be extremely impractical or would interfere substantially with the child's need for stability.[83] In addition, if a parent has abused or neglected a child or has inflicted domestic violence, a court should impose limits that are reasonably calculated to protect the child and the child's other parent from harm.[84]

The ALI's presumption of joint decision-making, and its reliance on past caretaking to allocate residential time, are consistent with the underlying policy goals of both the best interests standard and the new dispute resolution paradigm. The presumption in favor of joint decisionmaking recognizes that, in most circumstances, children benefit when both parents are involved in major decisions affecting their lives. The reliance on past parenting patterns to allocate residential time "promotes continuity and stability in the child's environment and relationships, preserving caretaking arrangements with which both the child and the parents are familiar."[85] In addition, by honoring an individual family's past caretaking patterns, the approximation standard allows for a range of parenting styles in different families rather than promoting one approach over others. At the same time, the standard "reduces the need for predictions about the future and thus the expenses and uncertainty produced by expert witnesses and psychological studies."[86] Moreover, unlike a primary caretaker preference, the approximation standard does not frame the custody decision as a zero-sum game in which one parent wins and the other loses.

The approximation standard is also dynamic. As fathers continue to assume a more active role in caring for children, the results produced by the approximation standard will look more and more like those produced by a norm of equally shared physical custody. Even today, application of an approximation approach would produce arrangements much closer to shared residential custody than to the traditional custody and visitation arrangements typical of adjudicated custody cases.[87] Thus, while the approximation standard "offers no windfall for a minimally involved parent," it honors the child's relationship with both parents and does not relegate either parent to second-class "visitor" status.[88]

Adoption of the ALI's approximation standard would also have beneficial systemic effects, for both litigated and non-litigated cases. In the context of adjudication, the standard relies on objective evidence of past behavior that is easier to evaluate and apply than the qualitative judgments and future predictions required by the current best interests approach. Reliance on past caretaking patterns also reduces the opportunity for judges to implement their own biases about child-rearing; further, it reduces the incentives for parents to engage experts to criticize one another and offer conflicting opinions about each parent's emotional bond with the child and the quality of their parenting.[89] Moreover, restricting the range of relevant evidence in disputed custody cases should discourage litigation and simplify proceedings, thereby reducing adjudication costs. It should also reduce the inclination of disputing parents to focus on each other's deficiencies—the dimension of custody adjudications that has the most costly repercussions for children.[90] Because of its greater determinacy, the approximation standard should also reduce the appeal of litigation and enhance the possibility of settlement. Finally, adoption of the approximation standard would eliminate the need for psychological evaluations in most disputed cases, which would reduce delays and conserve scarce family court resources.

Because doctrine matters, and because the legal norms embodied in the ALI's approach to parenting disputes are superior to the current, indeterminate best interests standard, reformers should endorse the ALI's emphasis on planning and its reliance on past caretaking patterns as a means of allocating custodial responsibility in cases where parents are unable to agree.

Conclusion

The late twentieth-century paradigm shift in family dispute resolution may represent an improvement over its more adversary predecessor. However, the current system fails to meet the diverse needs of today's disputing families. Implementing the recommendations in this chapter will strengthen the new paradigm and better align its lagging assumptions with the realities and needs of today's disputing families—rich and poor, marital and nonmarital, gay and straight, nuclear and extended. Moving non-adversarial processes and services from courts to communities will enhance access to these services and allow courts to focus on the critical functions that only courts can perform. Enhancing children's participation in non-adjudicative family dispute resolution processes will advance one of the core goals of the new paradigm—promoting the interests and welfare of children. Reforming legal practice and legal education will underscore the continuing importance of lawyers in helping families restructure and resolve disputes; it will also increase access to legal services, and equip lawyers with the skills and habits they need to serve clients effectively in the new paradigm. Finally, attending to legal doctrine and adopting an approach that emphasizes planning and past caretaking patterns recognizes the important expressive and channeling functions of family law; it also provides a clear legal framework both for out-of-court negotiation and for parties who are unable to settle and seek the authoritative guidance of a court. Taken together, these recommendations thus build on the valuable insights of the new paradigm in order to create a more just and effective twenty-first-century family dispute resolution regime.

NOTES

CHAPTER 1. HISTORICAL OVERVIEW

1 *See e.g.* Mary Ann Mason, *From Father's Property to Children's Rights* (New York: Columbia University Press, 1994), xii.

2 Michael Grossberg, *Governing the Hearth: Law and the Family in Nineteenth-Century America* (Chapel Hill: University of North Carolina Press, 1985), 5.

3 A number of feminist historians have challenged the accuracy of this legal depiction and have emphasized the important economic and community roles played by women in this era. *See e.g.* Martha Minow, "Forming Underneath Everything That Grows: Toward a History of Family Law," *Wisconsin Law Review* 1985 (1985): 865. ("Beneath the formal statements of treatises and judge-made law, some of the roles assumed by family members contested the formulations of historic family law cast in modern terms of dependency and authority, or subordination and authority.")

4 Grossberg, *Governing the Hearth*, 5.

5 Mason, *From Father's Property to Children's Rights*, 18–19.

6 *Ibid.* at 3.

7 *Ibid.* at 10.

8 *Ibid.* at 34.

9 Nancy Cott, *Public Vows: A History of Marriage and the Nation* (Cambridge, MA: Harvard University Press, 2000), 4.

10 *See generally* Carl Degler, *At Odds: Women and the Family in America from the Revolution to the Present* (New York: Oxford University Press, 1980), 26–30; Nancy Cott, *The Bonds of Womanhood* (New Haven, CT: Yale University Press, 1997), 64–98.

11 Degler, *At Odds*, 175.

12 Joel Bishop, *Commentaries on the Law of Marriage and Divorce* (Boston: Little, Brown, and Company, 1852), 517–518.

13 Grossberg, *Governing the Hearth*, 244.

14 *Ibid.* at 247.

15 *Ibid.*

16 Mason, *From Father's Property to Children's Rights*, 101–103.

17 *Ibid.* at 50.

18 Grossberg, *Governing the Hearth*, 38.

19 Mason, *From Father's Property to Children's Rights*, 68–70; *see* Grossberg, *Governing the Hearth*, 200–201.

20 Mason, *From Father's Property to Children's Rights*, 72.

21 Grossberg, *Governing the Hearth*, 244, 248.

22 *Ibid.* at 234.

23 Lynne Carol Halem, *Divorce Reform: Changing Legal and Social Perspectives* (New York: Free Press, 1980), 20.

24 Grossberg, *Governing the Hearth*, 251.

25 *Ibid.*, 250–251; *see* Andrew J. Cherlin, "American Marriage in the Early Twenty-First Century," *The Future of Children* 13 (2005): 36.

26 *See* Halem, *Divorce Reform*, 36–40.

27 George Squire, "The Shift from Adversary to Administrative Divorce," *Boston University Law Review* 33 (1953): 151–152.

28 J. Herbie DiFonzo, *Beneath the Fault Line: The Popular and Legal Culture of Divorce in Twentieth-Century America* (Charlottesville, VA: University of Virginia Press, 1997), 49.

29 *See* Jana Singer, "The Privatization of Family Law," *Wisconsin Law Review* 1992 (1992): 1470–1471.

30 Mason, *From Father's Property to Children's Rights*, 63.

31 *In re Gault*, 387 U.S. 1, 15 (1967).

32 Paul Lombard Sayre, *The Life of Roscoe Pound* (Littleton, CO: Rothman, 1948), 105.

33 Graham Parker, "The Juvenile Court Movement: The Illinois Experience," *University of Toronto Law Journal* 26 (1976): 253

34 For an introduction to the history and theory of the juvenile courts, *see* Janet E. Ainsworth, "Re-imagining Childhood and Reconstructing the Legal Order: The Case for Abolishing the Juvenile Court," *North Carolina Law Review* 69 (1991): 1083, 1096–1097; *see also* Barry C. Feld, "Violent Youth and Public Policy: A Case Study of Juvenile Justice Law Reform," *Minnesota Law Review* 79 (1995): 965, 969; David S. Tanenhaus, "The Evolution of the Juvenile Courts in the Early Twentieth Century: Beyond the Myth of Immaculate Construction," in Margaret K. Rosenheim, Franklin E. Zimring, David S. Tanenhaus, and Bernadine Dohrn, eds., *A Century of Juvenile Justice* (Chicago: University of Chicago Press, 2002), 42.

35 *In re Gault* at 15–16 (quoting Julian Mack, "The Juvenile Court," *Harvard Law Review* 23 [1909]: 104, 120).

36 "By design, the Cook County Juvenile Court was not supposed to be a criminal court at all. Instead, judges followed the more flexible procedure of a chancery court. . . . [T]he court heard cases informally, without the adversarial format, or the attention to due process rights, of an ordinary criminal proceeding." Michael Willrich, *City of Courts: Socializing Justice in Progressive Era Chicago* (Cambridge, UK: Cambridge University Press, 2003), 79–80. *But see* Sanford Fox, "Juvenile Justice Reform: An Historical Perspective," *Stanford Law Review* 22 (1970): 1187, 1192 (challenging the idea that informal procedures in criminal cases involving juveniles began with the establishment of juvenile courts).

37 Fox, "Juvenile Justice Reform," 1187, 1192; Marvin Ventrell, "Evolution of the Dependency Component of the Juvenile Court," *Juvenile and Family Court Journal* 49 (1998): 17.

38 Joel Handler, "The Juvenile Court and the Adversary System," *Wisconsin Law Review* 1965 (1965): 7, 9; *see* Fox, "Juvenile Justice Reform," 1187, 1192 (noting that the distinction between neglected children and delinquent children, which is of great importance today, had virtually no meaning to early juvenile court reformers).

39 Although preserving privacy of minors was a central theme of the theories underlying juvenile courts, the practice of closing hearings took some time to be established in the courts. David S. Tanenhaus, *Juvenile Justice in the Making* (New York: Oxford University Press, 2004), 25.

40 Although the Illinois Juvenile Court Act of 1899 guaranteed the right to a jury trial, it had to be requested. Many other state juvenile court statutes included no such guarantee. The broader issue of the role of juries in family law cases is discussed in Melissa Breger, "Introducing the Construct of the Jury into Family Violence Proceedings and Family Court Jurisprudence," *Michigan Journal of Gender and the Law* 13 (2006): 1.

41 Barbara Fedders, "Losing Hold of the Guiding Hand: Ineffective Assistance of Counsel in Juvenile Delinquency Representation," *Lewis and Clark Law Review* 14 (2010): 771, 779. *See also* Michael Willrich, "The Two Percent Solution: Eugenic Jurisprudence and the Socialization of American Law, 1900–1930," *Law and History Review* 16 (1998): 63. ("Defendants typically waived their rights to a jury trial, leaving all questions of fact and law to the judges.") Many in the early juvenile court movement viewed lawyers with suspicion. Even in the relatively few cases where children were represented, the broad power of the judges in juvenile courts and the lack of proce-dural protections limited the effectiveness of lawyers. Joseph M. Hawes, *The Children's Rights Movement* (New York: Twayne, 1991), 20.

42 Charles R. Henderson, "Juvenile Courts: Problems of Administration," *Charities and the Commons* 13 (1905), cited in Anthony Platt, *The Child Savers*, 2nd ed. (Chicago: University of Chicago Press, 1977), 144.

43 DiFonzo, *Beneath the Fault Line*, 152.

44 Platt, *The Child Savers*, 141 (discussing the juvenile court movement's "maximum dependency on extra legal resources"). *See also* Sanford J. Fox, "The Early History of the Court," *The Future of Children* 6 (1996): 36 (describing the role of nonlegal personnel, "With this development in Chicago, the reform of delinquents that was the core of the juvenile court moved a large step farther away from the judge and into the hands of other professionals").

45 As one commentator described the sentences imposed by the early juvenile courts, "Because a youth's offense was only a symptom of her 'real' needs, sentences were indeterminate, nonproportional, and potentially continued for the duration of minority." Barry C. Feld, "The Transformation of Juvenile Court," *Minnesota Law Review* 75 (1991): 695.

46 As Boston juvenile court Judge Harvey Baker explained it, "[A] boy who comes to court for some such trifle as failing to wear his badge when selling papers may be held on probation for months because of difficulties at school; and a boy who comes in for playing ball on the street may . . . be committed to a reform school because he is found to have habits of loafing, stealing, or gambling which cannot be corrected outside." "Procedure of the Boston Juvenile Court," *Survey* 23 (February 1910): 649.

47 Mason, *From Father's Property to Children's Rights*, 102. Indeed, the Illinois statute that created the first juvenile court was titled "An Act to Regulate the Treatment and Control of Dependent, Neglected and Delinquent Children." Act of April 21, 1899, Ill. Laws 131.

48 Katherine Lenroot and Emma O. Lundberg, *Juvenile Courts at Work: A Study of the Organization and Methods of Ten Courts* (New York: AMS Press, 1925, 1975), 1. Although they shared many characteristics, because they were creatures of state and local law, juvenile courts were diverse. As one scholar states, "The fact that juvenile courts have always been statutory creations, which state legislatures can alter at will, has contributed to many differences among these courts." Tanenhaus, *Juvenile Justice in the Making*, 179, n. 12.

49 *See e.g.* Solomon J. Greene, "Vicious Streets: The Crisis of the Industrial City and the Invention of Juvenile Justice," *Yale Journal of Law and Humanities* 15 (2003): 135, 136. For data on the migration of African Americans from rural areas of the country to the cities, *see e.g.* Elizabeth Anne Martin, "Detroit and the Great Migration," last modified July 5, 2007, http://bentley.umich.edu/research/publications/migration/ch1. php.

50 Halem, *Divorce Reform*, 118.

51 DiFonzo, *Beneath the Fault Line*, 151 (citing Report by the President's Commission on Law Enforcement and Administration of Justice, "The Challenge of Crime in a Free Society" [1967]).

52 Handler, "The Juvenile Court and the Adversary System," 7.

53 J. Herbie DiFonzo, "No-Fault Marital Dissolution: The Bitter Triumph of Naked Divorce," *San Diego Law Review* 31 (1994): 519.

54 DiFonzo, *Beneath the Fault Line*, 151.

55 Handler, "The Juvenile Court and the Adversary System," 7.

56 *In re Gault* at 17.

57 *Ibid.*

58 *Ibid.* at 18.

59 DiFonzo, *Beneath the Fault Line*, 152.

60 *Ibid.* at 113 (quoting Paul W. Alexander, "Is There a Divorce Evil?" *Ohio Magazine*, [April 1945]).

61 *Ibid.* at 117.

62 Paul W. Alexander, "Introduction to Symposium on Legal Science and the Social Sciences: The Family Court," *Missouri Law Review* 21 (1956): 105, 107.

63 *Ibid.* at 105, 109.

64 DiFonzo, *Beneath the Fault Line*, 120.

65 *See* Halem, *Divorce Reform*, 221–222.

66 DiFonzo, *Beneath the Fault Line*, 152.

67 Halem, *Divorce Reform*, 121.

68 Alexander, "Introduction to Symposium on Legal Science and the Social Sciences," 105, 106.

69 *Ibid.* at 105, 107.

70 Herma Hill Kay, "A Family Court: The California Proposal," *California Law Review* 56 (1968): 1205, 1228.

71 *Ibid.*

72 Halem, *Divorce Reform*, 116.

73 *See* Halem, *Divorce Reform*, 117 (describing inauguration of Hamilton County, Ohio, family court in 1914).

74 *Ibid.* at 118 (quoting Roger Baldwin and Bernard Flexner, *Juvenile Courts and Probation* [New York: Century, 1914], vii).

75 *Ibid.* at 126.

76 *See* Kay, "A Family Court," 1205, 1207 (acknowledging that "since the original family court idea was largely copied from the juvenile court model, it becomes necessary for modern advocates of the family court to reexamine their proposal in order to discover whether the common aspects of the two schemes are among those that have contributed to the present dissatisfaction with the juvenile court").

77 DiFonzo, *Beneath the Fault Line*, 122.

78 Halem, *Divorce Reform*, 124.

79 Herbert Jacobs, *Silent Revolution: The Transformation of Divorce Law in the United States* (Chicago: University of Chicago Press, 1988), 1–9.

80 See Singer, "The Privatization of Family Law," 1443, 1472.

81 *Ibid.* at 1443, 1471.

82 Andrew Schepard, "The Evolving Judicial Role in Child Custody Disputes: From Fault Finder to Conflict Manager to Differential Case Management," *University of Arkansas Little Rock Law Review* 22 (2000): 395–396.

83 Anna Freud, Joseph Goldstein, and Albert Solnit, *Beyond the Best Interests of the Child* (New York: Free Press, 1973), 37–40.

84 *Ibid.* at 38; *see* Andrew I. Schepard, *Children, Courts and Custody: Interdisciplinary Models for Divorcing Families* (Cambridge, UK: Cambridge University Press, 2004), 20.

85 Schepard, "The Evolving Judicial Role in Child Custody Disputes," 395, 402.

86 *See generally* Robert H. Mnookin, "Foreword: Symposium: Children, Divorce, and the Legal System, The Direction for Reform," *Law and Contemporary Problems* 19 (1985): 393, 394.

87 Schepard, "The Evolving Judicial Role in Child Custody Disputes," 395, 402; *see* Martha Fineman, "Dominant Discourse, Professional Language, and Legal Change in Child Custody Decisionmaking," *Harvard Law Review* 101 (1998): 727, 740 (with the removal of the tender years presumption, application of the best interests standard grew more complex and custody decisions became more difficult for judges).

88 Andre Derdeyn and Elizabeth Scott, "Rethinking Joint Custody," *Ohio State Law Journal* 45 (1984): 455, 456; *see* Schepard, *Children, Courts and Custody*, 46–48.

89 *See e.g.* Andrew Schepard, "Taking Children Seriously: Promoting Cooperative Custody after Divorce," *Texas Law Review* 64 (1985): 687, 770 ("The cooperative custody system symbolizes the inescapable reality that parents are forever, even if marriages are not."); Patrick Parkinson, *Family Law and the Indissolubility of Parenthood* (Cambridge, UK: Cambridge University Press, 2011), 41–42.

90 Parkinson, *Family Law and the Indissolubility of Parenthood*, 41.

91 *See e.g. McCarty v. McCarty*, 807 A.2d 1211 (2002) (neither a parent's objection to sharing custody nor the parents' current inability to communicate effectively should preclude an award of joint legal custody).

92 *See* Jana B. Singer, "Bargaining in the Shadow of the Best Interests Standard: The Close Connection between Substance and Process in Resolving Divorce-Related Parenting Disputes," *Law and Contemporary Problems* 77 (1) (2013): 191–193.

93 Andrew Schepard, "The Evolving Judicial Role in Child Custody Disputes," 396.

CHAPTER 2. THE CRITIQUE OF THE ADVERSARY SYSTEM AND THE
NEW PARADIGM AS A RESPONSE

1 Robert E. Emery, *Renegotiating Family Relationships: Divorce, Child Custody, and Mediation* (New York: Guilford Press, 2012), 100. *See generally* Paul Amato, *Children of Divorced Parents as Young Adults*, in E. M. Hetherington, ed., *Coping with Divorce, Single Parenting and Remarriage: A Risk and Resiliency Perspective* (New York: Psychology Press, 1999), 147–163; Joan Kelly, "Children's Adjustment in Conflicted Marriage and Divorce," *Journal of the American Academy of Child and Adolescent Psychology* 39 (2000): 963–973.

2 *See* Jana B. Singer, "Dispute Resolution and the Post-Divorce Family: Implications of a Paradigm Shift," *Family Court Review* 47 (2009): 363.

3 Solangel Maldonado, "Cultivating Forgiveness: Reducing Hostility and Conflict after Divorce," *Wake Forest Law Review* 43 (2008): 454 (quoting *Eldridge v. Eldridge*, 42 S.W.3d 82, 90 [Tenn. 2001]).

4 "Recommendation of the Law Revision Commission to the 1985 Legislature Relating to the Child Custody Decision-Making Process," *Columbia Journal of Law and Social Problems* 19 (1985): 120.

5 Eleanor E. Maccoby and Robert H. Mnookin, *Dividing the Child: Social and Legal Dilemmas of Custody* (Cambridge, MA: Harvard University Press, 1992), 31.

6 Janet R. Johnston, "High-Conflict Divorce," *The Future of Children* 4 (1994): 172; *see* Jessica J. Sauer, "Mediating Child Custody Disputes for High Conflict Couples: Structuring Mediation to Accommodate the Needs and Desires of Litigious Parents," *Pepperdine Dispute Resolution Law Journal* 7 (2007): 501. ("By encouraging parents to adopt polarized positions, the adversarial process weakens any remaining bonds between them and impairs their ability to provide a stable and nurturing environment for their children in both the present and the future.")

7 Hugh McIsaac, "Programs for High Conflict Families," *Willamette Law Review* 35 (1999): 580.

8 Janet Weinstein, "And Never the Twain Shall Meet: The Best Interests of Children and the Adversary System," *University of Miami Law Review* 52 (1997): 132–133.

9 Janet R. Johnston, "Building Multidisciplinary Professional Partnerships with the Court on Behalf of High-Conflict Divorcing Families and Their Children: Who Needs What Kind of Help?" *University of Arkansas Little Rock Law Review* 22 (2001): 453, 461.

10 *See e.g.* Emery, *Renegotiating Family Relationships*, 100–101 (citing sources); Weinstein, "And Never the Twain Shall Meet," 79.

11 Singer, "Dispute Resolution and the Post-Divorce Family," 365; *see generally* Patrick Parkinson, *Family Law and the Indissolubility of Parenthood* (Cambridge, UK: Cambridge University Press, 2011).

12 Marygold Melli, "Whatever Happened to Divorce?" *Wisconsin Law Review* 2000 (2000): 698.

13 Joan B. Kelly, "Psychological and Legal Intervention for Parents and Children in Custody and Access Disputes: Current Research and Practice," *Virginia Journal of Social Policy and Law* 10 (2000): 131; *see* Bill Ezzell, "Inside the Minds of America's Family Law Courts: The Psychology of Mediation versus Litigation in Domestic Disputes," *Law and Psychology Review* 25 (2001): 124 (noting that litigation "polarizes a divorcing couple, thus aggravating an already failed relationship").

14 *See* Emery, *Renegotiating Family Relationships*, 82.

15 Michael E. Lamb and Joan B. Kelly, "The Continuing Debate about Overnight Visitation: Using the Empirical Literature to Guide the Development of Parenting Plans for Young Children," *Family Court Review* 39 (2001): 366–367 (noting that many divorced fathers respond to adversary divorce proceedings "by drifting out of their children's lives, often failing to take advantage even of the limited opportunities for visitation afforded to them"); "Recommendation of the Law Revision Commission to the 1985 Legislature," 121. ("The non-custodial parent perceives himself as a loser, who can only see the child intermittently, and in order to protect himself, he may withdraw from the child both emotional and financial support.")

16 Emery, *Renegotiating Family Relationships*, 209–210. A recent study by several prominent demographers complicates this picture. Jacob Cheadle, Paul Amato, and Valerie King, "Patterns of Nonresident Father Contact," *Demography* 47 (2010): 205–225. The authors found that different groups of nonresident fathers exhibited distinct patterns of contact over time, and that only a minority of fathers followed a pattern of consistent and increasing disengagement from their children.

17 *See e.g.* Ross A. Thompson, "The Role of the Father after Divorce," *The Future of Children* 4 (1994): 222–224; Elizabeth Scott and Andre Derdeyn, "Rethinking Joint Custody," *Ohio State Law Journal* 45 (1984): 459–460; John Jacobs, "The Effect of Divorce on Fathers: An Overview of the Literature," *American Journal of Psychiatry* 139 (1982): 1235–1236.

18 *See* Andrew Schepard, "War and P.E.A.C.E.: A Preliminary Report and Model Statute on an Interdisciplinary Educational Program for Divorcing and Separating Parents," *University of Michigan Journal of Law Reform* 27 (1993): 146–147 (custody

litigation drains resources from limited marital assets at a time when those assets could better be used to preserve the family's standard of living).

19 *See* "Recommendation of the Law Revision Commission to the 1985 Legislature," 121.

20 *Ibid.*

21 Maldonado, "Cultivating Forgiveness," 450–451 (citing studies).

22 *See e.g.* Thomas E. Carbonneau, "A Consideration of Alternatives to Divorce Litigation," *University of Illinois Law Review* 1986 (1986) 1169 (positing that where custody outcomes are self-determined and the product of personal involvement by parents, the likelihood of continued compliance is enhanced and the possibility of reconsideration reduced).

23 Joan B. Kelly, "A Decade of Divorce Mediation Research, Some Answers and Questions," *Family and Conciliation Courts Review* 34 (1996): 377 (citing studies); *see* Kelly, "Psychological and Legal Intervention for Parents and Children in Custody and Access Disputes," 140. ("Relitigation rates are lower when mediation is used for solving parental disputes, and compliance with agreements occurs at higher rates among mediated samples.")

24 *See* Emery, *Renegotiating Family Relationships*, 103.

25 These findings are consistent with earlier studies. *See* Kelly, "A Decade of Divorce Mediation Research," 377 (noting that "parents using comprehensive divorce mediation reported significantly less conflict, more cooperation, more child-focused communication and more noncustodial parent participation in decision making about children, compared with the adversarial sample").

26 Lamb and Kelly, "The Continuing Debate about Overnight Visitation," 366–337 (citing studies).

27 Emery, *Renegotiating Family Relationships*, 214. ("With few exceptions, researchers have found no evidence of improved psychological well-being owing to mediation.")

28 *See e.g.* Schepard, "War and P.E.A.C.E.," 148 ("State court judges who preside over custody disputes commonly describe such cases as both frustrating and saddening, and as perhaps the hardest of all cases to decide."); Pauline H. Tesler, "Collaborative Law: A New Paradigm for Divorce Lawyers," *Psychology Public Policy and Law* 5 (1997): 969 (noting that "judges generally dislike handling domestic relations matters, are chronically understaffed and overworked, and lack specialized training in family systems and dynamics"); Andrew Kaplan, "The Advantages of Mediation in Resolving Child Custody Disputes," *Rutgers Law Review* 23 (1999): 7 ("judges are unhappy and uncomfortable making custody determinations"); Martha Fineman, "Dominant Discourse, Professional Language, and Legal Change in Child Custody Decisionmaking," *Harvard Law Review* 101 (1988): 740 (noting that judges feel ill equipped to make determinations about what placement will be in the "best interests" of children).

29 Mary R. Cathcart and Robert E. Robles, *Parenting Our Children: In the Best Interest of the Nation* (Washington, DC: U.S. Commission on Child and Family Welfare, 1996), 39.

30 Marsha Kline Pruett and Tamara D. Jackson, "The Lawyer's Role during the Divorce Process: Perceptions of Parents, Their Young Children, and Their Attorneys," *Family Law Quarterly* 33 (1999): 298.

31 Ezzell, "Inside the Minds of America's Family Law Courts," 124.

32 Emery, *Renegotiating Family Relationships*, 206.

33 *Ibid.* at 206–207.

34 *See e.g.* Kelly, "Psychological and Legal Intervention for Parents and Children in Custody and Access Disputes," 138 ("Empirical research in four countries demonstrates that a large majority of participants view custody mediation as quite satisfactory, including those that are mandated to attend mediation. Parents, and particularly men, are more satisfied with both mediation processes and outcomes, compared to control or comparison groups using adversarial processes to settle their divorce disputes."); Nancy Ver Steegh, "Family Court Reform and ADR: Shifting Values and Expectations Transform the Divorce Process," *Family Law Quarterly* 42 (2008): 662, n. 23 (noting that "[a]lthough satisfaction rates differ depending upon whether agreement is reached, participant satisfaction levels generally range from 60% to 93%").

35 Emery, *Renegotiating Family Relationships*, 207.

36 *See ibid.* at 207–208 (citing studies).

37 *See e.g.* Johnston, "Building Multidisciplinary Professional Partnerships with the Court on Behalf of High-Conflict Divorcing Families and Their Children," 470–471 ("solidly researched 'success rate' of mediation supports the philosophy that most couples have the capacity to re-order their lives in a private, confidential setting, according to their personal preferences, with the relatively limited help of a mediator who focuses on specific issues"); Kelly, "A Decade of Divorce Mediation Research," 375 ("Mediation research across countries indicate that clients reach agreement in divorce mediation 50% to 80% of the time, with most studies in the mid to upper range.")

38 *See* William J. Howe III, "Introduction to the Oregon Futures Report," *Family Law Quarterly* 40 (2002): 473 (reporting that many *pro se* litigants can afford counsel but do not seek representation "because they fear that to consult a lawyer would be to shake hands with the tar baby."); *but see* Julie Macfarlane, "Time to Shatter the Stereotype of the Self-Represented Litigants," *ABA Dispute Resolution Magazine* 20 (2013): 14 (summarizing research establishing "that the most significant reason for joining the ranks of the *pro se* litigants, who now constitute the majority in some family courts, is the high cost of legal services").

39 Pruett and Jackson, "The Lawyer's Role during the Divorce Process," 306.

40 Andrew I. Schepard, *Children, Courts and Custody: Interdisciplinary Models for Divorcing Families* (Cambridge, UK: Cambridge University Press, 2004), 43.

41 Ronald L. Solove, "Confessions of a Judicial Activist," *Ohio State Law Journal* 54 (1993): 807; *see* Julie Macfarlane, "Experiences of Collaborative Law: Preliminary Results from the Collaborative Lawyering Research Project," *Journal of Dispute Resolution* 2004 (2004): 181 (noting that "disillusionment and burn-out are legend among family lawyers").

42 *See generally* Weinstein, "And Never the Twain Shall Meet," 90–97.

43 *See* Macfarlane, "Experiences of Collaborative Law," 180.

44 *Ibid.*

45 *See generally* Pauline H. Tesler, "Collaborative Family Law," *Pepperdine Dispute Resolution Law Journal* 4 (2004): 317.

46 Jana B. Singer, "Dispute Resolution and the Post-Divorce Family: Implications of a Paradigm Shift," *Family Court Review* 47 (2009): 363, 364.

47 *See generally* Hon. Gerald Hardcastle, "Adversarialism and the Family Court: A Family Court Judge's Perspective," *Journal of Juvenile Law and Policy* 9 (2005): 57; Jane C. Murphy, "Revitalizing the Adversary System in Family Law," *University of Cincinnati Law Review* 78 (2010): 891.

48 Hardcastle, "Adversarialism and the Family Court," at 104–105 (footnote omitted).

49 *See* Anne H. Geraghty and Wallace J. Mlyniec, "Unified Family Courts: Tempering Enthusiasm with Caution," *Family Court Review* 40 (2002): 435, 441; Julie Doughty and Mervyn Murch, "Judicial Independence and the Restructuring of Family Courts and Their Support Services," *Child and Family Law Quarterly* 24 (2012): 333.

50 Murphy, "Revitalizing the Adversary System in Family Law," 891.

51 *See e.g.* Jane M. Spinak, "Romancing the Court," *Family Court Review* 46 (2008): 258; Timothy Casey, "When Good Intentions Are Not Enough: Problem-Solving Courts and the Impending Crisis of Legitimacy," *Southern Methodist Law Review* 57 (2009): 1459.

CHAPTER 3. EXPANDED COURTS WITH DIMINISHED LEGAL NORMS

1 Jana B. Singer, "Dispute Resolution and the Post-Divorce Family: Implications of a Paradigm Shift," *Family Court Review* 47 (2009): 363–364.

2 *Ibid.*, 364.

3 Andrew Schepard, "The Evolving Judicial Role in Custody Disputes: From Fault Finder to Conflict Manager to Differential Case Management," *University of Arkansas at Little Rock Law Review* 22 (2000): 395–396.

4 John Lande and Forrest S. Mosten, "Family Lawyering: Past, Present, and Future," *Family Court Review* 51 (2013): 20–21; Andrew I. Schepard, *Children, Courts and Custody: Interdisciplinary Models for Divorcing Families* (Cambridge, UK: Cambridge University Press, 2004), 38–40, 58–60, 68–78, 90–95, 100–124; Nancy Ver Steegh, "Family Court Reform and ADR: Shifting Values and Expectations Transform the Divorce Process," *Family Law Quarterly* 42 (2008): 659.

5 *See e.g.* Bruce J. Winick, "Therapeutic Jurisprudence and Problem-Solving Courts," *Fordham Urban Law Journal* 30 (2003): 1055; Marsha B. Freeman, "Love Means Always Having to Say You're Sorry: Applying the Realities of Therapeutic Jurisprudence to Family Law," *UCLA Women's Law Journal* 17, no. 2 (2008): 215.

6 Winick, "Therapeutic Jurisprudence and Problem-Solving Courts," 1055.

7 Jeffrey Kuhn, "A Seven-Year Lesson on Unified Family Courts: What We Have Learned since the 1990 National Family Court Symposium," *Family Law Quarterly* 32 (1998): 88; Sanford N. Katz and Jeffrey A. Kuhn, *Recommendations for a Model Family*

Court: A Report from the National Family Court Symposium (Reno, NV: National Council of Juvenile and Family Court Judges, 1991).

8 John Gibeaut, "ABA Backs Unified Family Courts," *ABA Journal* 83 (1997).

9 Susan Gamache, "Collaborative Practice: A New Opportunity to Address Children's Best Interest in Divorce," *Louisiana Law Review* 65 (2005): 1455.

10 *Ibid.*, 1459.

11 Solangel Maldonado, "Cultivating Forgiveness: Reducing Hostility and Conflict after Divorce," *Wake Forest Law Review* 43 (2008): 441.

12 Clare Huntington, "Repairing Family Law," *Duke Law Journal* 57 (2008): 1245, 1295.

13 Freeman, "Love Means Always Having to Say You're Sorry," 230–231.

14 *Ibid.*, 231 (arguing that the court system's failure to address these underlying needs "makes the courts major contributors to the cycle of continuous litigation that affects many families").

15 Singer, "Dispute Resolution and the Post-Divorce Family," 365.

16 Shirley Thomas, *Parents Are Forever: A Step-by-Step Guide to Becoming Successful Co-parents after Divorce* (Longmont, CO: Springboard, 2004); *see* Patrick Parkinson, *Family Law and the Indissolubility of Parenthood* (Cambridge, UK: Cambridge University Press, 2011). ("The history of family law reform in the last twenty years could be said to be the history of abandonment of the assumption . . . that divorce could dissolve the family as well as the marriage when there are children.")

17 Schepard, "The Evolving Judicial Role in Child Custody Disputes," 401–403.

18 *See* Linda D. Elrod and Milfred D. Dale, "Paradigm Shifts and Pendulum Swings in Child Custody: The Interests of Children in the Balance," *Family Law Quarterly* 42 (2008): 381, 388.

19 Robert E. Emery and Kimberly C. Emery, "Should Courts or Parents Make Child-Rearing Decisions? Married Parents as a Paradigm for Parents Who Live Apart," *Wake Forest Law Review* 43 (2008): 365.

20 Theresa Glennon, "Still Partners: Examining the Consequences of Post-dissolution Parenting," *Family Law Quarterly* 41 (2007): 105, 117 (noting that "assistance for post-divorce parenting has become a cottage industry").

21 *Ibid.*, 105.

22 *Ibid.*, 105–106.

23 Parkinson, *Family Law and the Indissolubility of Parenthood*, 14.

24 Glennon, "Still Partners," 106.

25 *Ibid.*, 123–125.

26 Linda D. Elrod, "A Move in the Right Direction? Best Interests of the Child Emerges as Standard for Relocation Cases," in Philip M. Stahl and Leslie Drozel, eds., *Relocation Issues in Child Custody Cases* (New York: Haworth Press, 2006), 29, 48.

27 Cynthia Grant Bowman, "The Legal Relationship between Cohabitants and Their Partner's Children," *Theoretical Inquiries in Law* 13 (2012): 127, 135.

28 J. Herbie DiFonzo and Ruth C. Stern, "Breaking the Mold and Picking Up the Pieces: Rights of Parenthood and Parentage in Nontraditional Families," *Family Court Review* 51 (2013): 109.

29 *A.H. v. M.P.*, 857 N.E.2d 1061 (Mass. 2006), quoting *Blixt v. Blixt*, 774 N.E.2d 1052 (Mass. 2002).

30 Michael Freeman, *Family Values and Family Justice* (Burlington, VT: Ashgate, 2010).

31 "Circuit Court Family Divisions and Family Services Programs," Department of Family Administrations, accessed October 25, 2014, http:www.courts.state.md.us/family/localcontacts.html; "Family Law Forms," Florida State Courts Self-Help, accessed June 7, 2012, http://www.flcourts.org/gen_public/family/forms_rules/index.shtml; "Domestic Relations Court," Courts and Court Services, accessed June 7, 2012, http://www.mcohio.org/government/domestic_relations_court/index.html.

32 Michael Willrich, *City of Courts: Socializing Justice in Progressive Era Chicago* (Cambridge, UK: Cambridge University Press 2003), 155.

33 Charles R. Henderson, "Juvenile Courts: Problems of Administration," *Charities* 13 (1905), cited in Anthony Platt, *The Child Savers*, 2nd ed. (Chicago: University of Chicago Press, 1977), 144.

34 Singer, "Dispute Resolution and the Post-Divorce Family," 363.

35 *See* discussion in chapter 2.

36 Linda Elrod, "Paradigm Shifts and Pendulum Swings in Child Custody: The Interests of Children in the Balance," *Family Law Quarterly* 42 (2008): 381.

37 T. J. Hester, "The Role of Mental Health Professionals in Child Custody Determinations Incident to Divorce," *Women's Law Reporter* 4 (1992): 109.

38 Martha Fineman, "Dominant Discourse, Professional Language, and Legal Change in Child Custody Decisionmaking," *Harvard Law Review* 101 (1988): 730.

39 Elizabeth S. Scott and Robert E. Emery, "Gender Politics and Child Custody: The Puzzling Persistence of the Best-Interests Standard," *Law and Contemporary Problems* 77 (2014): 69.

40 Barbara A. Babb, "Fashioning an Interdisciplinary Framework for Court Reform in Family Law: A Blueprint to Construct a Unified Family Court," *Southern California Law Review* 71 (1998): 469, 521.

41 *See e.g.* Office of the State Courts Administrator Florida Supreme Court, A National Conference on *Pro Se* Litigation Florida Team Report (January 3, 2000), app. A (surveying various states' efforts to use court staff to assist unrepresented parties in court).

42 The AFCC Task Force on Parenting Coordination, "Guidelines for Parenting Coordination," *Family Court Review* 44 (2006): 165. (The Association of Family and Conciliation Courts [AFCC] has been particularly active in establishing standards of practice for these new participants in family dispute resolution.).

43 Daniel B. Pickar and Jeffrey J. Kahn, "Settlement-Focused Parenting Plan Consultations: An Evaluative Mediation Alternative to Child Custody Evaluations," *Family Court Review* 49 (2011): 59–71.

44 Mary E. O'Connell and J. Herbie DiFonzo, "The Family Law Education Reform Project Final Report," *Family Court Review* 44 (2006): 524–525. *See also* Lynne Kenney Markan and David K. Weinstock, "Expanding Forensically Informed Evaluations and

Therapeutic Interventions in Family Court," *Family Court Review* 43 (2005): 466 (reviewing various types of evaluations, including dispute assessments, child developmental evaluations, child forensic interviews, and emergency case stabilizations, as well as different types of therapeutic interventions in the twenty-first-century family court).

45 O'Connell and DiFonzo, "The Family Law Education Reform Project Final Report," 524–525. For further discussion of the changing nature of the lawyer's role in the new paradigm, *see* chapter 5.

46 In response to this concern, the American Bar Association added language to its Comments to Model Rule 2.1, Scope of Advice, suggesting that lawyers may be obligated to advise clients about the availability of alternative dispute resolution. *See* Model Rules of Professional Conduct R. 2.1 cmt. 5 (2002) (noting that "when a matter is likely to involve litigation, it may be necessary . . . to inform the client of forms of dispute resolution that might constitute reasonable alternatives to litigation").

47 There has been some recognition of the important role lawyers can play in mediation. *See e.g.* Jean R. Sternlight, "Lawyerless Dispute Resolution: Rethinking a Paradigm," *Fordham Urban Law Journal* 37 (2010): 381 (identifying roles of lawyers in mediation, including advising clients about law as well as balancing power and providing emotional support); Stephen Landsman, "Nothing for Something: Denying Legal Assistance to Those Compelled to Participate in ADR Proceedings," *Fordham Urban Law Journal* 37 (2010): 273. For an empirical study of the impact of lawyer participation in divorce mediation, *see* Craig A. McEwen *et al.*, "Bring in the Lawyers: Challenging the Dominant Approaches to Ensuring Fairness in Divorce Mediation," *Minnesota Law Review* 79 (1995): 1317 (analyzing a study of lawyer participation in divorce mediation in Maine and concluding that such participation protects clients and otherwise improves the quality of the mediation process).

48 Mark C. Rutherford, "Lawyers and Divorce Mediation: Designing the Role of 'Outside Counsel," *Mediation Quarterly* 12 (1986): 17, 27. ("For mediation to succeed as a profession and to reach its highest objectives, advocacy has no place in any part of the process. For outside counsel to advocate a client's interest contradicts the very essence of mediation and can produce inequitable results."); Uniform Mediation Act §10 (2001); "Model Standards of Practice for Family and Divorce Mediation," *Family and Conciliation Courts Review* 39 (2001): 121–134.

49 Louise de Koven Bowen, *Safeguards for City Youth: At Work and at Play* (New York 1914), 128.

50 Andrew Schepard and Peter Salem, "Foreword to the Special Issue on the Family Law Education Reform Project," *Family Court Review* 44 (2006): 513, 516.

51 Jay Folberg, *et al.*, eds., *Divorce and Family Mediation: Models, Techniques, and Applications* (New York: Guilford Press, 2004), 3–22; Jane Murphy and Robert Rubinson, *Family Mediation: Theory and Practice* (New Providence, NJ: LexisNexis Matthew Bender, 2009), 109–110.

52 Christine A. Coates, "A Brief Overview of Parenting Coordination," *Colorado Law Review* 38 (2009): 61.

53 Marsha Pruett *et al.*, "Therapeutic Mediation with High-Conflict Parents: Effective Models and Strategies," in Jay Folberg *et al.*, eds., *Divorce and Family Mediation: Models, Techniques, and Applications* (New York: Guilford Press, 2004), 92–111.

54 Yvonne Pearson, "Early Neutral Evaluations: Applications to Custody and Parenting Time Cases Program Development and Implementation in Hennepin County, Minnesota," *Family Court Review* 44 (2006): 674.

55 Arnold Shienvold, "Hybrid Processes," in Jay Folberg *et al.*, eds., *Divorce and Family Mediation: Models, Techniques, and Applications* (New York: Guilford Press, 2004), 112–126.

56 Murphy and Rubinson, *Family Mediation*, 12.

57 Jonathan Hyman and Lela Love, "If Portia Were a Mediator: An Inquiry into Justice in Mediation," *Clinical Law Review* 9 (2002): 157, 161.

58 Leonard Marlow and S. Richard Sauber, *The Handbook of Divorce Mediation* (New York: Plenum Press, 1990), 41.

59 Marilyn S. McKnight *et al.*, "The Plan to Separately Parent Children after Divorce," in Jay Folberg *et al.*, eds., *Divorce and Family Mediation: Models, Techniques, and Applications* (New York: Guilford Press, 2004), 129–133.

60 Elizabeth S. Scott, "Parental Autonomy and Children's Welfare," *William and Mary Bill of Rights Journal* 11 (2003): 1089.

61 American Law Institute, *Principles of the Law of Family Dissolution: Analysis and Recommendations* (St. Paul, MN: American Law Institute Publishers, 2002), "Overview of the Principles of Chapter 2."

62 American Psychological Association, "Guidelines for Child Custody Evaluations in Family Law Proceedings," *American Psychologist* 65 (2010): 863.

63 John Lande, "The Movement Toward Early Case Handling in Courts and Private Dispute Resolution," *Ohio State Journal on Dispute Resolution* 24 (2008): 81; Forrest S. Mosten, "Confidential Mini Child-Custody Evaluations: Another ADR Option," *Family Law Quarterly* 45 (2011): 119.

64 *Annual Report of Family Divisions and Family Law Services* (Annapolis, MD: Administrative Office of the Courts, Department of Family Administration, 2005), 8–11.

65 Jonathan Lippman, "Achieving Better Outcomes for Litigants in the New York State Courts," *Fordham Urban Law Journal* 34 (2007): 813, 815; James R. Holbrook, "The Effects of Alternative Dispute Resolution on Access to Justice in Utah," *Utah Law Review* 1017 (2006): 1021–1025; Robert E. Emery *et al.*, "Divorce Mediation: Research and Reflections," *Family Court Review* 43 (2005): 22–37.

66 Jennifer McIntosh "Guest Editor's Introduction to Special Issue on Attachment Theory, Separation, and Divorce: Forging Coherent Understandings for Family Law," *Family Court Review* 49 (2011): 418.

67 Andrew Schepard, "Preface to the Draft Model Standards," *Family Court Review* 38 (2000): 106.

68 Melanie B. Jacobs, "My Two Dads: Disaggregating Biological and Social Paternity," *Arizona State Law Journal* 38 (2006): 809; Theresa Glennon, "Still Partners?

Examining the Consequences of Post-Dissolution Parenting," 41 *Family Law Quarterly* 41 (2007): 105; Sheelagh McGuinness and Amel Alghrani, "Gender and Parenthood: The Case for Realignment," *Medical Law Review* 16 (2008): 261.

69 "Task Force on Preservation of the Justice System," National Center for State Courts, accessed June 10, 2014, http://www.ncsc.org/information-and-resources/budget-resource-center/analysis_strategy/economic-impact/archive-aba-task-force-0511-nh.aspx. *But see* Carl Tobias, "Executive Branch Civil Justice Reform," *American University Law Review* 42 (1993): 1521 (questioning whether ADR programs reduce costs).

70 Deborah Chase and Hon. Peggy Fulton Hora, "The Best Seat in the House: The Court Assignment and Judicial Satisfaction," *Family Court Review* 47 (2009): 209–238; *see* Richard Boldt and Jana Singer, "Juristocracy in the Trenches: Problem-Solving Judges and Therapeutic Jurisprudence in Drug Treatment Courts and Unified Family Courts," *Maryland Law Review* 65 (2006): 82, 87 (discussing judicial satisfaction from engagement and "empathetic connection" in drug treatment courts); *but see* Hon. Gerald W. Hardcastle, "Adversarialism and the Family Court: A Family Court Judge's Perspective." *Journal of Juvenile Law and Policy* 9 (2005): 92. He expresses skepticism about the competence of judges who are "redefined from a neutral judge to a 'healer' or 'participant in the process' or a 'sensitive, empathetic counselor.'"

71 *See* discussion in chapter 7.

72 Russell Engler, "And Justice For All—Including the Unrepresented Poor: Revisiting the Roles of the Judges, Mediators, and Clerks," *Fordham Law Review* 67 (2007): 201–211 (arguing for changing the role of mediator when one or both parties are unrepresented to include providing legal information); *see also* Ellen A. Waldman, "Identifying the Role of Social Norms in Mediation: A Multiple Model Approach," *Hastings Law Journal* 48 (1997): 703, 708 (proposing a "norm educating" or even "norm advocating" role for mediators in some situations, including certain types of family mediation). But the vast majority of mediators reject such a role; *see* Lela P. Love, "The Top Ten Reasons Why Mediators Should Not Evaluate," *Florida State University Law Review* 24 (1997): 937.

73 Richard Delgado *et al.*, "Fairness and Formality: Minimizing the Risk of Prejudice in Alternative Dispute Resolution," *Wisconsin Law Review* 1985 (1985): 1359.

74 One of the earliest articulations of this position is the oft-cited article by Trina Grillo, "The Mediation Alternative: Process Dangers for Women," *Yale Law Journal* 100 (1991): 1581. More recently, a number of scholars have addressed the dangers of power imbalance in mediation, often in the context of court-based child welfare mediation. *See e.g.* Amy Sinden, "'Why Won't Mom Cooperate?': A Critique of Informality in Child Welfare Proceedings, *Yale Journal of Law and Feminism* 11 (1999): 351–352.

75 Michael Lang, "Understanding and Responding to Power in Mediation," in Jay Folberg *et al.*, eds., *Divorce and Family Mediation: Models, Techniques, and Applications* (New York: Guilford Press, 2004), 209.

76 The Model Standards of Practice for Family and Divorce Mediation, endorsed by, among others, the American Bar Association and the Association of Family and

Conciliation Courts, include provisions defining domestic violence, requiring domestic violence training for mediators, screening, and setting forth steps to ensure safety during mediation. "Model Standards of Practice for Family and Divorce Mediation," 121, 127. The Model Standards also recognize that some cases should not be mediated "because of safety, control, or intimidation issues." *Ibid.*, 132. The American Law Institute takes the position that the risks of coercion and intimidation in mediation for victims of domestic violence require that all mediation programs be voluntary. American Law Institute, *Principles of the Law of Family Dissolution*, §2.07(2).

77 *See* Jane Murphy and Robert Rubinson, "Domestic Violence and Mediation: Responding to the Challenges of Creating Effective Screens," *Family Law Quarterly* 39 (2005): 53.

78 *Ibid.*

79 Fineman, "Dominant Discourse, Professional Language, and Legal Change in Child Custody Decisionmaking," 727, 730–731. ("[S]ocial workers and other members of the helping professions . . . present themselves as neutral, nonadversarial decision makers in contrast to attorneys, whom they characterize as both adversarial and combative. Yet social workers are not neutral; they have a professional bias in favor of a specific substantive result. That result benefits their profession by creating the need for mediation and counseling. It is this bias and self-interest that makes the process one for political consideration. The bias inherent in mediation is different from, but no less suspect than, the bias that can result from overt favoritism of one party over another.")

80 *Ibid.*, 770–774.

81 For further discussion of the "primary caretaker standard," and another standard based, in part, on past caretaking, the American Law Institute endorsed the "approximation standard." *See* chapter 7.

82 Timothy M. Tippins and Jeffrey P. Wittmann, "Empirical and Ethical Problems with Custody Recommendations: A Call for Clinical Humility and Judicial Vigilance," *Family Court Review* 43 (2005): 193, 214–215. This article generated vigorous debate about the role of custody evaluation. *See e.g.* Joan B. Kelly and Janet R. Johnston, "Commentary on Tippins and Wittmann's 'Empirical and Ethical Problems with Custody Recommendations: A Call for Clinical Humility and Judicial Vigilance,'" *Family Court Review* 43 (2005): 233. For a more recent critique of the role of mental health professionals in child custody cases, *see* Elizabeth S. Scott and Robert E. Emery, "Gender Politics and Child Custody: The Puzzling Persistence of the Best Interest Standard," *Law and Contemporary Problems* 77 (2014): 69–108.

83 Kelly and Johnston, "Commentary," 233.

84 Jennifer McIntosh, "Attachment, Separation, and Divorce: Forging Coherent Understandings for Family Law," *Family Court Review* 49 (2011): 418, 419.

85 Lisa Merkel-Holguin, "Sharing Power with the People: Family Group Conferencing as a Democratic Experiment," *Journal of Sociology and Social Welfare* 31 (2004): 155.

86 Kimberlee K. Kovach, *Mediation: Principles and Practice* (New York: West, 2004), 429–478.

87 For a discussion of the damage that poor mediators can cause in family law mediation, *see* Penelope Eileen Bryan, "Reclaiming Professionalism: The Lawyer's Role in Divorce Mediation," *Family Law Quarterly* 28 (1994): 177. For a rare instance where an alleged bad mediator was subjected to judicial scrutiny, albeit unsuccessfully, *see Allen v. Leal*, 27 F. Supp. 2d 945 (S.D. Tex. 1998) (plaintiffs alleged that mediator coerced settlement).

88 *See* Merkel-Holguin, "Sharing Power with the People," 161.

89 Deborah J. Chase, *"Pro Se* Justice and Unified Family Courts," *Family Law Quarterly* 37 (2003): 403–430.

90 *Ibid.*

91 *See* Catherine J. Ross, "The Failure of Fragmentation: The Promise of a System of Unified Family Courts," *Family Law Quarterly* 32, no.1 (1998): 3, 13.

92 *Ibid.* at 17.

93 Gloria Danziger, "Delinquency Jurisdiction in a Unified Family Court: Balancing Intervention, Prevention, and Adjudication," *Family Law Quarterly* 37 (2003): 381, 394.

94 Anne H. Geraghty and Wallace J. Mlyniec, "Unified Family Courts: Tempering Enthusiasm with Caution," *Family Court Review* 40 (2002): 435, 439.

95 Boldt and Singer, "Juristocracy in the Trenches," 82, 96; *see* Winick, "Therapeutic Jurisprudence and Problem-Solving Courts," 1060.

96 *See e.g.* Md. Code Ann., Fam. Law §7–103.2 (LexisNexis 2009); Alicia M. Hehr, "A Child Shall Lead Them: Developing and Utilizing Child Protection Mediation to Better Serve the Interests of the Child," *Ohio State Journal on Dispute Resolution* 22 (2007): 443, 455.

97 *See e.g.* Md. Rule 16–204(a)(3).

98 *Ibid.*

99 Md. Rule 9–205.

100 The Women's Law Center of Maryland, "Custody and Financial Distribution in Maryland: An Empirical Study of Custody and Divorce Cases Filed in Maryland during Fiscal Year 1999" (April 2004), at 21–22, accessed October 8, 2014, http://www.wlcmd.org/wp-content/uploads/2013/06/Custody-and-Financial-Distribution-in-Maryland.pdf. Statistics from one court system support the need for concern that court-sponsored "services" are being utilized disproportionately by low-income families); *see* Robert Rubinson, "A Theory of Access to Justice," *Journal of the Legal Profession* 90 (2005): 89, 119 (noting that "[m]ost of these mandatory [court-based] mediation programs are for family law cases in which the vast majority of disputants are low income").

101 Jeanne F. Allegra, "Elements of a Custody Evaluation," *Family Law News* (February 2009), 12. As one custody evaluator described the process, "when [custody evaluation is warranted] the couple might agree to a private Custody Evaluation, performed by a psychologist, retained for this purpose. The clients' attorneys are often instrumental in helping their clients identify a psychologist, who is experienced in performing this type of evaluation. When there is no agreement to perform a private custody evaluation, but the psychological issue still exists as an impediment to custody-visitation arrangements, the court steps in and orders its own Custody Evaluation."

102 Jane C. Murphy, "Legal Images of Motherhood: Conflicting Definitions from Welfare 'Reform,' Family, and Criminal Law," *Cornell Law Review* 83 (1998): 688, 707–709. Analyzing the treatment of mothers in a range of legal proceedings involving children and noting that "because mothers overwhelmingly are the custodians and caretakers of children, they are, in most cases, the focus of the state's intervention in cases of allegations of child abuse or neglect. As noted, from their inception, child welfare programs focused on poor children."

103 *See* Nancy E. Dowd, *In Defense of Single-Parent Families* (New York: New York University Press, 1997) (arguing that there is an inherent bias against poor and single-parent families in the legal system).

104 Zorza, "Specialty and Problem-Solving Courts," 47.

105 *Ibid.*

106 Carrie Menkel-Meadow, "The Trouble with the Adversary System in a Postmodern, Multicultural World," *William and Mary Law Review* 38 (1996): 5, 7.

107 *See* Geraghty and Mlyniec, "Unified Family Courts," 441.

108 *Ibid.*, "Task Force on Preservation of the Justice System," Nation Center for State Courts, accessed April 14, 22014, http://www.ncsc.org/information-and-resources/budget-resource-center/analysis_strategy/economic-impact/archive-aba-task-force-0511-nh.aspx; John Lande, "How Much Justice Can We Afford? Defining the Court's Roles and Deciding the Appropriate Number of Trials, Settlement Signals, and Other Elements Needed to Administer Justice," *Journal of Dispute Resolution* 2006 (2006): 213.

109 Hazel Genn, "What Is Civil Justice For? Reform, ADR, and Access to Justice," *Yale Journal of Law and Humanities* 24 (2012): 397–417 (analyzing the trend to replace adjudication with mediation in the English legal system and concluding that "even though most disputes settle without the need for trial, a flow of adjudicated cases is necessary to provide guidance on the law and, occasionally, to make new leaps").

110 Jana Singer, "The Privatization of Family Law," *Wisconsin Law Review* 1992 (1992): 1557, 1559; *see* Owen Fiss, "Against Settlement," *Yale Law Journal* 93, no. 6 (1984): 1073.

111 Singer, "The Privatization of Family Law," 1557, 1559.

CHAPTER 4. THE NEW VISION MEETS THE NEW FAMILY

1 Natalie Angier, "The Changing American Family," *New York Times* (November 25, 2013) (quoting Andrew Cherlin), accessed November 2, 2014, http://www.nytimes.com/2013/11/26/health/families.html.

2 J. Herbie DiFonzo, "How Marriage Became Optional: Cohabitation, Gender, and the Emerging Functional Norms," *Rutgers Journal of Law and Public Policy* 8 (2011): 522.

3 Pew Research Center, "Barely Half of All Adults Are Married: A Record Low" (December 14, 2011).

4 U.S. Census Bureau, "U.S. Census Bureau Reports Men and Women Wait Longer to Get Married," (2010), accessed October 25, 2014, http://www.census.gov/newsroom/

releases/archives/families_households/cb10–174.html; *see* Pew Research Center, "The Decline of Marriage and Rise of New Families" (November 18, 2010), 2.

5 DiFonzo, "How Marriage Became Optional," 527.

6 Jana Singer, "The Privatization of Family Law," *Wisconsin Law Review* 1992 (1992): 1453; *see* Andrew Cherlin, *The Marriage-Go-Round (New York: Vintage Books 2010), 27.* ("What we have witnessed over the past half century is, at its core, the unprecedented decline of marriage as the only acceptable arrangement for having sexual relations and for raising children.")

7 *See* Pew Research Center, "For Millennials, Parenthood Trumps Marriage" (March 9, 2011) (noting that young adults have "delinked" marriage and parenthood and that they value parenthood much more than marriage).

8 Centers for Disease Control and Prevention, "FastStats: Unmarried Childbearing," (2011), http://www.cdc.gov/nchs/fastats/unmarry.htm; *see* DiFonzo, "How Marriage Became Optional," 538.

9 DiFonzo, "How Marriage Became Optional," 522.

10 Cynthia Grant Bowman, "The Legal Relationship between Cohabitants and Their Partners' Children," *Theoretical Inquiries* 13 (2012): 135.

11 *Ibid.* (noting that "children live in about forty percent of all cohabiting households").

12 Kevin Hartnett, "When Having Babies Beats Marriage," *Harvard Magazine* (July–August 2012) (quoting Harvard Kennedy School professor Kathryn Edin). For an extensive and illuminating discussion of the causes and implications of these class-based differences, *see* June Carbone and Naomi Cahn, *Marriage Markets: How Inequality Is Remaking the American Family* (New York: Oxford University Press, 2014).

13 *See e.g.* Brookings Institution, "Marriage and the African-American Community" (November 28, 2006), accessed October 25, 2014, http://www.brookings.edu/events/2006/11/28children-families; Richard Banks, *Is Marriage for White People? How the African American Marriage Decline Affects Everyone* (2011), 6.

14 Pew Research Center, "Women, Men, and the New Economics of Marriage" (January 19, 2010), 4–5.

15 June Carbone and Naomi Cahn, *Red Families v. Blue Families: Legal Polarization and the Creation of Culture* (2011), 2 (noting that, for African American women who do not finish high school, 96 percent of births take place outside of marriage).

16 *Ibid.*

17 *Ibid.* at 7.

18 *See* Jason DeParle, "Two Classes, Divided by 'I Do,'" *New York Times* (July 15, 2012), accessed October 25, 2014, *http://www.nytimes.com/2012/07/15/us/two-classes-in-america-divided-by-i-do.html?_r=0.* A study of nearly two thousand mothers in their mid to late twenties found that a third of those with high school degrees or less already had children with multiple men, as did 12 percent of mothers with some post–high school training. By contrast, none of the women in the study who had finished college before giving birth had children with multiple men.

19 *See* Elizabeth S. Scott, "A World without Marriage," *Family Law Quarterly* 41 (2007): 548 (arguing that cohabitation relationships are less stable and enduring than marriage because they are not supported legally or socially); Clare Huntington, "Postmarital Family Law," *Stanford Law Review* 67 (2015): 167, 171 (arguing that "the fundamental mismatch between marital family law and nonmarital family life undermines relationships in nonmarital families").

20 *See* Princeton University and Columbia University, "Fragile Families and Child Wellbeing Study Fact Sheet" (n.d.), http://www.fragilefamilies.princeton.edu/documents/FragileFamiliesandChildWellbeingStudyFactSheet.pdf (noting that while one-half of unmarried parents are living together at the time of their child's birth, most of those relationships do not last).

21 *See* Jason DeParle and Sabrina Tavernise, "For Women under 30, Most Births Occur outside Marriage," *New York Times* (February 17, 2012), http://www.nytimes.com/2012/02/18/us/for-women-under-30-most-births-occur-outside-marriage.html?pagewanted=all.

22 *See* Cynthia Osborne & Sara McLanahan, "Partnership Instability and Child Well-Being," *Journal of Marriage and Family* 69 (2007): 1079.

23 *See* Linda D. Elrod and Robert G. Spector, "A Review of the Year in Family Law: Numbers of Disputes Increase," *Family Law Quarterly* 45 (2012): 444 (noting that disputes between unmarried parents are responsible for a significant increase in state custody litigation). For example, in Baltimore in FY 2013, 86 percent of the custody and visitation cases involved parents who had never been married. Circuit Court for Baltimore City, "Annual Report of the Family Division Fiscal Year 2013" (2013), 6.

24 *See* Stacy Brustin and Lisa Vollendorf Martin, "Engineering the Low Income Family: Welfare, Child Support, and the Fatherhood Initiative" (2014), 3 (on file with authors).

25 *Ibid.* at 6–9; *see* U.S. Department of Health and Human Services, Administration for Children and Families, Office of Child Support Enforcement, "Child Support and Parenting Time: Improving Coordination to Benefit Families" (July 2013).

26 U.S. Department of Health and Human Services, Administration for Children and Families, Office of Child Support Enforcement, "Child Support and Fatherhood Initiative in the Administration's FY 2014 Budget" (April 15, 2013).

27 DiFonzo, "How Marriage Became Optional," 527, n. 24.

28 *Ibid.*

29 *Ibid.* at 528.

30 Cherlin, *The Marriage Go-Round*, 20.

31 *Ibid.*

32 J. Herbie DiFonzo and Ruth C. Stern, "Breaking the Mold and Picking Up the Pieces: Rights of Parenthood and Parentage in Nontraditional Families," *Family Court Review* 51 (2013): 109.

33 Pew Research Center, "A Portrait of Stepfamilies" (January 13, 2011).

34 DiFonzo and Stern, "Breaking the Mold and Picking Up the Pieces," 109.

35 *Ibid.*

36 Francis Goldscheider and Sharon Sassler, "Creating Stepfamilies: Incorporating Children into the Study of Union Formation," *Journal of Marriage and Family* 68 (2006): 277.

37 American Law Institute, *Principles of the Law of Family Dissolution: Analysis and Recommendations* (St. Paul, MN: American Law Institute Publishers, 2002), §2.03(b) and (c).

38 *Ibid.*, cmts. (b) and (c).

39 DiFonzo and Stern, "Breaking the Mold and Picking Up the Pieces," 110.

40 *See* William C. Duncan, "The Legal Fiction of De Facto Parenthood," *Journal of Legislation* 36 (2010): 263 (arguing that, by limiting the number of persons who could claim parental status, the law achieved a measure of predictability and certainty that benefited children and parents).

41 Robin Fretwell Wilson, "Undeserved Trust: Reflection on the ALI's Treatment of De Facto Parents," in Robin Fretwell Wilson, ed., *Reconceiving the Family: Critique on the American Law Institute's Principles of the Law of Family Dissolution* (2006), 99–100.

42 Pew Research Center, "Since the Start of the Great Recession, More Children Raised by Grandparents" (September 9, 2010).

43 *Ibid.*

44 *Ibid.*

45 *See* Jane E. Cross, Nan Palmer, and Charlene L. Smith, "Families Redefined: Kinship Groups That Deserve Benefits," *Mississippi Law Journal* 78 (2009): 802.

46 *Troxel v. Granville*, 530 U.S. 57 (2000).

47 Gary P. Gates, "Same-Sex Couples in Census 2010: Race and Ethnicity." *The Williams Institute* (2012), 1. For a thoughtful discussion of the difficulties of attempting to measure the size of the LGBT population, *see* Gary J. Gates, "LGBT Identity: A Demographer's Perspective," *Loyola of Los Angeles Law Review* 45 (2012): 693.

48 Gates, "Same-Sex Couples in Census 2010," p. 4 and fig. 5 (reporting that 20.6 percent of same-sex couples are interracial or interethnic, compared to 18.3 percent of different-sex unmarried couples and just 9.5 percent of different-sex married couples).

49 *See* Gary J. Gates, "Family Formation and Raising Children among Same-Sex Couples," *National Council on Family Relations* 51 (2012): F1. Earlier estimates, based on data collected in 2000 and 2008, indicated that roughly 30 percent of lesbian couples and 17 percent of gay male couples were rearing children. Nanette Gartrell *et al.*, "Family Characteristics, Custody Arrangements, and Adolescent Psychological Well-Being after Lesbian Mothers Break Up," *Family Relations* 60 (2011): 572.

50 Williams Institute, "Census Snapshot 2010" (2011), http://williamsinstitute.law. ucla.edu/research/census-lgbt-demographics-studies/us-census-snapshot-2010 (noting that 31 percent of same-sex couples who identified as spouses and 14 percent of same-sex unmarried partners are raising children).

51 Movement Advancement Project, Family Equality Council, and Center for American Progress, "All Children Matter: How Legal and Social Inequalities Hurt LGBT Families" (October 2011), 7.

52 Gates, "Family Formation and Raising Children among Same-Sex Couples," F3.

53 *Ibid.*

54 Judith Daar, "Physician Duties in the Face of Deceitful Gamete Donors, Disobedient Surrogate Mothers, and Divorcing Parents," *Virtual Mentor* 16 (2014): 42.

55 Lori B. Andrews and Nanette Elster, "Regulating Reproductive Technologies," *Journal of Legal Medicine* 21 (2000): 36.

56 *Ibid.*

57 *See e.g. Frazier v. Goudschaal*, 26 Kan. 730, 295 P.2d 542 (2013) (applying statutory parentage presumption to nonbiological co-parent of child conceived by artificial insemination during nonmarital relationship); *In re Parentage of M.J.*, 203 Ill. 2d 526, 787 N.E.2d 144 (2003) (mother may pursue child support from her former unmarried partner for child conceived through artificial insemination with his consent); *see generally* Nancy Polikoff, "A Mother Should Not Have to Adopt Her Own Child: Parentage Laws for Children of Lesbian Couples in the Twenty-First Century," *Stanford Journal of Civil Rights and Civil Liberties* 5 (2009): 201.

58 *See* DiFonzo, "How Marriage Became Optional," 532.

59 Naomi Cahn, "The New Kinship," *Georgetown Law Journal* 100 (2012): 368–369.

60 DiFonzo, "How Marriage Became Optional," 532–533.

61 *N.A.H. v. S.L.S.*, 3 P.3d 354–359 (Colo. 2000).

62 DiFonzo, "How Marriage Became Optional," 560.

63 *Ibid.* at 561; *see also* DiFonzo and Stern, "Breaking the Mold and Picking Up the Pieces," 106–107.

64 Connie J. A. Beck *et al.*, "Divorce Mediation with and without Legal Representation," *Family Court Review* 48 (2010): 632; *see* Hon. Randall T. Shepard, "The Self-Represented Litigant: Implications for the Bench and Bar," *Family Court Review* 48 (2010): 611 (noting that "some reports estimate that 80 to 90 percent of family law cases involve at least one self-represented litigant"). The percentage of cases in which one or both parties appears *pro se* is significantly higher in family law cases than in any other area of law. Nancy Ver Steegh, Gabrielle Davis, and Loretta Frederick, "Look before You Leap: Court System Triage of Family Law Cases Involving Intimate Partner Violence," *Marquette Law Review* 95 (2012): 957.

65 *See e.g.* Circuit Court for Baltimore City, "Annual Report of the Family Division Fiscal Year 2013," 5 (reporting that at least one *pro se* litigant appeared in 90 percent of all cases in the Family Division). *See also* Legal Services Corporation, "Documenting the Justice Gap in America: The Current Unmet Civil Legal Needs of Low-Income Americans" (2007), 18, accessed October 25, 2014, http://lsc.gov/sites/default/files/LSC/images/justicegap.pdf.

66 Andrew Schepard, "Editorial Notes," *Family Court Review* 40 (2002): 6.

67 *See* William J. Howe III, "Introduction to the Oregon Futures Report," *Family Law Quarterly* 40 (2002): 473

68 *See* Julie Macfarlane, "ADR and the Courts: Renewing Our Commitment to Innovation," *Marquette Law Review* 95 (2012): 930.

69 Constance L. Shehan, "*Pro Se* Divorce," in Robert E. Emery, ed., *Cultural Sociology of Divorce: An Encyclopedia* (2013), 992.

70 Julie Macfarlane, "Time to Shatter the Stereotype of the Self-Represented Litigants," *ABA Dispute Resolution Magazine* 20 (2013): 14 (summarizing her research, which she feels "makes it clear beyond doubt that the most significant reason for joining the ranks of the *pro se* litigants, who now constitute the majority in some family courts, is the high cost of legal services").

71 David Udell and Rebekah Diller, *Access to Justice: Opening the Courthouse Door* (New York: Brennan Center for Justice at New York University School of Law, 2007), 4–5.

72 *Turner v. Rogers*, 131 S.Ct. 2507, 2512 (2011).

73 Ver Steegh, Davis, and Frederick, "Look Before You Leap," 957.

74 "Judges' Views of *Pro Se* Litigants' Effect on Courts," *Clearinghouse Review Journal of Poverty Law and Policy* (July–August 2006) (reprinting portions of an amicus brief describing the ways in which *pro se* litigants burdened the courts, written by eleven state court judges in Wisconsin).

75 See *Turner*, 131 S.Ct. at 2521 (finding that procedural safeguards to ensure due process for unrepresented litigant might include "greater judicial engagement"); Russell Engler, "*Turner v. Rogers* and the Essential Role of the Courts in Delivering Access to Justice," *Harvard Law and Policy Review* 7 (2013): 31; C. D. Schwarz, "*Pro Se* Divorce Litigants: Frustrating the Traditional Role of the Trial Court Judge and Court Personnel," *Family Court Review* 42 (2004): 4.

76 "Meeting the Challenges of Self-Represented Litigants: A Bench Book for General Sessions Judges of the State of Tennessee" (May 2013); *see also* Rebecca A. Albrecht *et al.*, "Judicial Techniques for Cases Involving Self-Represented Litigants," *Judges Journal* 42 (2003): 17–19.

77 American Arbitration Association *et al.*, "Model Standards of Conduct for Mediators, Preamble" (2005), *accessed October 25, 2014*, http://www.abanet.org/dispute/documents/model_standards_conduct_april2007.pdf. As with other players in the court system, many commentators think that the traditional role of mediator poses serious risks for *pro se* parties. See Russell Engler, "Revising the Role of the Court-Connected Mediator to Achieve Fairness for Unrepresented Litigants," accessed October 25, 2014, http://www.neacr.org/Resources/Documents/2000–2007%20 newsletters/11–1.pdf; *see also* Stephen Landsman, "Nothing for Something? Denying Legal Assistance to Those Compelled to Participate in ADR Proceedings," *Fordham Urban Law Journal* 37 (2010): 285. But the vast majority of mediators reject a more active role. *See e.g.* Lela P. Love, "The Top Ten Reasons Why Mediators Should Not Evaluate," *Florida State University Law Review* 24 (1997): 938.

78 Kimberlee K. Kovach, *Mediation: Principles and Practice* (New York: West, 2004), 211 (discussing the centrality of neutrality to mediation process).

79 Landsman, "Nothing for Something?" 291.

80 *See* Ellen B. Langan, "We Can Work It Out: Using Cooperative Mediation—a Blend of Collaborative Law and Traditional Mediation—to Resolve Divorce Disputes," *Review of Litigation* 30 (2011): 267.

81 *Ibid.* at 272–273 ("The presence of counsel to provide legal advice, including an explanation of rights and obligations arising as a matter of law, and the practical and

legal implications if these are altered by an agreement, is essential to ensuring that a party who settles at mediation does so with informed consent, and not merely as a result of a bargaining disadvantage.")

82 Landsman, "Nothing for Something?" 273.

83 *Ibid.* at 297.

84 Russell Engler, "And Justice For All—Including the Unrepresented Poor: Revisiting the Roles of the Judges, Mediators, and Clerks," *Fordham Law Review* 67 (2007): 201–211 (arguing that the role of mediators should be changed when mediation involves unrepresented parties).

85 Amy Applegate and Connie Beck, "Self-Represented Parties in Mediation: Fifty Years Later It Remains the Elephant in the Room," *Family Court Review* 51 (2013): 87.

86 John Bingham, "Family Courts Risk 'Collapse' as Surge in Custody Cases Follows Legal Aid Cuts," *The Telegraph* (June 11, 2013), accessed October 25, 2014, http://www. telegraph.co.uk/news/uknews/law-and-order/10111462/Family-courts-risk-collapse-as-surge-in-custody-cases-follows-legal-aid-cuts.html (describing the threats to access to justice for families in Britain's family law courts because "the withdrawal of public funding for most types of cases has meant court potentially now being the first and only option considered by those now having to represent themselves").

87 *See generally* Patrick Parkinson, *Family Law and the Indissolubility of Parenthood* (Cambridge, UK: Cambridge University Press, 2011); Robert Emery, *Renegotiating Family Relationships* (2012), 62–64.

88 Parkinson, *Family Law and the Indissolubility of Parenthood*, 176.

89 *Ibid.*

90 *See* Sasha Aslanian, "Never-Married Parents Get Help from Special Court," *NPR* (May 7, 2012), accessed October 25, 2014, http://www.npr.org/2012/05/07/152157287/never-married-parents-get-help-from-special-court (discussing Minneapolis co-parent court for unmarried parents involved in paternity establishment and child support proceedings).

91 Marian Roberts, *Mediation in Family Disputes: Principles of Practice* (2008), 9.

92 *Ibid.*

93 *See e.g.* Nancy A. Welsh, "The Current Transitional State of Court-Connected ADR," *Marquette Law Review* 95 (2012): 880 (noting that faith in the principle of self-determination "continues to animate the field of ADR").

94 Nancy A. Welsh, "Reconciling Self-Determination, Coercion, and Settlement in Court-Connected Mediation," in Jay Folberg, *et al.*, eds., *Divorce and Family Mediation: Models, Techniques, and Applications* (New York: Guilford Press, 2004), 421.

95 *Ibid.*; *see* Roberts, *Mediation in Family Disputes*, 1–2 (describing party competence and control as the distinguishing characteristics of mediation).

96 *See* Welsh, "Reconciling Self-Determination, Coercion, and Settlement in Court-Connected Mediation," 420 (citing codes).

97 Richard W. Shields, Judith R. Ryan, and Victoria Smith, *Collaborative Family Law: Another Way to Resolve Family Disputes* (Toronto: Carswell, 2003), vi.

98 *Ibid.*, 74; *see* Pauline H. Tesler, *Collaborative Law: Achieving Effective Resolution in Divorce without Litigation*, 2nd ed. (Chicago: American Bar Association, 2008), 339.

99 Shields, Ryan, and Smith, *Collaborative Family Law*, 39.

100 Tesler, *Collaborative Law*, 40.

101 Shields, Ryan, and Smith, *Collaborative Family Law*, 55.

102 Bernard S. Mayer, *Beyond Neutrality: Confronting the Crisis in Conflict Resolution* (2004), 53.

103 *See e.g.* Md. Rule, 17–103, Committee Note.

104 *See e.g.* Nancy Ver Steegh, "Yes, No, and Maybe: Informed Decision Making about Divorce Mediation in the Presence of Domestic Violence," *William and Mary Journal of Women and the Law* 9 (2003): 147; Jane C. Murphy and Robert Rubinson, "Domestic Violence and Mediation: Responding to the Challenges of Crafting Effective Screens," *Family Law Quarterly* 39 (2005): 53.

105 *See* Noel Semple, "Mandatory Mediation and the Settlement Mission: A Feminist Critique," *Canadian Journal of Women and the Law* 24 (2012): 207; Noel Semple, "The Settlement Mission in Custody and Access Cases" (2013), accessed October 25, 2014, http://ssrn.com/abstract=2101819.

106 Anne H. Geraghty and Wallace J. Mlyniec, "Unified Family Courts: Tempering Enthusiasm With Caution," *Family Court Review* 40 (2002): 437.

107 According to a recent law review article, forty-six states now offer parent education classes. Tali Schaefer, "Saving Children or Blaming Parents? Lessons from Mandated Parenting Classes," *Columbia Journal of Gender and Law* 19 (2010): 491, 495. In forty-one of these forty-six states, at least some parents seeking a divorce or involved in custody proceedings are legally required to attend these classes, either by state statute (twenty-seven states), by judicial rules (six states), by county- and district-based mandates (five states), or by individual judges' decrees (three states). *Ibid.*; *see also* Susan L. Pollet and Melissa Lombreglia, "A Nationwide Survey of Mandatory Parent Education" *Family Court Review* 46 (2008): 375, app. A (finding that forty-six states now offer parent education programs).

108 Most programs focus on the children's reactions to divorce and parental reactions to children, with secondary attention to parental adjustment, parenting issues, and co-parenting. Jessica Pearson, "Court Services: Meeting the Needs of Twenty-First Century Families," *Family Law Quarterly* 33 (1999): 622–623 (noting the need to create materials for parent education programs for never-married populations).

109 *See* Janet R. Johnston, "Building Multidisciplinary Professional Partnerships with the Court on Behalf of High-Conflict Divorcing Families and Their Children: Who Needs What Kind of Help?" *University of Arkansas Little Rock Law Review* 22 (2000): 468. ("There is growing awareness that one size does not fit all in approaches to parenting education."); Susan L. Pollet and Melissa Lombreglia, "A Nationwide Survey of Mandatory Parent Education," *Family Court Review* 46 (2008): 385 ("there needs to be special educational programs for various groups beyond children, including never-married parents, various ethnic groups, and high-conflict, violent, and chronically litigating families").

110 Over thirty of the states now specifically provide for parenting plans, also known as parenting agreements and parental responsibility plans. A few states require them in every case, a number of other states require them when shared or joint custody is sought or ordered, and several more permit courts, at their discretion, to require parenting plans, or provide for parents to prepare them voluntarily. Elizabeth S. Scott, "Parental Autonomy and Children's Welfare," *William and Mary Bill of Rights Journal* 11 (2003): 1089.

111 Jana B. Singer, "Bargaining in the Shadow of the Best Interests Standard: The Close Connection between Substance and Process in Divorce-Related Parenting Disputes," *Law and Contemporary Problems* 77 (2014): 192–194.

112 Jane W. Ellis, "Plans, Protections, and Professional Intervention: Innovations in Divorce Custody Reform and the Role of Legal Professionals," *University of Michigan Journal of Law Reform* 24 (1990): 82–86 (quoting from Washington statute).

113 June Carbone and Naomi Cahn, "Marriage, Parentage, and Child Support," *Family Law Quarterly* 45 (2011): 219.

114 Constance Ahrons, "Redefining the Divorced Family: A Conceptual Framework," *Social Work* 25 (1981): 437.

115 Constance Ahrons, *The Good Divorce: Keeping Your Family Together When Your Marriage Comes Apart* (HarperCollins 1994), 120–124.

116 *See e.g.* Emery, *Renegotiating Family Relationships*, 79 (asserting that "the ultimate objective of mediation" is to help parents find ways "to raise their children effectively alone and across two households").

117 Sara McLanahan and Audrey Beck, "Parental Relationships in Fragile Families," *The Future of Children* 20 (2010): 121.

118 Sara S. McLanahan and Irvin Garfinkel, "Fragile Families: Debates, Facts, and Solutions," in Marsha Garrison and Elizabeth S. Scott, eds., *Marriage at a Crossroads: Law, Policy, and the Brave New World of Twenty-First Century Families* (2012): 153.

119 *Ibid.*

120 McLanahan and Beck, "Parental Relationships in Fragile Families," 122.

121 Rose M. Kreider, United States Census Bureau, "Remarriage in the United States," presentation at the American Sociological Association annual meeting (August 10–14, 2006), accessed October 25, 2014, http://www.census.gov/hhes/socdemo/marriage/data/sipp/us-remarriage-poster.pdf.

122 *Ibid.*

123 Emery, *Renegotiating Family Relationships*, 96.

124 Cherlin, *The Marriage Go-Round*, 5.

125 Relocation disputes have risen sharply in recent years. *See* Theresa Glennon, "Still Partners? Examining the Consequences of Post-Dissolution Parenting," *Family Law Quarterly* 41 (2007): 118; Parkinson, *Family Law and the Indissolubility of Parenthood*, 150–152.

126 Glennon, "Still Partners?" 105–106.

127 *See* Parkinson, *Family Law and the Indissolubility of Parenthood*, 150–151.

128 Glennon, "Still Partners?" 119.

129 *Ibid.* at 123–125 (reporting on results of a study of reported cases between 2001 and 2006 finding that courts granted permission to relocate in fewer than half of the cases in which a final decision was made).

130 *See* Merle H. Weiner, "Inertia and Inequality: Reconceptualizing Disputes over Parental Relocation," *University of California Davis Law Review* 40 (2007): 1750.

131 Catherine Ross, "The Failure of Fragmentation: The Promise of Unified Family Courts," *Family Law Quarterly* 32 (1998): 15–16.

132 *See* Princeton University and Columbia University, "Fragile Families and Child Wellbeing Study Fact Sheet" (noting that unmarried parents are much more likely than married parents to rely on public assistance and income-tested programs).

133 Tali Schaefer, "Saving Children or Blaming Parents? Lessons from Mandated Parenting Classes," *Columbia Journal of Gender and Law* 19 (2010): 491, 537.

134 Clare Huntington, *Failure to Flourish: How Law Undermines Family Relationships* (New York: Oxford University Press, 2014).

135 Jane Murphy, "Revitalizing the Adversary System in Family Law," *University of Cincinnati Law Review* 78 (2010): 919.

CHAPTER 5. FROM GLADIATORS AND UMPIRES TO PROBLEM-SOLVERS AND MANAGERS

1 Stephen A. Landsman, "A Brief Summary of the Development of the Adversary System," *Ohio State Law Journal* 44 (1983): 713–714 (describing the development of the adversarial system).

2 The term "zealous," often a flashpoint for debates about the value of the adversary system, was included in the original American Bar Association Canon of Ethics, Canon 7, which states, "A lawyer shall represent a client zealously within the bounds of the law." For thorough and enthusiastic defenses of the lawyer's role in the adversary system *see* Monroe Freedman, *Lawyers' Ethics in an Adversary System* (Indianapolis: Bobbs-Merrill, 1975); Charles Fried, "The Lawyer as Friend: The Moral Foundations of the Lawyer–Client Relation," *Yale Law Journal* 84 (1976): 1060.

3 Julie Macfarlane, *The New Lawyer: How Settlement Is Transforming the Practice of Law* (Vancouver: UBC Press, 2008), 49.

4 *Ibid.*

5 "ABA Model Code of Judicial Conduct," American Bar Association Center for Professional Responsibility, accessed December 20, 2013, http://www.americanbar.org/groups/professional_responsibility/publications/model_code_of_judicial_conduct.html.

6 Edward Wright, "Courtroom Decorum and the Trial Process," *Judicature* 51 (1968): 378, 382.

7 Model Rules of Professional Conduct R. 1.1 (the word "zealous" was removed from the current Model Rules of Professional Conduct and replaced with "competence"); Model Rules of Professional Conduct R. 1.3 (when describing a lawyer's obligation to

her client, advising that the lawyer must also act with "reasonable diligence and promptness"); Model Rules of Professional Conduct R. 1.3, cmt. 1. (The comments to the rules still advise that a "lawyer must also act with commitment and dedication to the interests of the client and with zeal in advocacy upon the client's behalf," and also caution that "the lawyer is not bound . . . to press for every advantage that might be realized for a client.") The rules can be found at *http://www.americanbar.org/groups/ professional_responsibility/publications/model_rules_of_professional_conduct/model_ rules_of_professional_conduct_table_of_contents.html*, accessed November 2, 2014.

8 Richard Maiman, Lynn Mather, and Craig McEwen, *Divorce Lawyers at Work: Varieties of Professionalism in Practice* (New York: Oxford University Press, 2001), 112.

9 William L. F. Felstiner and Austin Sarat, *Divorce Lawyers and Their Clients: Power and Meaning in the Legal Process* (New York: Oxford University Press, 1997), 53–58 (finding that clients generally promote adversarial behavior more than lawyers, and describing strategies that lawyers use to persuade clients to accept "reasonable" settlements in light of existing law).

10 *See* Maiman, Mather, and McEwen, *Divorce Lawyers at Work*, 118 (in a study of 163 interviews with Maine and New Hampshire divorce lawyers, researchers concluded that family lawyers are likely to "dampen legal conflict far more than they exacerbate it and generally try to avoid adversarial actions").

11 "Bounds of Advocacy: Goals for Family Lawyers," American Academy of Matrimonial Lawyers, accessed December 23, 2013, http://www.aaml.org/library/ publications/19/bounds-advocacy; Nancy Ver Steegh and Clare Dalton, "Report from the Wingspread Conference on Domestic Violence and Family Courts," *Family Court Review* 46 (2008): 460.

12 Pauline H. Tesler, "Collaborative Law: What It Is and Why Family Law Attorneys Need to Know about It," *American Journal of Family Law* 13 (1999): 215.

13 Hon. Sonia Sotomayor and Judge Mario G. Olmos, "Memorial Lecture: Latina Judge's Voice," *La Raza Law Journal* 13 (2002): 92 (a speech in which Justice Sotomayor explains how "our gender and national origins may and will make a difference in our judging"); *see also* Hon. Arrie W. Davis, "The Richness of Experience, Empathy, and the Role of a Judge: The Senate Confirmation Hearings for Judge Sonia Sotomayor," *University of Baltimore Law Forum* 40 (2009): 38.

14 Consistent with our focus on intra-family disputes in which the state is not a party, our discussion of new roles for lawyers in this chapter focuses on nongovernment lawyers.

15 Macfarlane, *The New Lawyer*, 54.

16 Model Rules of Professional Conduct R. 1.2(a). (This traditional division of roles is embodied in the ABA's Model Rules, which require a lawyer to "abide" by the "client's decisions concerning the objectives of representation," while limiting the lawyer's responsibility to "consult[ing] with the client as to the means by which [the objectives] are to be pursued.")

17 Of course, such a discussion won't always be appropriate and in the client's and children's interest. *See e.g.* Barry Goldstein and Mo Therese Hannah, *Domestic*

Violence, Abuse, and Child Custody Legal Strategies and Policy Issues (Kingston, NJ: Civic Research Institute, 2010). *See also* Janet R. Johnston, "A Child-Centered Approach to High-Conflict and Domestic Violence Families: Differential Assessment and Interventions," *Journal of Family Studies* 12 (2006): 15.

18 This conception of the lawyer's role in promoting non-adversarial resolution processes was encouraged by the likes of Chief Justice Warren Burger, who feared that the inefficiency of and acrimony fostered by the adversarial system would result in a "society overrun by hordes of lawyers, hungry as locusts and brigades of judges in numbers never before contemplated." Bryan Clark, *Lawyers and Mediation* (New York: Springer, 2012), 2.

19 The question of how to address domestic violence and mediation has been the subject of extensive scholarship. *See e.g.* Janet R. Johnston and Nancy Ver Steegh, "Historical Trends in Family Court Response to Intimate Partner Violence: Perspectives of Critics and Proponents of Current Practices," *Family Court Review* 51 (2013): 63. For a discussion of the range of power imbalances between couples that may interfere with mediation, *see* Gretchen Walther, "Power Imbalances and Divorce Mediation," *American Journal of Family Law* 14 (2000): 95; *see also* Michael P. Johnson and Joan B. Kelly, "Differentiation among Types of Intimate Partner Violence: Research Update and Implications for Interventions," *Family Court Review* 46 (2008): 476.

20 *See generally* John Lande, "Helping Lawyers Help Clients Make Good Decisions about Dispute Resolution," *Dispute Resolution Magazine* 17 (2010): 14. *See also* Amy Applegate, Connie Beck, and Amy Holtzworth-Munroe, "The Mediator's Assessment of Safety Issues and Concerns (MASIC): A Screening Interview for Intimate Partner Violence and Abuse Available in the Public Domain," *Family Court Review* 48 (2010): 646; Jane Murphy and Robert Rubinson, "Screening in Mediation for Domestic Violence," *ABA Family Law Quarterly* 39 (2005): 56; Gregg Herman and John Lande, "Fitting the Forum to the Family Fuss," *Family Court Review*, 42 (2004): 280–291.

21 Mary Pat Treuhart, "In Harm's Way? Family Mediation and the Role of the Attorney Advocate," *Golden Gate University Law Review* 717 (1993): 744–745.

22 Macfarlane, *The New Lawyer*, 24.

23 *Ibid.*, 23.

24 *Ibid.*

25 *Ibid.*

26 *Ibid.*, 24.

27 *See* Felstiner and Sarat, *Divorce Lawyers and Their Clients*, 56–57; Robert F. Cochran Jr., "Legal Ethics and Collaborative Ethics," *Hofstra Law Review* 38 (2009): 542. ("In theory, the client sets the goal of the representation and must approve any settlement offers, but studies of negotiation practices suggest that in fact lawyers are in control all the way through.")

28 Roselle L. Wissler, "Party Participation and Voice in Mediation," *Dispute Resolution Magazine* 18 (2011): 20 (citing Nancy A. Welsh, "Making Deals in Court-Connected Mediation: What's Justice Got to Do with It?" *Washington University Law Quarterly* 79 [2001]: 817–820).

29 Leonard L. Riskin, "Understanding Mediators' Orientations, Strategies, and Techniques: A Grid for the Perplexed," *Harvard Negotiation Law Review* 1 (1996): 24; *but see* Jean Sternlight, "Lawyerless Dispute Resolution: Rethinking a Paradigm," *Fordham Urban Law Journal* 37 (2009): 381, 407–408 (noting that lawyers can play an important role in providing emotional support to clients in mediation). Some lawyers have argued for a more active but non-adversarial role in mediation that still preserves the core values of client self-determination. *See* Harold Abramson, *Mediation Representation: Advocating in a Problem-Solving Process* (South Bend, IN: National Institute for Trial Advocacy, 2004).

30 Pauline H. Tesler, *Collaborative Law: Achieving Effective Resolution in Divorce without Litigation*, 2nd ed. (Chicago: American Bar Association, 2008), 70.

31 Robert F. Cochran Jr., "Legal Ethics and Collaborative Ethics," *Hofstra Law Review* 38 (2009): 543.

32 The term "mediation" covers a broad range of processes. But the most commonly used in family law, particularly court-based child access mediation, is facilitative mediation. *See* Armand H. Matheny Antommaria, "Alternative Dispute Resolution and Pediatric Clinical Ethics Consultation: Why the Limits of Ethical Expertise and the Indeterminacy of the Best Interests Standard Favor Mediation," *Ohio State Journal of Dispute Resolution* 17 (2007): 32. This discussion of the lawyer's role assumes a facilitative approach.

33 Richard M. Calkins, "A Revolutionary Process That Is Replacing the American Judicial System," *Cardozo Journal of Conflict Resolution* 13 (2011): 15. ("An important consideration is that mediation enables the parties to take control of their cases and resolve them any way they wish. They are no longer passive bystanders buffeted by attorneys in a courtroom.")

34 One articulation of this view can be found in Mark C. Rutherford, "Lawyers and Divorce Mediation: Designing the Role of 'Outside Counsel,'" *Mediation Quarterly* 12 (1986): 17, 27. ("For mediation to succeed as a profession and to reach its highest objectives, advocacy has no place in any part of the process. For outside counsel to advocate a client's interests contradicts the very essence of mediation and can produce inequitable results.")

35 Roselle L. Wissler, "Representation in Mediation: What We Know from Empirical Research," *Fordham Urban Law Journal* 37 (2010): 470.

36 Richard Shields, Judith P. Ryan, and Victoria Smith, *Collaborative Family Law: Another Way to Resolve Disputes* (Ontario: Thomson, 2003), iv.

37 *See generally* Forrest S. Mosten, *Unbundling Legal Services: A Guide to Delivering Legal Services a la Carte* (Chicago: American Bar Association, 2000); Andrew Schepard, "Special Issue: Unbundled Legal Services and Unrepresented Family Court Litigants," *Family Court Review* 40 (2002): 5; "Standing Committee on the Delivery of Legal Services," Resource Center, accessed August 7, 2013, http://www.americanbar.org/groups/delivery_legal_services/resources.html (articles, books and reports, cases, court rules, ethics opinions, and information about self-service centers).

38 M. Sue Talia, *Reinventing the Practice of Law: Emerging Models to Enhance Affordable Legal Services* (Chicago: ABA Standing Committee on the Delivery of Legal Services, 2014), 4.

39 *See e.g.* Kathryn Alfisi, "Access to Justice: Helping Litigants Help Themselves," *Washington Lawyer* (January 2010); Mary C. Ashcroft, "Unbundling Legal Services: Delivering What Your Client Wants at a Price She Can Afford," *Vermont Bar Journal* (Winter 2010); J. Timothy Eaton and David Holtermann, "Expanding Access to Justice: Limited Scope Representation is Here," *CBA Record* 36–41 (April 2010).

40 "Limited Representation in Maryland: A White Paper of the Maryland Access to Justice Commission" (September 2009), 1.

41 *Ibid.*

42 American Bar Association, "Resolution 108" (adopted by the House of Delegates February 11, 2013). Over forty states and territories have adopted some form of ABA Model Rule 1.2(c), which authorizes lawyers to engage in limited representation. Talia, *Reinventing the Practice of Law. But see* Michele N. Struffolino, "Taking Limited Representation to the Limits: The Efficacy of Using Unbundled Legal Services in Domestic Relations Matter Involving Litigation," *St. Mary's Journal on Legal Malpractice and Ethics* 2 (2012): 166 (discussing the ways in which limited representation "causes difficulties for litigants, attorneys, and the court").

43 Jeffrey W. Stempel, "Theralaw and the Law-Business Paradigm Debate," *Psychology, Public Policy, and Law* 5 (1999): 851.

44 *Ibid.* at 849.

45 Donna Beck Weaver, "The Collaborative Law Process for Prenuptial Agreements," *Pepperdine Dispute Resolution Law Journal* 4 (2004): 337 (citing data that demonstrates that the use of premarital agreements has quintupled in the last twenty years).

46 *Ibid.*

47 Arizona Board of Regents *et al.*, "Legal Planning for Unmarried Committed Partners: Empirical Lessons for a Preventative and Therapeutic Approach," *Arizona Law Review* 41 (1999): 417. Preventive law has also provided a mechanism for gay and lesbian couples and families to provide for family transitions where the law and courts do not offer the range of options needed for such families. *See e.g.* Denis Clifford, Emily Doskow, and Frederick Hertz, *A Legal Guide for Lesbian and Gay Couples* (Berkeley, CA: Nolo, 2010).

48 Marjorie A. Silver, "Love, Hate, and Other Emotional Interference in the Lawyer/Client Relationship," *Clinical Law Review* 6 (1999): 284 (noting that Erwin Griswold, dean of Harvard Law School from 1946 to 1967, criticized law schools for spending too much time on teaching doctrinal law and not enough time on developing students' interpersonal and psychological skills); Warren Burger, "Address to the American Bar Association Mid-Year Meeting" (address, Las Vegas, February 12, 1984). ("The entire legal profession—lawyers, judges, law teachers—have become so mesmerized with the stimulation of the courtroom contest that we tend to forget that we ought to be

healers—healers of conflicts . . .") Gandhi was an even earlier proponent of the lawyer as healer, writing, "My joy was boundless. I had learnt the true practice of law. I had learnt to find out the better side of human nature . . . I realized the true function of a lawyer was to unite parties driven asunder." Mahatma Gandhi, *An Autobiography: The Story of My Experiments with the Truth* (Auckland: Floating Press, 2009), 220.

49 Susan Daicoff, "Law as a Healing Profession: The 'Comprehensive Law Movement,'" *Pepperdine Dispute Resolution Law Journal* 6 (2005): 1–2. The comprehensive law movement distinguishes itself from the formality and adversarial nature of traditional law practice in its search for "more collaborative, comprehensive, healing, and humane forms of law practice." Marjorie A. Silver, "Lawyering and Its Discontents: Reclaiming Meaning in the Practice of Law," *Touro Law Review* 19 (2004): 773.

50 Pauline H. Tesler, *Collaborative Law: Achieving Effective Resolution in Divorce without Litigation*, 2nd ed. (Chicago: American Bar Association, 2008), 19.

51 Hon. Michael A. Town, "The Unified Family Court: Preventative, Therapeutic, and Restorative Justice for America's Families," *ABA Child Law Practice* 21 (2002): 109.

52 Daicoff, "Law as a Healing Profession," 5.

53 Della Noce *et al.*, "Clarifying the Theoretical Underpinnings of Mediation: Implications for Practice and Policy," *Pepperdine Dispute Resolution Law Journal* 3 (2002): 39–65.

54 Robert A. Baruch Bush and Sally Ganong Pope, "Changing the Quality of Conflict Interaction: The Principles and Practice of Transformative Mediation," *Pepperdine Dispute Resolution Law Journal* 3 (2002): 67–96.

55 Thomas Porter, "The Spirit and the Law," *Fordham Urban Law Journal* 26 (1999): 1155.

56 Pauline H. Tesler, "Collaborative Law: A New Paradigm for Divorce Lawyers," *Journal of Psychology, Public Policy, and Law* 5 (1999): 967, 989.

57 *Ibid.* at 990, n. 57.

58 Pauline H. Tesler, *Collaborative Law: Achieving Effective Resolution in Divorce without Litigation*, 2nd ed. (Chicago: American Bar Association, 2008), 5.

59 *See generally* Marjorie A. Silver, *The Affective Assistance of Counsel: Practicing Law as a Healing Profession* (Durham, NC: Carolina Academic Press, 2006).

60 Debra Berman and James Alfini, "Lawyer Colonization of Family Mediation: Consequences and Implications," *Marquette Law Review* 95 (2012): 887, 890.

61 *Ibid.* at 891.

62 *Ibid.*

63 *Ibid.* at 895 (quoting interview with Bernard Mayer).

64 Andrew I. Schepard, *Children, Courts, and Custody: Interdisciplinary Models for Divorcing Families* (Cambridge, UK: Cambridge University Press, 2004).

65 "Task Force on Parenting Coordination, Guidelines for Parenting Coordination," Association of Family and Conciliation Courts, accessed November 1, 2014, http://www.afccnet.org/Resource-Center/Practice-Guidelines-and-Standards; *see also* Semple, "The Settlement Mission in Custody and Access Cases."

66 *See generally* Jordan Leigh Santeramo, "Early Neutral Evaluation in Divorce Cases," *Family Court Review* 42 (2004): 321; Yvonne Pearson, "Early Neutral Evaluations: Applications to Custody and Parenting Time Cases Program Development and Implementation in Hennepin County, Minnesota," *Family Court Review* 44 (2006): 672; John Lande, "The Movement Toward Early Case Handling in Courts and Private Dispute Resolution," *Ohio State Journal on Dispute Resolution* 24 (2008): 81, 99–101.

67 *See e.g.* "Family Court Process: Early Neutral Evaluation," Mid-Minnesota Legal Aid and Legal Services, accessed December 27, 2013, http://www.lawhelpmn.org/files/1765CC5E-1EC9–4FC4–65EC-957272D8A04E/attachments/06F9454A-F896-E521–812D-3436DF8A70BB/f-9-enes.pdf.

68 *See* George K. Walker, "Arbitrating Family Law Cases by Agreement," *Journal of the American Academy of Matrimonial Lawyers* 18 (2003): 431; "Model Family Law Arbitration Act," American Academy of Matrimonial Lawyers (2004), accessed November 1, 2014, http://www.aaml.org/library/publications/21215/model-family-law-arbitration-act.

69 Sheila Nagaraj, "The Marriage of Private Judging and Family Law in California," *Yale Law Journal* 116 (2007): 1615.

70 Court decisions and state laws may limit the power of parties to submit final decisions about child access to arbitration, viewing the authority to resolve issues relating to children as resting exclusively with the courts. *See e.g. Toiberman v. Tisera*, 998 So.2d 4 (Fla. App. 2008). But even in jurisdictions where these prohibitions exist, courts give great deference to parents' agreements about child custody and visitation.

71 Anne H. Geraghty and Wallace J. Mlyniec, "Unified Family Courts: Tempering Enthusiasm with Caution," *Family Court Review* 40 (2002): 437.

72 *Ibid.*

73 Victor E. Flango, "Problem-Solving Courts under a Different Lens," in *Future Trends in State Courts* (Williamsburg: National Center for State Courts, 2007),42, accessed November 8, 2014, http://cdm16501.contentdm.oclc.org/cdm/ref/collection/spcts/id/177.

74 *Ibid.*

75 *Ibid.*

76 *See* Leslie Eaton and Leslie Kaufman, "In Problem-Solving Court, Judges Turn Therapist," *New York Times* (April 26, 2005), accessed November 8, 2014, http://www.nytimes.com/2005/04/26/nyregion/26courts.html (one court-watcher, commenting on the new role of judges in one kind of problem-solving court, drug treatment courts).

77 *Ibid.*

78 *Ibid.*

79 Gerald Hardcastle, "Adversarialism and the Family Court: A Family Court Judge's Perspective," *Journal of Juvenile Law and Policy* 9 (2005): 57; Timothy Casey, "When Good Intentions Are Not Enough: Problem-Solving Courts and the Impending Crisis of Legitimacy," *SMU Law Review* 57 (2004): 1482–1483.

80 Deborah J. Chase and Peggy Fulton Hora, "The Implications of Therapeutic Jurisprudence for Judicial Satisfaction," Court *Review* (Spring 2000): 12.

81 Deborah J. Chase and Hon. Peggy Fulton Hora, "The Best Seat in the House: The Court Assignment and Judicial Satisfaction," *Family Court Review* 47 (2009) 234.

82 James L. Nolan Jr., "Therapeutic Adjudication," *Society* 39 (2002): 38; *see* Richard Boldt and Jana Singer, "Juristocracy in the Trenches: Problem-Solving Judges and Therapeutic Jurisprudence in Drug Treatment Courts and Unified Family Courts," *Maryland Law Review* 65 (2006): 86–90.

83 Noel Semple, "Judicial Settlement-Seeking in Parenting Disputes: Consensus and Controversy," *Conflict Resolution Quarterly* 29 (2012): 309, 327.

84 *Ibid.* at 309.

85 This model is less common in large jurisdictions, but some jurisdictions have one judge or a "one judge, one family" model. Noel Semple, "Judicial Settlement in Parenting Cases: A Mock Trial," *Journal of Dispute Resolution* 2 (2013): 24–25.

86 *Ibid.*, 25.

87 Semple, "Judicial Settlement-Seeking in Parenting Disputes," 324.

88 *Ibid.* at 322–323.

89 Many of these programs measure their success based on the number of cases resolved by agreement. *See e.g.* Carol J. King, "Burdening Access to Justice: The Cost of Divorce Mediation on the Cheap," *St. John's Law Review* 375 (1999): 438. ("The justification offered for mandating mediation has been that the process promotes judicial economy. Theoretically, if cases awaiting trial can be diverted through settlement, backlogs will be reduced and cases that cannot—or should not—be settled will go to trial more quickly. Cases that do not require trial will also save the cost of providing the services of a presiding judge.") Welsh, "Making Deals in Court-Connected Mediation," 787.

90 For example, when a party's lawyer raises the issue of domestic violence, most judges have the authority to exclude the case from mediation. *See e.g.* Md. Rule, 9–205(b)(2) (a court shall not order mediation in cases where physical or sexual abuse has been alleged in good faith).

91 Uniform Collaborative Rules and Act §6(a) (rev. 2010).

92 Donna J. Hitchens, "Family Law Judge for the Twenty-First Century," *Collaborative Quarterly* 2 (2000): 1–2.

93 Andrew Schepard, "The Evolving Judicial Role in Child Custody Disputes: From Fault Finder to Conflict Manager to Differential Case Management," *University of Arkansas at Little Rock Law Review* 22 (2000): 395. Similar changes to the judicial role have occurred in other family court systems. *See e.g.* Julie Doughty and Mervyn Murch, "Judicial Independence and the Restructuring of Family Courts and Their Support Services," *Child and Family Law Quarterly* 24 (2012): 333–354 (discussing changes to the role of family court judges in England).

94 Schepard, "The Evolving Judicial Role in Child Custody Disputes," 397.

95 *Ibid.*

96 Peter Salem, "The Emergence of Triage in Family Court Services: The Beginning of the End of Mandatory Mediation?" *Family Court Review* 47 (2009): 373.

97 *Ibid.*

98 Gabrielle Davis, Loretta Frederick, and Nancy Ver Steegh, "Look before You Leap: Court System Triage of Family Law Cases Involving Intimate Partner Violence," *Marquette Law Review* 95 (2012): 956.

99 Frank E. A. Sander, *Varieties of Dispute Processing* (St. Paul, MN: West Publishing, 1976), 131.

100 Salem, "The Emergence of Triage in Family Court Services," 381.

101 Davis, Frederick, and Ver Steegh, "Look Before You Leap," 956.

102 Barbara Glesner Fines, "Fifty Years of the Family Law Practice: The Evolving Role of the Family Law Attorney," *Journal of the American Academy of Matrimonial Lawyers* 24 (2012): 391.

103 Semple, "The Settlement Mission in Custody and Access Cases" (arguing against the involvement of judges in conducting settlement conferences in family law cases); Nancy Ver Steegh, "Family Court Reform and ADR: Shifting Values and Expectations Transform the Divorce Process," *Family Law Quarterly* 42 (2008): 669; *but see* Kevin McGrath, "Settling Dissolution Cases: Court Rules and Judges' Roles," *Family Law Quarterly* 45 (2011): 37 (defending the role of judge as settlement facilitator based on experiences in one family court in Minnesota).

104 Geraghty and Mlyniec, "Unified Family Courts," 438–440.

105 Model Rules of Professional Conduct R 1.1; 1.2(c) (2009).

106 *Ibid.*, R. 1.2(c); 1.7 cmt. 6 (2009).

107 *Ibid.*, R. 1.16 cmt. 7 (2009) (the lawyer may not withdraw if it would be materially adverse to the client's interests); *Ibid.*, R. 1.2 cmt. 7, requires agreements limiting the scope of representation to be reasonable because limited representation may not further clients' goals or even help them under some circumstances. For example if "a client's objective is limited to securing general information . . . in order to handle a common and typically uncomplicated legal problem, the lawyer and client may agree that the lawyer's services will be limited to a brief telephone consultation. Such a limitation, however, would not be reasonable if the time allotted was not sufficient to yield advice upon which the client could rely." *Ibid. See also* R. 8.4(c) (identifying types of behavior that constitute "professional misconduct" involving "dishonesty, fraud, deceit, or misrepresentation" as including in some jurisdictions "ghostwriting and undisclosed assistance to *pro se* litigants"). *Annotated Model Rules of Professional Conduct*, 7th ed.(Chicago: American Bar Association, 2011), 616–617.

108 Model Rules of Professional Conduct R. 6.5 (Nonprofit and Court-Annexed Legal Services Programs).

109 *Ibid.*, R. 4.2 (Communication Between Lawyer and Person Represented by Counsel).

110 American Bar Association Section of Litigation, "Handbook on Limited Scope Legal Assistance: A Report of the Modest Means Task Force" (2003), 44.

111 Model Rules of Professional Conduct R. 1.16 (governing termination of client representation). Motions to withdraw are also governed in some jurisdictions by the Rules of Civil Procedure.

112 *Ibid.*

113 *See* Scott R. Peppet, "The (New) Ethics of Collaborative Law," *Dispute Resolution Magazine* 14 (2008): 23, 24–25.

114 Cochran, "Legal Ethics and Collaborative Ethics," 537, 545.

115 Model Rules of Professional Conduct R. 1.6 (2009).

116 *Ibid.*, 5.4(d), cmt. to R. 2.1. Although the Model Rules recognize that lawyers may "refer to moral and ethical considerations when giving advice," the rules are also clear that "matters that go beyond strictly legal questions may also be in the domain of another profession." Cmt. to 2.1(2) and (4). Rather than fostering collaboration among the professions to address a client's problems, the rules suggest the lawyer should refer clients to other professionals in some circumstances while retaining the prerogative to "recommend a course of action" when the experts conflict. Cmt. to 2.1(4).

117 *Ibid.*, R. 1.12 and 2.4. Cmts. 3 and 4 to R. 2.4 discuss the unique problems presented to lawyers as third-party neutrals and the potential conflicts of interest created by that role. Cmt. 3 notes that the potential for confusion regarding the lawyer's role can become particularly confusing when the parties are not represented by counsel. It emphasizes the importance for the lawyer to explain his role both as a neutral and as an advocate. Cmt. 4 addresses the conflict of interest that will arise when the lawyer serves as a third-party neutral and is later asked to represent one of the clients if the matter goes to trial.

118 *See e.g.* Patricia Weaver, "Alternative Dispute Resolution and Ethics," *Maryland Bar Journal* 44 (2011): 20–23; Robert Rubinson, "The New Maryland Rules of Professional Conduct and Mediation: Perplexing Questions Answered and Perplexing Questions Remain," *University of Baltimore Law Forum* 36 (2005): 1.

119 Bruce J. Winick and David B. Wexler, *Judging in a Therapeutic Key: Therapeutic Jurisprudence and the Courts* (Durham, NC: Carolina Academic Press, 2003), 298–299.

120 *Ibid.* at 288. Some commentators have noted, however, that the real issue here is judicial *engagement*, not neutrality. The fact that judges in problem-solving courts might be more engaged with the parties and conflict before them than their counterparts in traditional courts does not interfere with the judge's obligation to be neutral and, in fact, improves judicial performance. *See* Richard Zorza, "The Disconnect between the Requirements of Judicial Neutrality and Those of the Appearance of Neutrality When Parties Appear *Pro Se*: Causes, Solutions, Recommendations, and Implications," *Georgetown Journal of Legal Ethics* 23 (2004): 423, 430, nn. 17–18, 448–452, nn. 47–65.

121 "Canon 3 of the Model Code of Judicial Conduct," ABA Model Code of Judicial Conduct, accessed August 18, 2013, http://www.americanbar.org/content/dam/aba/migrated/judicialethics/ABA_MCJC_approved.authcheckdam.pdf.

122 "Canon 1 of the Model Code of Judicial Conduct," *ibid.*

123 "Model Code of Judicial Conduct Rule 2.6(B) (2007)," *ibid.*

124 *See e.g.* ABA Model Code of Judicial Conduct, cmt. to R. 2.6. (Cautioning judges to be careful "that efforts to further settlement do not undermine any parties' right to be heard according to law," and referring to "lawyers and parties" throughout the comment. *Pro se* parties are only mentioned as a factor urging judicial caution when pursuing settlement.)

125 Model Rules of Professional Conduct R. 1.2(c) (2013); 1.2(c) (Scope of Representation) states, "A lawyer may limit the scope of the representation if the limitation is reasonable under the circumstances and the client gives informed consent." For a state-by-state listing of rules regarding unbundling, *see* "Unbundling Rules," National Center for State Courts, accessed June 11, 2014, http://www.ncsc.org/ Topics/Access-and-Fairness/Self-Representation/State-Links.aspx?cat=unbundling%20 Rules; "Standing Committee on the Delivery of Legal Services: *Pro Se* Unbundling Resource Center, Court Rules," American Bar Association, accessed June 11, 2014, http://www.americanbar.org/delivery_legal_services/resoruces/pro_se_unbundling_ resource_center/court_rules.html.

126 Model Rules of Professional Conduct R. 6.5 (Nonprofit and Court-Annexed Legal Services Programs).

127 "Family Law Limited Scope Representation: Risk Management Materials" (California Commission on Access to Justice) (January 12, 2004), accessed November 8, 2014, http://calbar.ca.gov/LinkClick.aspx?fileticket=BpsuqBowlBM=; *see also* reports and articles found at http://www.americanbar.org/groups/delivery_legal_services/ resources/pro_se_unbundling_resource_center/books_reports.html (accessed June 11, 2014).

128 *An Analysis of Rules that Enable Lawyers to Serve Self Represented Litigants: A White Paper by the ABA Standing Committee on the Delivery of Legal Services* (Chicago: American Bar Association, 2014), accessed November 8, 2014, http://www.american-bar.org/content/dam/aba/administrative/delivery_legal_services/ ls_del_unbundling_white_paper_2014.authcheckdam.pdf.

129 *Ibid.*

130 *Ibid.* at 12–16.

131 Model Rule 2.4, Reporter's Explanation of Changes, Report 401 on Amendments to Model Rules of Professional Conduct (Ethics 2000) to the House of Delegates of the American Bar Association (2002).

132 Model Rules of Professional Conduct R. 2.4.

133 Robert Rubinson, "The New Maryland Rules of Professional Conduct and Mediation: Perplexing Questions Answered and Perplexing Questions Remain," *University of Baltimore Law Forum* 36 (2005): 1.

134 Model Rules of Professional Conduct R. 1.12 (2005). The rule addresses ethical issues when an attorney seeks to assume the role of client representative with one of the parties to the mediation after the mediation is concluded. It prohibits an attorney–mediator from "represent[ing] anyone in connection with a matter" in which the attorney–mediator had previously acted as a mediator absent "informed consent, confirmed in writing" from all parties. Model Rules of Professional Conduct 1.12(a)

(2005). This disqualification is "imputed" to the attorney-mediator's firm unless the attorney-mediator is properly "screened" from participation in the case. Model Rules of Professional Conduct R. 1.12(c) (2005). A comment to the rule acknowledges that "[o]ther . . . codes of ethics governing third-party neutrals may impose more stringent standards of personal or imputed disqualification." Model Rules of Professional Conduct R. 1.12, cmt. 3 (2005). The rule also prohibits an attorney-mediator from negotiating for employment with a party or with an attorney representing a party in mediation. Model Rules of Professional Conduct R. 1.12(b) (2005).

135 *See* Uniform Collaborative Law Act, Prefatory Note at 16 (discussing state ethics opinions). A Colorado Ethics Opinion is the lone dissenting view, and that view was specifically rejected by the American Bar Association. *Ibid.*

136 *Ibid.* at 18.

137 *Ibid.*, cmt. to sec. 17; *see* Prefatory Note at 35–36. ("Without assurances that communications made during the collaborative process will not be used to their detriment later, parties, collaborative lawyers, and non-party participants such as mental health and financial professions will be reluctant to speak frankly, test out ideas and proposals, or freely exchange information.")

138 *Ibid.* at 14.

139 Section 10(b) of the Uniform Collaborative Law Act, sec. 10(b).

140 *Ethical Considerations for Attorneys and Judges in Drug Court*, National Drug Court Institute (2001).

CHAPTER 6. THE INFLUENCE OF COMPARATIVE AND INTERNATIONAL FAMILY LAW

1 *See* Jana B. Singer, "Dispute Resolution and the Post-Divorce Family: Implications of a Paradigm Shift," *Family Court Review* 47 (2009): 363 (discussing "velvet revolution" in family conflict resolution).

2 For example, *Family Court Review*, the journal of the Association of Family and Conciliation Courts, recently published a special issue focused on Australia's Family Relationship Centres. *See Family Court Review* 51 (April 2013).

3 Patrick Parkinson, "The Idea of Family Relationship Centres in Australia," *Family Court Review* 51 (2013): 195.

4 *Ibid.*

5 *Ibid.* at 197.

6 Andrew Schepard and Robert Emery, "Editorial Notes: The Australian Family Relationship Centres and the Future of Services for Separating and Divorcing Families," *Family Court Review* 51 (2013): 180.

7 *Ibid.*

8 *Ibid.*

9 *Ibid.* at 181. The organizations compete for funding and operational authority through a rigorous, renewable application process based on criteria established by the government.

10 *Ibid.* at 180–181.

11 Parkinson, "The Idea of Family Relationship Centres in Australia," 196; *see* Sue Pidgeon, "From Policy to Implementation: How Family Relationship Centres Became a Reality," *Family Court Review* 51 (2013): 226 (noting that "the FRCs' referral role was particularly important where families were not separating or separated, but were going through relationship difficulties or simply wanted to improve their relationship").

12 Parkinson, "The Idea of Family Relationship Centres in Australia," 195.

13 *Ibid*. at 206.

14 *Ibid*. at 196.

15 Lawrie Moloney, "From Helping Court to Community-Based Services: The 30-Year Evolution of Australia's Family Relationship Centres," *Family Court Review* 51 (2013): 214.

16 Parkinson, "The Idea of Family Relationship Centres in Australia," 202.

17 *Ibid*. at 212.

18 Pidgeon, "From Policy to Implementation," 228.

19 Parkinson, "The Idea of Family Relationship Centres in Australia," 210.

20 *Ibid*. at 197.

21 *Ibid*. at 181.

22 *Ibid*. at 181.

23 *Ibid*. at 199.

24 *Ibid*.; *see* Helen Rhoades, "Legislating to Promote Children's Welfare and the Quest for Certainty," *Child and Family Law Quarterly* 24 (2012): 164.

25 Pidgeon, "From Policy to Implementation," 231.

26 Parkinson, "Family Relationship Centres in Australia," 208; *see* Lawrie Moloney *et al*., "Evaluating the Work of Australia's Family Relationship Centres: Evidence From the First 5 Years," *Family Court Review* 51 (2013): 238 (noting that approximately two-thirds of required Family Dispute Resolution takes place at FRCs).

27 Parkinson, "The Idea of Family Relationship Centres in Australia," 210.

28 Moloney, "From Helping Court to Community-Based Services," 220.

29 Lawrie Moloney *et al*., "Family Relationship Centres: Partnerships with Legal Assistance Services," *Family Court Review* 51 (2013): 250.

30 Schepard and Emery, "Editorial Notes," 182.

31 Moloney *et al*., "Family Relationship Centres," 250.

32 *Ibid*. at 251.

33 *Ibid*.

34 *Ibid*. at 256–258.

35 Moloney, "From Helping Court to Community-Based Services," 220.

36 *Ibid*.

37 Jennifer E. McIntosh, Hon. Diana Bryant, and Kristen Murray, "Evidence of a Different Nature: The Child-Responsive and Less Adversarial Initiatives of the Family Court of Australia," *Family Court Review* 46 (2008): 129.

38 *Ibid*. at 130–131. In addition, at the same time that the FRCs were being rolled out, a national Family Relationship Advice Line and a comprehensive website were established. *See* Pidgeon, "From Policy to Implementation," 228. These resources are

particularly important in providing services to families in rural and remote communities who may not have access to a "brick and mortar" FRC. *Ibid.* at 230.

39 Parkinson, "The Idea of Family Relationship Centres in Australia," 182.

40 Moloney *et al.*, "Evaluating the Work of Australia's Family Relationship Centres," 242.

41 *Ibid.*

42 Moloney, "From Helping Court to Community-Based Services," 220; *see* Moloney *et al.*, "Evaluating the Work of Australia's Family Relationship Centres," 235.

43 Moloney *et al.*, "Evaluating the Work of Australia's Family Relationship Centres," 235.

44 Moloney, "From Helping Court to Community-Based Services," 215.

45 Moloney *et al.*, "Evaluating the Work of Australia's Family Relationship Centres," 242–243.

46 *Ibid.* at 243.

47 *Ibid.*

48 Moloney, "From Helping Court to Community-Based Services," 220; *see* Moloney *et al.*, "Evaluating the Work of Australia's Family Relationship Centres," 236–237.

49 Moloney *et al.*, "Evaluating the Work of Australia's Family Relationship Centres," 237.

50 *Ibid.*

51 *Ibid.*

52 Moloney, "From Helping Court to Community-Based Services," 214.

53 Pidgeon, "From Policy to Implementation," 229.

54 Moloney *et al.*, "Evaluating the Work of Australia's Family Relationship Centres," 236.

55 *Ibid.*

56 Australian Government Attorney General's Department, "Family Violence Act: Frequently Asked Questions," accessed November 2, 2014, http://www.ag.gov.au/FamiliesAndMarriage/Families/FamilyViolence/Documents/Family%20Violence%20Act%20FAQ.pdf.

57 *Ibid.*

58 Lola Akin Ojelabi *et al.*, "A Cultural Assessment of Family Dispute Resolution: Findings about Cultural Appropriateness from the Evaluation of a Family Relationship Centre," *Journal of Family Studies* 18 (2012): 78.

59 *Ibid.*

60 *Ibid.* at 80.

61 *Ibid.* at 81–82.

62 Satoshi Minamikata, "Resolution of Disputes over Parental Rights and Duties in a Marital Dissolution Case in Japan: A Nonlitigious Approach to Chotei (Family Court Mediation)," *Family Law Quarterly* 39 (2005): 490–491.

63 Xia Yinlan, "The Legal System of Guardianship over Minors in the People's Republic of China," *Family Law Quarterly* 39 (2005): 482.

64 *See* Nandita Bhatla and Anuradha Rajan, "Private Concerns in Public Discourse: Women-Initiated Responses to Domestic Violence," *Economic and Political Weekly* (April 26, 2003), 1658.

65 Susan Zaidel, "Taking Divorce out of the Context of Dispute Resolution," *Family Court Review* 42 (2004): 679.

66 *Ibid.*

67 *See* N. W. Lowe, "The Allocation of Parental Rights and Responsibilities: The Position in England and Wales," *Family Law Quarterly* 39 (2005): 272–274.

68 *Ibid.* at 273; *see* D. Marianne Blair *et al.*, *Family Law in the World Community* (Durham, NC: Carolina Academic Press, 2009), 390.

69 Lowe, "The Allocation of Parental Rights and Responsibilities," 273.

70 Mervyn Murch, "The Voice of the Child in Private Family Law Proceedings in England and Wales," *International Family Law* (March 2005), 14.

71 Nina Dethloff, "Parental Rights and Responsibilities in Germany," *Family Law Quarterly* 39 (2005): 319.

72 Hugues Fulchiron, "Custody and Separated Families: The Example of French Law," *Family Law Quarterly* 39 (2005): 305.

73 The other non-signatory member state is Somalia. UNICEF, "Convention on the Rights of the Child: Frequently Asked Questions" (2005), accessed November 2, 2014, http://www.unicef.org/crc/index_30229.html.

74 UNICEF, "Protecting and Realizing Children's Rights" (2005), accessed November 2, 2014, http://www.unicef.org/crc/index_protecting.html.

75 Convention on the Rights of the Child, Art. 12, Para. 2 (November 20, 1989), 1577 U.N.T.S. 3.

76 *Ibid.*, Art. 12, Para. 1.

77 United Nations Committee on the Rights of the Child, "General Comment No. 12: The Right of the Child to Be Heard" (2009): 5, accessed November 2, 2014, http://tbinternet.ohchr.org/_layouts/treatybodyexternal/TBSearch.aspx?Lang=en&TreatyID=5&DocTypeID=11.

78 *Ibid.*

79 *Ibid.* at 11, 15.

80 *Ibid.* at 11.

81 *Ibid.* at 15.

82 *Ibid.* at 13.

83 *See e.g.* African Charter on the Rights and Welfare of the Child, Art. 4(2) (July 1, 1980), OAU Doc. CAB/LEG/153/Rev 2 (1990) ("In all judicial or administrative proceedings affecting a child who is capable of communicating his/her own views, an opportunity shall be provided for the views of the child to be heard either directly or through an impartial representative as a party to the proceedings . . ."); European Convention on the Exercise of Children's Rights (January 25, 1996), Europ. T.S. No. 160, Art. 3 (articulating child's right "to receive all relevant information" and "to be consulted and express his or her views" in all judicial proceedings affecting him).

84 Nigel Lowe and Mervyn Murch, "Children's Participation in the Family Justice System: Translating Principles into Practice," *Child and Family Law Quarterly* 13 (2001): 138; *see* Nicola Taylor, "What Do We Know about Involving Children and Young

People in Family Law Decision-Making? A Research Update," *Australian Journal of Family Law* 20 (2006): 14–18.

85 *See* "United Nations Committee on the Rights of the Child, General Comment No. 12" at 5 ("[s]ince the adoption of the Convention in 1989, considerable progress has been achieved at the local, national, regional and global levels in the development of legislation, policies and methodologies to promote the implementation of article 12"); Joan B. Kelly, "Psychological and Legal Interventions for Parents and Children in Custody and Access Disputes: Current Research and Practice," *Virginia Journal of Social Policy and Law* 10 (2002): 148–149 (noting that Article 12 has stimulated debate in England, Canada, and Australia regarding the most appropriate procedures for encouraging children's participation in custody and access disputes).

86 Department of Justice, Canada, "Research Report: The Voice of the Child in Separation/Divorce Mediation and Other Alternative Dispute Resolution Processes: A Literature Review" (June 2009).

87 *See generally* Michelle Fernando, "Family Law Proceedings and the Child's Right to Be Heard in Australia, the United Kingdom, New Zealand, and Canada," *Family Court Review* 52 (2014): 46; D. Marianne Blair and Merle H. Weiner, "Resolving Parental Custody Disputes—A Comparative Exploration: Symposium on Comparative Custody Law: Introduction," *Family Law Quarterly* 39 (2005): 247.

88 *See* Adrian L. James *et al.*, "The Voice of the Child in Family Mediation: Norway and England," *International Journal of Children's Rights* 18 (2010): 324 (describing Norwegian Children's Act); Taylor, "What Do We Know about Involving Children and Young People in Family Law Decision-Making?" 32–34 (discussing legislation in Scotland and New Zealand).

89 Branka Rešetar and Robert Emery, "Children's Rights in European Legal Proceedings: Why Are Family Practices So Different from Legal Theories," *Family Court Review* 46 (2008): 69–70.

90 *See e.g.* Patrick Parkinson and Judy Cashmore, *The Voice of a Child in Family Law Disputes* (New York: Oxford University Press 2009); Maria Coley, "Children's Voices in Custody and Access Decisions: The Need to Reconceptualize Rights and Effect Transformative Change," *Appeal* 12 (2007): 48 (noting that Canada's international commitments, including the CRC, "provide justification for involving children meaningfully in custody and access decisions"); Murch, "The Voice of the Child in Private Family Law Proceedings in England and Wales," 10.

91 Lowe, "The Allocation of Parental Rights and Responsibilities," 276–277.

92 *Ibid.* at 278.

93 James *et al.*, "The Voice of the Child in Family Mediation," 318.

94 Eva Ryrstedt, "Custody of Children in Sweden," *Family Law Quarterly* 39 (2005): 400.

95 *Ibid.*

96 *Ibid.* at 402.

97 *See* James *et al.*, "The Voice of the Child in Family Mediation," 313.

98 *Ibid.* at 325.

99 Barbara Ann Atwood, "The Uniform Representation of Children in Abuse, Neglect, and Custody Proceedings: Bridging the Divide Between Pragmatism and Idealism," *Family Law Quarterly* 42 (2008): 75.

100 Barbara A. Atwood, "The Child's Voice in Custody Litigation: An Empirical Survey and Suggestions for Reform," *Arizona Law Review* 45 (2003): 630–631; Jacqueline Clarke, "Do I Have A Voice? An Empirical Analysis of Children's Voices in Michigan Custody Litigation," *Family Law Quarterly* 47 (2013) 457–458.

101 Atwood, "The Uniform Representation of Children in Abuse, Neglect, and Custody Proceedings," 65 (noting that "statutory provisions and procedural rules for children's lawyers and guardians ad litem vary dramatically from state to state").

102 *Ibid.* at 72.

103 American Bar Association Section of Family Law, "Standards of Practice for Lawyers Representing Children in Custody Cases," *Family Law Quarterly* 37 (2003): 137; American Academy of Matrimonial Lawyers, "Representing Children: Standards for Attorneys for Children in Custody or Visitation Proceedings with Commentary," *Journal of the American Academy of Matrimonial Lawyers* 22 (2009): 227. In addition, the National Conference of Commissioners on Uniform State Laws has approved a Uniform Act governing the representation of children in abuse, neglect, and custody proceedings; the act was designed, in part, to implement the ABA standards. *See* Atwood, "The Uniform Representation of Children in Abuse, Neglect, and Custody Proceedings," 66.

104 As part of the lawyer's "pretrial responsibilities," the ABA standards specify that the lawyer should "[p]articipate in, and, when appropriate, initiate, negotiations and mediation." The commentary to this section notes that "[t]he lawyer should attempt to resolve the case in the least adversarial manner possible, considering whether therapeutic intervention, parenting or co-parenting education, mediation, or other dispute resolution methods are appropriate." "Standards of Practice for Lawyers Representing Children in Custody Cases," Section III (F).

105 Donald Saposnek, "Working with Children in Mediation," in Jay Folberg, Ann Milne, and Peter Salem, eds., *Divorce and Family Mediation: Models, Techniques, and Applications* (New York: Guilford Press, 2004), 155.

106 *Ibid.* at 155–156.

107 Model Standards of Practice for Family and Divorce Mediators §VIII (D), *Family and Conciliation Courts Review* 39 (2001): 131.

108 Melissa J. Schoffer, "Bringing Children to the Mediation Table: Defining a Child's Best Interest in Divorce Mediation," *Family Court Review* 43 (2005): 326.

109 *See ibid.* at 326–327.

110 *See* Saposnek, "Working with Children in Mediation," 157.

111 Dona Lansky *et al.*, "The Role of Children in Mediation," *Mediation Quarterly* 14 (1996): 147.

112 Jennifer E. McIntosh *et al.*, "Child-Focused and Child-Inclusive Divorce Mediation: Comparative Outcomes from a Prospective Study of Post-separation Adjustment," *Family Court Review* 46 (2008): 105.

113 Robin H. Ballard *et al.*, "A Randomized Controlled Trial of Child-Informed Mediation," *Psychology, Public Policy, and Law* 19 (2013): 272.

114 McIntosh *et al.*, "Child-Focused and Child-Inclusive Divorce Mediation," 110–111; *see* Ballard *et al.*, "A Randomized Controlled Trial of Child-Informed Mediation," 272.

115 Ballard *et al.*, "A Randomized Controlled Trial of Child-Informed Mediation," 272.

116 Jennifer McIntosh, Caroline M. Long, and Yvonne D. Wells, "Children beyond Dispute: A Four-Year Follow-Up Study of Outcomes from Child-Focused and Child-Inclusive Post-separation Family Dispute Resolution" (2009), accessed November 2, 2014, http://apo.org.au/node/18667; *see* Ballard *et al.*, "A Randomized Controlled Trial of Child-Informed Mediation," 272 (discussing follow-up study).

117 Ballard *et al.*, "A Randomized Controlled Trial of Child-Informed Mediation," 272.

118 *Ibid.* (noting concerns about possible conflicts of interest if mediators step outside of a neutral role to take the position of the child during the mediation).

119 *Ibid.* at 280.

120 *Ibid.* at 278.

121 Saposnek, "Working with Children in Mediation," 158; *see* Atwood, "The Child's Voice in Custody Litigation," 660–662 (discussing research).

122 Saposnek, "Working with Children in Mediation," 158–159.

123 Kelly, "Psychological and Legal Interventions for Parents and Children in Custody and Access Disputes," 151–152.

124 Taylor, "What Do We Know about Involving Children and Young People in Family Law Decision-Making?" 18–19; Jonathan W. Gould and David A. Martindale, "Including Children in Decision Making about Custodial Placement," *Journal of the American Academy of Matrimonial Law* 22 (2009): 304–305.

125 Mervyn Murch, "The Voice of the Child in Private Family Law Proceedings: Time to Rethink the Approach," *Seen and Heard* 20 (2010): 38–40.

126 Kelly, "Psychological and Legal Interventions for Parents and Children in Custody and Access Disputes," 149–150.

127 *Ibid.*

128 Taylor, "What Do We Know about Involving Children and Young People in Family Law Decision-Making?" 23–24.

129 *See e.g.* Murch, "The Voice of the Child in Private Family Law Proceedings in England and Wales," 10 (discussing studies).

CHAPTER 7. CREATING A TWENTY-FIRST-CENTURY FAMILY DISPUTE RESOLUTION SYSTEM

1 *See generally* Anne H. Geraghty and Wallace J. Mlyniec, "Unified Family Courts: Tempering Enthusiasm with Caution," *Family Court Review* 40 (2002): 435–447.

2 Resolution, "'Worrying Lack of Awareness' about Divorce Process Risks Increasing Cost and Stress of Break-Ups," last modified November 25, 2013, http://www.resolution.org.uk/news-list.asp?page_id=228&page=1&n_id=208.

3 *Ibid.*

4 *Ibid.*

5 Jessica Pearson, "An Evaluation of Alternatives to Court Adjudication," *Justice Systems Journal* 7 (1982): 420, 426–429.

6 Andrew Schepard, "Center for Separating Families and Children," *New York Law Journal* (January 23, 2014), 4.

7 The model for RCSDF was developed by the Honoring Families Initiative of the Institute for the Advancement of the American Legal System, the goal of which is to offer new models of service delivery and facilitate dialogue on how courts and communities can better meet the needs of families and children affected by divorce and separation. *See* Rebecca Love Kourlis *et al.*, "IAALS's Honoring Families Initiative: Courts and Communities Helping Families in Transition Arising from Separation or Divorce," *Family Court Review* 51 (2013): 351.

8 Rachel Birnbaum, "The Voice of the Child in Separation/Divorce Mediation and Other Alternative Dispute Resolution Processes: A Literature Review" (Canada, Department of Justice, 2009), 61.

9 *See* Susan Hansen, Jeanne Schroeder, and Kathy Gehl, "The Child Specialist Role in Client Choice of Process," *Collaborative Review* 13 (2013): 13.

10 Nicola Taylor, "What Do We Know about Involving Children and Young People in Family Law Decision-Making A Research Update," *Australian Journal of Family Law* 20 (2006): 27.

11 Jan Gilman, Dana Schneider, and Rebecca Shulak, "Children's Ability to Cope Post-divorce: The Effects of the Kids' Turn Intervention Program on 7 to 9 Year Olds," *Journal of Divorce and Remarriage* 42 (2005): 109–126. A more recent evaluation focusing on parent participants showed similar positive effects on reducing inter-parental conflict and ameliorating anxiety and depression among children. Jeffrey T. Cookston and Wenson W. Fung, "The Kids' Turn Program Evaluation: Probing Change within a Community-Based Intervention for Separating Families," *Family Court Review* 49 (2010): 348–363.

12 Taylor, "What Do We Know about Involving Children and Young People in Family Law Decision-Making?" 47–48.

13. This is particularly true in large urban jurisdictions. *See e.g.* Circuit Court for Baltimore City, *Annual Report of the Family Division Fiscal Year 2013* at 7 (noting that, in FY 2013, "eighty-six percent [86%] of custody and visitation case involved parents who had never been married").

14 Lamar Clarkson, "Divorce Rates Falling, Reports Find," *CNN Living* (May 19, 2011), accessed November 5, 2014, http://www.cnn.com/2011/LIVING/05/19/divorce. rates.drop.

15 *See generally* Jane C. Murphy, "Legal Images of Fatherhood: Welfare Reform, Child Support Enforcement, and Fatherless Children," *Notre Dame Law Review* 81 (2005): 325, 344–365.

16 For example, since 1996, the federal Office of Child Support Enforcement (OCSE) has provided annual grants of more than $10 million to support programs that

assist noncustodial parents in gaining access to and visitation with their children. More recently, in 2012, the OCSE established an additional grant program designed to expand opportunities for unmarried parents to create legally binding parenting time agreements at the time an initial child support order is entered. National Child Support Enforcement Association Parenting Time Order (July 13, 2013), accessed November 5, 2014, http://www.ncsea.org/documents/Parenting-Time-Order_7.31.13.pdf.

17 *See* Clare Huntington, "Postmarital Family Law," *Stanford Law Review* 67 (2015): __ (forthcoming) (noting that legal institutions governing family dissolution are designed for marital families); Jana B. Singer, "Dispute Resolution and the Post-Divorce Family: Implications of a Paradigm Shift," *Family Court Review* 47 (2009): 364.

18 Tali Schaefer, "Saving Children or Blaming Parents? Lessons from Mandated Parenting Classes," *Columbia Journal of Gender and Law* 19 (2010): 493. *See also* Peter Salem, Irwin Sandler, and Sharlene Wolchik, "Taking Stock of Parent Education in the Family Courts: Envisioning a Public Health Approach," *Family Court Review* 51 (2013): 131.

19 *See* Peter Salem, "The Emergence of Triage in Family Court Services: The Beginning of the End for Mandatory Mediation," *Family Court Review* 47 (2009): 373–374 (describing mediation as being "at the heart of the tiered service model for nearly three decades" and citing an Association of Family and Conciliation Courts" survey which found that 92 percent of family court service agencies offered mediation). *See also* Carrie-Ann Tondo *et al.*, "Mediation Trends: A *e*Survey of the States," *Family Court Review* 39 (2011): 431–453.

20 All forms of "mediation, combined with parenting plans, can offer families a private, perhaps less costly, setting to plan for parenting of children after breakup. Mediation helps parties avoid the public acrimony of a trial and focus on common ground, thus preserving family relationships. Mediation may also offer a better alternative than the adversary system for accommodating diverse family traditions. Mediation's informality gives it the potential to address cultural differences in ways litigation may not." Jane C. Murphy, "Revitalizing the Adversary System in Family Law," *University of Cincinnati Law Review* 78 (2010): 923–924.

21 Yishai Boyarin, "Court-Connected ADR: A Time of Crisis, a Time of Change," *Marquette Law Review* 85 (2012): 1018.

22 Daniel B. Pickar and Jeffrey J. Kahn, "Settlement-Focused Parenting Plan Consultation: An Evaluative Mediation Alternative to Child Custody Evaluations," *Family Court Review* 49 (2011): 59 (citing L. R. Lowry, "Evaluative Mediation," Jay Folberg, t alt., eds., *Divorce and Family Mediation: Models, Techniques, and Applications* [New York: Guilford Press, 2004], 72–91).

23 Pickar and Kahn, "Settlement-Focused Parenting Plan Consultation."

24 Boyarin, "Court-Connected ADR," 1018. One particularly promising approach, the settlement-focused parenting plan consultation, "combines traditional facilitative and interest-based mediation, with its emphasis on self-determination and confidentiality, with an evaluative process that provides parents with expertly gathered

information to be utilized in devising a parenting plan that meets their children's best interests." Pickar and Kahn, "Settlement-Focused Parenting Plan Consultation," 60.

25 Clare Huntington, "Rights Myopia in Child Welfare," *UCLA Law Review* 53 (2006): 674.

26 Peter Salem, "The Emergence of Triage in Family Court Services: The Beginning of the End for Mandatory Mediation?" *Family Court Review* 47 (2009): 371–388; Timothy Hedeen, "Remodeling the Multi-door Courthouse to 'Fit the Forum to the Folks': How Screening and Preparation Will Enhance ADR," *Marquette Law Review* 95 (2012): 944.

27 Gabrielle Davis, Loretta Frederick, and Nancy Ver Steegh, "Look before You Leap: Court System Triage of Family Law Cases Involving Intimate Partner Violence," *Marquette Law Review* 95 (2012): 961.

28 *Ibid.* at 988.

29 *Ibid.* at 990–991.

30 Stacy Brustin and Lisa Vollendorf Martin, "The Parenting Time Imperative," *Indiana Law Review* 48 (2015) (forthcoming).

31 *Ibid.* at 28.

32 Legal Services Corporation, "Documenting the Justice Gap in America: The Current Unmet Civil Legal Needs of Low-Income Americans" (September 10, 2009), accessed November 5, 2014, http://www.lsc.gov/sites/default/files/LSC/pdfs/documenting_the_justice_gap_in_america_2009.pdf (collecting data finding, among other things, that for every client served by an LSC-funded program in 2009, one person who seeks help is turned down because of insufficient resources and that only a small fraction of the legal problems experienced by low-income people [less than one in five] are addressed with the assistance of either a legal services lawyer or a private attorney, pro bono or paid).

33 *See e.g.* Bonnie Rose Hough and Pamela Cardullo Ortiz, eds., *Innovations for Self-Represented Litigants* (Madison, WI: Association of Family and Conciliation Courts, 2013); Bonnie Hough, "Self-Represented Litigants in Family Law: The Response of California's Courts," *California Law Review Circuit* 1 (2010): 15; Richard Zorza, *The Self-Help Friendly Court: Designed from the Ground Up to Work for People without Lawyers* (Williamsburg, VA: National Center for State Courts, 2002), 7–8 (describing efforts to improve *pro se* court access, including a nine-hundred-page self-help guide on the book's accompanying website for *pro se* litigants, which is visited over one hundred thousand times per month) The American Judicature Society has an online forum dedicated to *pro se* issues. *See "Pro Se* Forum," *American Judicature Society* (2012), accessed November 5, 2014, http://216.36.221.170/prose/home.asp.

34 James E. Cabral *et al.*, "Using Technology to Enhance Access to Justice," *Harvard Journal of Law and Technology* 26 (2012): 241, 248–252.

35 *See e.g.* "One Day Divorce Program," Superior Court of California County of Sacramento, accessed November 5, 2014, http://www.saccourt.ca.gov/family/one-day-divorce.aspx. *See also* Ann Carrns, "California Pioneers the Court-Aided One-Day Divorce," *New York Times* (June 7, 2014), accessed November 5, 2013, http://www.

nytimes.com/2014/06/07/your-money/court-aided-one-day-divorces-may-be-wave-of-the-future.html?_r=0.

36 Rachel M. Burns, Ateev Mehrotra, and Robin M. Weinick, "How Many Emergency Department Visits Could Be Managed at Urgent Care Centers and Retail Clinics?" *Health Affairs* 29 (2010): 1630.

37 Carol J. Williams, "Another Sign of Tough Times: Legal Aid for the Middle Class," *Los Angeles Times* (March 10, 2009), at 6. (describing Legal Grind, a storefront "cafe–legal clearinghouse" in Santa Monica, California, where "those facing court dates to deal with divorce, custody matters, driving offenses and debt can find out for $45 how best to tackle their problems without plunking down a $5,000 retainer and $400 an hour for a lawyer."

38 "Clinic," Target, accessed July 7, 2014, http://www.target.com/pharmacy/clinic-services; "Minute Clinic," CVS, accessed July 7, 2014, http://www.cvs.com/minuteclinic.

39 Debra Cassens Weiss, "Is Wal-Mart Law Coming to the U.S.? Retailer Adds Lawyers on Site for Toronto-Area Shoppers," *ABA Journal* (May 8, 2014), accessed November 5, 2014, http://www.abajournal.com/news/article/is_walmart_law_coming_to_the_us_retailer_adds_lawyers_on_site_for_canadian_.

40 Adam Cohen, "Just How Bad Off Are Law School Graduates?" *Time* (March 11, 2013), accessed July 7, 2014, http://ideas.time.com/2013/03/11/just-how-bad-off-are-law-school-graduates/.

41 *See* American Academy of Matrimonial Lawyers. "Bounds of Advocacy: Goals for Family Lawyers (Standard 3.1)" (2009), http://www.aaml.org/library/publications/19/bounds-advocacy/3-conflict-interest (a matrimonial lawyer should not attempt to represent both husband and wife, even with the consent of both); Kristi N. Saylors, "Conflicts of Interest in Family Law," *Family Law Quarterly* 28 (1994); 451, 453 (dual representation in contested divorce creates a *per se* conflict of interests and is prohibited by the Rules of Professional Conduct even where both parties consent).

42 *See* Geoffrey C. Hazard Jr., "Lawyer for the Situation," *Valparaiso University Law Review* 39 (2004): 377, 383–384 (noting that the ethical rules concerning conflicts of interest in transactional practice permit almost any multiple representation as long as there is adequately informed consent of all affected clients).

43 Rebecca Aviel, "Counsel for the Divorce," *Boston College Law Review* 55 (2014): 1099.

44 *Ibid.* at 1124.

45 *Ibid.* at 1146–1147.

46 John Nethercut, "'This Issue Will Not Go Away': Continuing to Seek the Right to Counsel in Civil Cases," *Clearinghouse Review* 38 (2004): 481.

47 Rebecca Aviel, "Why Civil Gideon Won't Fix Family Law," *Yale Law Journal* 122 (2013): 2112 (citing Rachel Kleinman, "Housing *Gideon*: The Right to Counsel in Eviction Cases," *Fordham Urban Law Journal* 31 [2004]: 1507, 1508).

48 Russell Engler, "Reflections on a Civil Right to Counsel and Drawing Lines: When Does Access to Justice Mean Full Representation by Counsel, and When Might Less Assistance Suffice?" *Seattle Journal for Social Justice* 9 (2010): 113–115.

49 Aviel, "Why Civil Gideon Won't Fix Family Law," at 2109. Aviel estimates that between 85 and 90 percent of cases "can and should be resolved by simple, cheap, and cooperative procedures." *Ibid.* at 2122. The authors suggest that Aviel may underestimate the number of cases where full traditional representation is needed, particularly in large urban courts, but agree with the larger point she makes about the importance of differentiating among cases and legal services needed.

50 John Lande and Jean Sternlight, "The Potential Contribution of ADR to an Integrated Curriculum," *Ohio State Journal on Dispute Resolution* 25 (2010): 255.

51 Barbara Glesner Fines, "Out of the Shadows: What Legal Research Instruction Reveals about Incorporating Skills throughout the Curriculum," *Journal of Dispute Resolution* (Spring 2013), 178.

52 *Ibid.*

53 William M. Sullivan *et al.*, *Educating Lawyers: Preparation for the Practice of Law* (San Francisco: Jossey-Bass, 2007), 6.

54 *Ibid.* at 12–13.

55 Roy Stuckey *et al.*, *Best Practices for Legal Education* (Columbia, SC: Clinical Legal Education Association, 2007), 8–9, accessed November 6, 2014, http://cleaweb.org/Resources/Documents/best_practices-full.pdf.

56 *See* Carrie Menkel-Meadow, "Crisis in Legal Education or the Other Things Law Students Should Be Learning and Doing," *McGeorge Law Review* 45 (2013): 155–156; Carrie Menkel-Meadow, "Doing Good Instead of Doing Well? What Lawyers Could Be Doing in a World of 'Too Many' Lawyers," *Oñati Socio-Legal Series* 3 (2013): 391–392.

57 Mary E. O'Connell and J. Herbie DiFonzo, "The Family Law Education Reform Project Final Report," *Family Court Review* 44 (2006): 524.

58 American Bar Association, "A Survey of Law School Curricula: 2002–2010," last modified 2010, http://www.americanbar.org/content/dam/aba/publications/misc/legal_education/2012_survey_of_law_school_curricula_2002_2010_executive_summary.authcheckdam.pdf.

59 *See* Lande and Sternlight, "The Potential Contribution of ADR to an Integrated Curriculum," 247.

60 Committee on Family Court and Family Law, "Survey of Family Law Curricula in New York City and Long Island Law Schools," *New York City Bar Association* (January 2010), 22.

61 *Ibid.* at 23.

62 *Ibid.*

63 Mervyn Murch, "The Voice of the Child in Private Family Law Proceedings in England and Wales," *International Family Law* (March 2005), 10, 13.

64 Taylor, "What Do We Know about Involving Children and Young People in Family Law Decision-Making?" 39.

65 Robert Mnookin and Lewis Kornhauser, "Bargaining in the Shadow of the Law: The Case of Divorce," *Yale Law Journal* 88 (1979): 968.

66 Elizabeth S. Scott and Robert E. Emery, "Gender Politics and Child Custody: The Puzzling Persistence of the Best Interests Standard," *Law and Contemporary Problems* 77 (2014): 72.

67 *See* Carol Weisbrod, "On the Expressive Functions of Family Law," *University of California Davis Law Review* 22 (1989): 991.

68 Martha Fineman, "Dominant Discourse, Professional Language, and Legal Change in Child Custody Decisionmaking," *Harvard Law Review* 101 (1988): 727.

69 Scott and Emery, "Gender Politics and Child Custody," at 69. For earlier critiques of the best interests standard, *see* Robert Mnookin, "Child Custody Adjudication: Judicial Functions in the Face of Indeterminacy," *Law and Contemporary Problems* 26 (1975): 226; Rena Uviller, "Fathers' Rights and Feminism: The Maternal Presumption Revisited," *Harvard Women's Law Journal* 1 (1978): 107; Jon Elster, "Solomonic Judgments: Against the Best Interest of the Child," *University of Chicago Law Review* 54 (1987): 1.

70 *See* Scott and Emery, "Gender Politics and Child Custody," at 71.

71 *Ibid.* at 69. Scott and Emery attribute the entrenchment of the best interests standard to two factors: a political deadlock in state legislatures between advocates for fathers and for mothers, and a misplaced faith in the ability of mental health professionals to evaluate families and advise courts about which custodial arrangements will promote children's interests.

72 *See* David Chambers, "Rethinking the Substantive Rules for Custody Disputes in Divorce," *Michigan Law Review* 83 (1984): 477, 527–532; Fineman, "Dominant Discourse, Professional Language, and Legal Change in Child Custody Decisionmaking," at 770–774.

73 American Law Institute, *Principles of the Law of Family Dissolution: Analysis and Recommendations* (San Francisco: LexisNexis, 2002), at 1.

74 *Ibid.* at 7

75 *Ibid.*

76 *Ibid.*

77 Jana B. Singer, "Bargaining in the Shadow of the Best Interest Standard: The Close Connection between Substance and Process in Resolving Divorce-Related Parenting Disputes," *Law and Contemporary Problems* 77 (2014): 188; *see* American Law Institute, *Principles of the Law of Family Dissolution*, §2.06, cmt. A.

78 *See* American Law Institute, *Principles of the Law of Family Dissolution*, §2.05, cmt. A ("The parenting plan concept presupposes a diverse range of childrearing arrangements, and rejects any pre-established set of statutory choices about what arrangements are best for children").

79 *Ibid.* at §2.09(2).

80 *Ibid.* at §2.09(2), §2.09(2), cmt. A.

81 *Ibid.* at §2.08(1).

82 *Ibid.* at 9. For a recent defense of the approximation standard, and its focus on past caretaking, *see* Katherine T. Bartlett, "Prioritizing Past Caretaking in Child-Custody Decisionmaking," *Law and Contemporary Problems* 77 (2014): 29–67.

83 American Law Institute, *Principles of the Law of Family Dissolution*, at §2.08(1)(b)–(f).

84 *Ibid.* at §2.08, §2.11.

85 Scott and Emery, "Gender Politics and Child Custody," at 101.

86 American Law Institute, *Principles of the Law of Family Dissolution*, at 8.

87 Scott and Emery, "Gender Politics and Child Custody," at 103. Current research indicates that fathers perform about one-third of child care in marital families. *See ibid.* at n. 178.

88 Scott and Emery, "Gender Politics and Child Custody," 103.

89 Bartlett, "Prioritizing Past Caretaking in Child Custody Decisionmaking," 32.

90 Scott and Emery, "Gender Politics and Child Custody," 102.

INDEX

AAML. *See* American Academy of Matrimonial Lawyers

ABA. *See* American Bar Association

Abuse. *See* Child abuse; Domestic violence

Addams, Jane, 12

Adoption, 67

Adversary system: assumptions of, 83–84; children harmed by, 26–28; courts on, 128; critique of, 26–36; critique of the critique of, 35; family harmed by, 28–29; financial harm from, 29; judges on, 31, 164n28; judicial system harmed by, 31–33; lawyers harmed by, 33–34; legal system harmed by, 33–34; paradigm shift from, 34–36, 128–29; parents harmed by, 28–31; *pro se* litigants in, 33

African Americans: births and, 61, 175n15; in colonial America, 7; education and, 61, 175n15

Ahrons, Constance, 77

Alexander, Paul W., 16

ALI. *See* American Law Institute

American Academy of Matrimonial Lawyers (AAML), 84–85

American Bar Association (ABA), 17; on ethical rules, 105–7; on lawyer-mediators, 94–95; on litigation alternatives, 169n46

American Law Institute (ALI): approximation standard, 152–54; *Principles of the Law of Family Dissolution*, 48, 64, 151–54

Approximation standard, 152–54

ART. *See* Assisted reproductive technology

Assisted reproductive technology (ART), 67–68

Association of Family and Conciliation Courts, 168n42, 194n2, 202n19, 203n33

Assumptions of new paradigm: on disputants' relationships, 72–73; on economic means, 73–76; on parental conflict and disputes, 79–81; on parental status, 76–77; on static post-separation family, 77–79; in twenty-first-century American families, 71–81

Attachment theory, 54

Attorneys. *See* Lawyers/attorneys

Australia, 110, 134. *See also* Family Relationship Centres

Aviel, Rebecca, 143–44, 205n49

Best interests standard: alternative proposals, 151–52; child welfare relating to, 44–45; critique of, 150–51, 206n71; fault relating to, 20; grandparents relating to, 65; Tippins and Wittmann on, 53, 172n82

Binuclear family, 77–78

Births: African Americans and, 61, 175n15; education and, 61, 175n15, 175n18; non-marital, 61, 78; socioeconomic status relating to, 61; for women under thirty, 176n21

Bishop, Joel, 8

Burger, Warren, 92, 185n18

Therapeutic divorce: divorce counseling, 18; judges for, 17–18; juvenile justice relating to, 16–19; mission of, 16–17; proponents of, 16–17
Therapeutic ideal, 12–16
Therapeutic jurisprudence, 38, 93, 105
Third-party caretakers, 64–65. *See also* Grandparents
Tippins, Timothy M., 53, 172n82
Training, lawyer, 144–48
Triage model, 100–101, 138
Twenty-first-century American families: assumptions, of new paradigm, 71–81; decoupling of marriage and parenthood, 60–63, 73; gay and lesbian families, 66–68, 177n48; multi-generational families and third-party caretakers, 64–65; *pro se* litigants' prevalence, 68–71; reproductive technology's impact, 67–68; stepfamilies' prevalence, 63–64
Twenty-first-century dispute resolution and reform: best interests standard for, 150–52, 206n71; children's voices in, 132–34; doctrinal changes, 148–54; lawyer training, 144–48; legal norms for, 148–50; legal services, through new lawyering models, 139–44; overview, 128–30; paradigm shift, from courts to communities, 130–32; processes and services, to needs of all families, 134–39

UCLA. *See* Uniform Collaborative Law Act
UK. *See* United Kingdom

Unbundled legal representation. *See* Limited scope representation/unbundled legal representation
Unified family courts, 55, 80. *See also* Family court
Uniform Collaborative Law Act (UCLA), 99, 107–8
United Kingdom (UK), 131–32; children's voices in, 118, 121
United Nations Convention on the Rights of the Child (CRC): Article 12 and participation mandate, 119–23; child-informed mediation relating to, 123–26; on children's voices, 119–23
Unrepresented parties. See *Pro se* litigants/unrepresented parties

Ver Steegh, Nancy, 101, 138
Violence. *See* Domestic violence
Visitation: noncustodial parents and, 29, 163n15; for non-marital families, 62, 176n23; for stepparents, 42

Wittmann, Jeffrey P., 53, 172n82
Women: births, for women under thirty, 176n21; in colonial America, 6, 157n3; domesticity relating to, 7–9, 10; gender equality and gender roles, 21–22; maternal custody rights, 8; mothers, child welfare, and state intervention, 56, 174n102; non-marital births, 61, 78; sole custody, gender roles, and, 21–22

Zealous advocacy, 83–85, 183n2, 183n7

ABOUT THE AUTHORS

JANE C. MURPHY is Laurence M. Katz Professor of Law at the University of Baltimore School of Law. She teaches family law, alternative dispute resolution, and clinical courses and has served as Associate Dean for Academic Affairs and Director of Clinical Education. Professor Murphy is the co-editor of *Resolving Family Conflicts* (2008) and co-author of *Family Mediation: Theory and Practice* (2009) as well as numerous articles on the law's treatment of families, conflict resolution, and access to justice in both the academic and popular press.

JANA B. SINGER is Professor of Law at the University of Maryland Francis King Carey School of Law, where she teaches family law, contracts, and constitutional law. She has written widely on family and children's issues and on family dispute resolution and is the co-editor of *Resolving Family Conflicts* (2008). Professor Singer is a member of the American Law Institute and a past Chair of the Family and Juvenile Law Section of the American Association of Law Schools. She currently serves on the editorial board of the *Family Court Review* and on the Divorce Roundtable, an interdisciplinary group of lawyers, judges, mediators, and mental health professionals.